NEWS AND THESE UNITED STATES

NEWS

AND THESE UNITED STATES

BY EDITH MERWIN BARTOW ★ ★ ★

FUNK & WAGNALLS COMPANY ★ ★ ★

NEW YORK 1952

PREFACE

IT WAS ONLY YESTERDAY THAT—"IT PLEASED GOD TO put a Period to the life of Oliver, the Lord Protector"; a London Copheehouse could advertise "that excellent, and by all physicians approved, China Drink called by the Chineans Tcha, by other Nations Tay, or Tee"; and the newspaper, come of age, was welcomed into dynamic partnership by common men.

Grown strong in the restrictive environs of towns and cities and of regions defined by topography and the means of transportation, the newspapers of these United States—the stout voices of their subscribers —were in the vanguard in the building of the country. In this informal tracing, from the files of two hundred and fifty years, is underscored that intimate association which has so strongly marked the changing course of the news. Within the fabric of the news can be discerned the challenge that may well subvert the advocates of the new aristocracy of total politics, who rely alone on a total ignorance of voter and taxpayer.

To the readers of tomorrow's newspapers this book, *News and These United States*, is offered.

For many courtesies, thanks are due to the New York Public Library, the Library of Congress, the New-York Historical Society, the John Carter Library of Brown University, the Bancroft Library of the University of California, and other libraries for the privilege of the use of their newspaper files and the manifest help of their librarians. To Mr. Clarence S. Brigham and Mrs. Dorothy Spears of the American Antiquarian Society of Worcester, and to Mr. E. J. Brehaut of the Boston Chamber of Commerce appreciation is here expressed.

Particular thanks must certainly be given to Mr. Lewis M. Stark, Mr. Percy E. Clapp, Mrs. Philomena S. Houlihan, Mr. Gerald McDonald, Mr. Robert W. Henderson, and Mr. Louis H. Fox of New York; to Mr. John H. Thaxter, Mr. Clyde S. Edwards, and Mr. Jacob Kainen of Washington; and to the many secretaries of local and regional historical societies and those many others who have been so helpful.

E. M. B.

March 15, 1952

CONTENTS

	PREFACE	v
1	FIRST PRESSES	5
2	EARLY NEWSPAPERS	17
3	THE BRIGHT MORNING STAR OF FREEDOM	31
4	DRUMS OF REVOLUTION	47
5	THE DAILIES	57
6	THE PIONEERS	71
7	COCKADES TO COCKED HATS	83
8	TO THE TERRAPIN WAR	101
9	PUBLISHERS' PROGRESS	115
10	THE STEAMBOAT WHISTLES	127
11	LOW BRIDGE	137
12	THE PENNY DREADFULS	151
13	"WHAT HATH GOD WROUGHT?"	163
14	THE WESTERNS	177
15	TRAMP, TRAMP, TRAMP	189
16	PEANUTS, PIE, AND GUTTA-PERCHA	205
17	NEW NEWS FRONTIERS	215
18	ON THE BREEZY SIDE	229
19	IN THE GRASSROOTS	241
20	THE ETHICAL PRESS	249
21	CRY CENSOR!	259
22	TO THE SKYWAYS	267
	BIBLIOGRAPHY	271
	INDEX	273

Illustrations

Decorative eagle mounted on the Columbian Press of George
  Clymer, 1818   Title page
The Coranto, English forerunner of the newspaper, printed in
  Holland, 1620   2 – 3
Nameplate, *Boston Gazette*, 1719   16 – 17
Cartoon, "Join or Die," *Pennsylvania Gazette*, 1754   30
Nameplate, *The Massachusetts Spy or, Thomas's Boston Journal*,
  1776   46 – 47
Cartoon, "Federal Edifice," *The Massachusetts Sentinel* 1788   56
Nameplate, *The New Hampshire Mercury and The General Ad-
  vertiser*, 1799   70 – 71
Nameplate, *Greenleaf's New Daily Advertiser*, New York, 1797   82 – 83
Advertisement for soldiers, *Independent Chronicle*, Boston, 1813   100
Nameplate, *Manufacturers' and Farmers' Journal, Providence
  and Pawtuckett Advertiser*, 1820   114
Advertisement of tours, *Niagara Journal*, Buffalo, 1819   126
Nameplate, *New York Enquirer*, 1826   136 – 137
Nameplate, *The Sun*, New York, 1835   150 – 151
Nameplate, *Evening Gazette*, Boston, 1833   162 – 163
Nameplate, *Alta California*, Steamer Edition, 1860   176 – 177
Nameplate, *The Liberator*, Boston, 1831   188 – 189
Map, "The Cable Celebration Number," *Frank Leslie's Illus-
  trated Newspaper*, New York, 1858   204 – 205
Nameplate, *Trans-Continental*, En route at Omaha, 1870   214
Nameplate and Editorial, *The World*, New York, 1883   228 – 229
Small-town dailies, 1952. *The Delta Democrat-Times*, Green-
  ville, Mississippi; *The Madisonian*, Virginia City, Montana;
  New Canaan Advertiser, New Canaan, Connecticut   240
Cartoon, "Presidential Equestrianism," *The Times*, Los Angeles,
  1885   248
The effects of censorship. Nameplates: *Russkiya Vedomosti*,
  Moscow, 1917; *Novoye Vremya*, Petrograd, 1917; *Frank-
  furter Zeitung und Handelsblatt*, Frankfurt-am-Main, 1943;
  Vossische Zeitung, Berlin, 1934; *La Prensa*, Buenos Aires,
  1951   258
News item giving readership statistics, *The New York Times*,
  1952   266

NEWS AND THESE UNITED STATES

Out of Weenen, the 6 November.

THe French Ambassadour hath caused the Earle of Dampier to be buried stately at Presburg In the meane vvhile hath Bethlem Gabor cited all the Hungerish States, to com together at Presburg the 5. of this present, to discourse aboute the Crovvning & other causes concerning the same Kingdom.

The Hungatians continue vvith roveing against these Lands. In like manner those of Moravia, vvhich are fallen uppon the Cosackes yester night by Hotleyn, set them on fire, and slaine many dead, the rest vvill revenge the same.

Heere is certaine nevves com, that the Crabats, as also the Lord Budean, are fallen unto Betlem Gabor.

The Emperour sends the Earle of Altheim, as Ambassadour to Crackovv in Polen, to appeare upon the same meeting-day.

Novv comes tidings, that Betlem Gabor is at Thurna, there doe gather to gether great store of States.

The Emper. Maj. hath appoynted heere a meeting-day upon the 1. of Decemb. thereupon should appeare the 4. Proclaimed States. The appoynted taxing shall bring up a great som of money.

Out of Prage, the 5 of November.

Three dayes agone are passed by, 2. mile from this Cittie 6000 Hungarians (chosen out Soldiers) under the General Rediferens, vvhich are gon to our Head-camp, & the Enimie lieth yet near unto ours by Rackonits, though the crie goeth, that the enimie caused all his might to com togither, to com this vvayes against Prage, if that comes to passe, it shall not run of vvithout blovves, the vvhich might be revealed vvith in sevv dayes.

It coutinues, that in the Satser Crais are gathered togither 10000 Contrie-men, most high-dutch-men, against Meisslen, & no Bohemians, they vvill help the King, to drive the enimie out of the Land. In like manner som certaine 1000 Contrie-men rebel in the Lentmaritscher Crais, but it is feared that those Countrie-men are starred up, through practise of the Adversarie, that the enimie in the meane vvhile might com to Prage. Wee understand, that Bucquoy hath not been in the Camp, but by the Duke of Saxen som certaine dayes, therefore vve are to looke to our selves, for feare of Trecherie. And it is thonght that the Emperour vvill leave Austria to the Hungorians, & see to effect his intention only uppon Praghe.

Out of Ceulen, the 2 1. Novemb.

Writing from Marpurg in Hessen, that the Earle of the same Land, doth cause the foresaid Cittie to be strongly fortified, there on doe vvorke many 100 men dayly, and there is mustered in the Earleship Zigenheym not long since 1. Government of foote-men, & 6. Cornets of horse-men, the foote-men are sent to Marpurg & Rijnsels. But the horse-men are lodged in the Villages about the Cittie, & thereafter are also mustered the Duke of Saxen Lauvvenburgs Governement in Tries-Zigenheym, novv further vvhere they shallbe laid & used, is yet unknovvn. The sames Brothers Governement, there quarter is laid by Cassel, the Souldiers vvhich are taken on about Hamburg. Lubeck, in the Dukeship of Holsteen, & Meckelenburg, should also be mustered about Cassel, & be used vvhere neede shall require.

Since the last vve cannot enquire, that there is any thing of any importaunce passed betvvixt the Marquis Spinola & the Vnited Princes. We understand that the foresaid Spinola vvil lay his Souldiers in Garnisson vvith the first, & deale them unto divers places, on part to Oppenheym, Altzey, Ingelheym & Cruijssnach, the other part at Summeren & Bacharacht, the speech goeth that there shalbe layed vvith in Ments a good Company in Garnisson.

The Bishop at Halberstadt, Duke Christiaen at Bruynsvvyck, doth cause to be taken on 2000 Musquetters, to send to the Vnited Princes.

Heere is tydings, that betvveen the King of Bohemia & the Emperours folke hath beene a great Battel about Prage, but because there is different vvriting & speaking thereuppon, so cannot for this time any certainety thereof be vvritten, but must vvayte for the next Post. As also of the Cittie Pilsen, vvhich the Earle of Mansvelt (so the speech goeth) should have delivered into the Emperours hands.

From Cadan in Bohemia, 4. mile from Raconits, the 12. November.

From Solts is certaine advise that the Emperours folk have made them selves vvith all theire might out of theire Camp, & taken their vvay to vvards Praghe, like as they vveare then com to the long mile, but as the King understand such, he is broken up vvith his armey, and com to the lóg mile beforen the enimie, vvhere they have had a very strong Battelle & on both sides more then 6000 men slaine, though most on the Kings side, also hath the enimie gotten of the King som peeces of Ordenuaunce and vvaggens vvith amunitie, so that the King must retire back to Praghe, and the enimie to the Weissenberg, there he lies yet and roves from thence to the Lout Maritscher Crais unto Brix, hath taken in, Trebnits, Pielan & Dux, also laid folk upon Leutmarifcher Slainer, and Launer paffages, that the Paffage upon Prage is vvholy taken avvay, and this day is com heere in a certain Perfon that brings tydinghs unto our Magiftrat, that bervvixt Sonnevveid and Patronit, vvhere the enimie hath lien are found fom certaine 1000 dead Bodies, & on the other fide there King lay alfo fom certaine 1000. dead bodies, vvhat is com to paffe betvvixt both vve fhal fhortly heare.

Out of Amberghe, in the Vpper-Pallatine, the 17. ditto.

Here hath h . . . . . om tne Beyerens by . . f R . . . ne vvhole day togither, that . . c flaine aboute 8000 men, and very many fhould be hurt. Our King, vvith the Lord General the Earle of Hohento, alfo the vvhole army arervvith in Prage, & the Duke of

Beyeren uppon the Weyffenbergh & Stern; vve hoope that they fhall fhortly be driven from thence. Whatfurther is done betvvixt them, vve look for every houre to enquire further thereof & it feemes none can com from Prage, becaufe the paffages are every vvhere fhut.

Out of Cealen, the 24 of November.

Letters out of Neurenburghe of the 20 of this prefent, make mentio- --at they had advife from the Bord-

. . . re upon, and fo provio. . .he vvhole vvinter. And are not long ni.te in the night 500 Souldiers paffed by Dure out of Gulik, fo the fpeech goerh, there meaning fhoulde be to build a nievv Sch. ntfe by Flammerfheym, to take avvay the paffag- from the Marquis Spinola.

Imprinted at Amfterdam by George Vefeler, Ao. 1620. The 2. of Decemember.
And are to be foulde by Petrus Keerius, dvvelling in the Calverftreete, in the uncertaine time.

A Coranto of December 2, 1620. From Van Stockum's The First Newspapers of England, Printed in Holland. Courtesy of New York Public Library.

For when news is printed,
It leaves, sir, to be news; while 'tis but written
Tho' it be ne'er so false, it runs news still . . .
See diversmen's opinions! unto some
The very printing of 'em makes them news;
That have not the heart to believe anything
But what they see in print.
The Staple of News—BEN JONSON

FIRST PRESSES

IT'S THE NEWS!

"Mrs. Theodore W. Jones's little boy, William, fell off the drawbridge twice last Thursday. He was rescued both times by Harbor-Master Capt. Charles V. Lacey who warned Willie to stay away from the drawbridge in the future."

"The Ladies of the Grange will hold a food sale in Green's Olde Corner Drug-Store next Saturday morning. Don't forget your cakes, Girls! (Jim Green does NOT expect to sell any more bi-carb than usual on Saturday night. Ye Ed.)"

"Extra! Extra! Extra! Read about State Executives charged with illegal use of publicly owned automobiles and gasoline for trips to Kentucky, Florida and California racetracks! (From Our Exclusive Capital Correspondent.)"

"The President Addresses the Congress on the State of the Nation. (By Special Wire from Washington.)"

News from home and news from abroad; news of familiar, friendly little worlds at our doors and news of strange lands far beyond our horizons. News of the world of art, music, and letters. News of trade and commerce and transportation by land, sea, and air. News of science, invention, manufacture, engineering, and agriculture. News of help and healing and news of death, disaster, and man's new cruelties to man. News of politics and governments, of presidents, kings, and dictators. News in endless streams that vanish almost as swiftly as they come, leaving readers sometimes happier, sometimes sadder, but always a little wiser and better informed about this changing universe and its changeling peoples.

News of births, deaths, marriages, divorces, accidents, murders, fires, floods, bankruptcies, horse races, baseball games, basement bargain sales, new hats, the antics of café society, the prices of food, stocks, bonds, steel, coal, and the labor of men and women—all this, and more, is in the news of today and tomorrow for the fifty-odd millions of Americans daily reading one or more of the thousands of daily, weekly, twice- and three-times weekly newspapers of the land.

Today's newspaper readers know what they want. First they want home-town news: laudatory obituaries of saints and sinners, descriptions of weddings, news of churches, schools, clubs, and stores. News of Washington and other world capitals looms up as news of importance to the truth-seeking public. Voters expect news of legislative debates under the domes of forty-eight state capitals. And all want news—foreign, domestic, local—while it is still news and as accurate as if written from prolonged research.

Patrons of the press turn to Walter Lippmann, David Lawrence, Mark Sullivan, and other trusted commentators on the news. In the columns of Frank Kent, Ray Tucker, Robert S. Allen, Drew Pearson, Peter Edson, and other writers, they search for sparks to light tomorrow's headlines and news with humor, philosophy, and personal experiences that they find under by-lines including H. I. Phillips, Leonard Lyons, and Mrs. Eleanor Roosevelt. Even the acidulous wares of Westbrook Pegler, the sackcloth-swathed brickbats of Robert C. Ruark, and the amiable raillery of Frederick C. Othman contribute to news understanding.

Readers relish the spice of airy hints and mysterious rumors in local news columns as keenly as the stylized gossip of Walter Winchell. Daily they chuckle over favorite comics sometimes far from funny. Old-timers welcome the Katzenjammer Kids created in 1897 by Rudolph Dirks, Mutt and Jeff first from the pen of Bud Fisher in 1907, and the Toonerville Folks, gift of Fontaine Fox in 1908, all of them still sharing expensive newsprint with newcomers including Gus Edson's Andy Gump, Frank Willard's Moon Mullins, Chic Young's Blondie, Arthur Folwell and Kin Platt's Mr. and Mrs., Al Capp's L'il Abner, Dan Spiegle's Hopalong Cassidy, Wayne Boring's Superman, E. Rice Burroughs' aging but ageless Tarzan, and almost innumerable denizens of the "strips" and "panels."

Avidly armies of fans reach for the crisp, zesty news from the Kingdom of Swat, the stadia, prize rings, racetracks, tennis courts, golf links, and bridge tables; eagerly they read the critics of opera, symphony, drama, movie, painting, sculpture, new books. They collect and use the fashion hints, cooking recipes, patterns for sewing and crochet. Articles on home-decoration, child-rearing, medicine, and etiquette are all popular. There is comfort in the columns for teen-agers and the lovelorn. Features such as these and many other specialized departments are sought and found in almost every newspaper's every issue.

The country's citizenry demands of its press that editorial policies and opinions remain consistent with those professed by the publishers. Readers adopt them as their own, or measure them smugly against the "erroneous" convictions of the opposition.

Changing newspapers is a serious matter for the reader. He is too intelligent to believe literally all he reads in the papers but he recognizes and respects high standards of editorial intent and accomplished reporting. Readers resent any attempt to color or distort the news or slant it. Editorial shallowness or the carelessness of lazy newsmen is spotted and long remembered. Facile syndicated "stars" who blow hot today and cold tomorrow or bludgeon the reader with propaganda severely strain the public confidence. But an actual change of paper usually marks progress on the part of the reader from a desire for sensational to serious news treatment, or for more local news. But only rarely will readers follow editors, favorite columnists, or even pet comics to new mastheads.

The modern newspaper developed as slowly as the literacy to which it owes existence, and its future will reflect the demands of the public to whose maturity it is a necessity. Opinions as to what constitutes news, the most perishable of essential commodities, will probably always be contradictory—a fact which is fortunate for both press and public. Every detail of today's newspapers (format, news evaluations, entertainment, editorials, reporting, and advertising) is the result of the past successes and failures of countless pioneers whose early imprints still influence every page. Today's leaders are shaping tomorrow's newspapers, and tomorrow's press—fluid, flexible, and sensitive to change—will employ new techniques to increase the already uncanny speed with which news is gathered from local, national, and international sources.

In the curiously intimate relationship persisting between Americans and their newspapers for well over two centuries, battles have been many. More than a few times they have reached the heat that drove mobs of infuriated subscribers into print-shops to destroy presses, hurl types into streets, burn buildings, and kill or maim offending publishers. Egged on by the public, editors have fought each other until the two proverbial shots fired into frosty morning air became so frequent as to be ridiculous. Many a pair of pearl-handled duelling pistols, once considered essential to all well-appointed newspaper offices, now lie on exhibition in velvet-lined cases. Well-meaning outside interference in brawls between press and public has been met with the closed ranks of an instinctive partnership: the balanced responsibility that, since the days of John Peter Zenger, has been the potent guardian of freedom. To its press America looks with confidence for protection of the "American way" and preservation of the Constitution it so effectively promoted; and, in turn, not a newspaper can live free to print the news of its choice without this confidence.

The first American newspapers were produced by tough-fibered printers who shared with their subscribers an aversion to censorship. They refused to truckle to any so-called "Authority" as being opposed to human progress. Just as vain was the opposition to Johann Gansefleisch of Gutenberg when he succeeded in printing from movable types the Latin Grammar of Ælius Donatus.

Gutenberg's press was adapted from the one back-saving device of medieval households where it was used to make wine, cider, and cheese. The frame of two heavy wooden uprights supported two crossbeams, through the upper of which passed a wooden screw operated by a lever in a socket, and from which suspended the platen. On the lower beam rested the type-bed. Matrices were cut in tempered steel and hardened in heat for the molten casting-mixture, and the metal letters were dressed and sorted into the trays of upper and lower cases. Each line of text was set in hand-held composing sticks, transferred to galleys, and locked in type-beds with blanks. Inked with a mixture of soot or lampblack and boiled linseed oil applied with leather-covered wool balls on short sticks, a dampened sheet of paper was placed on top and the platen lowered to make a single impression on one side of the page. Each printed page was hung to dry while the process was repeated to complete editions of books of yet unsurpassed printing perfection.

The art that thrilled the intellectuals of the Continent was held secret until carried to Europe's cities by workmen fleeing Mainz (stormed, sacked and fired in the Archbishop's War). Everywhere the printing press was recognized as dangerous, and its regulation became the urgent concern of both church and state.

William Caxton, linguist and dealer in silks, learned to print with Colard Mansion in Cologne. In Bruges in 1474, he published the first book printed in English, his own translation of Raoul le Fèvre's *Le Recueil des Histoires de Troyes*. He returned to his native country and set up its first press at the Signe of the Red Pale in the almonry of Westminster, and here, three years later, issued England's first dated volume in print, *The Dictes and Sayengis of the Phylosophers* of The Earl of Rivers. Printers, many from Normandy, followed Caxton to England, and a native press established the allied crafts of type cutting and casting, bookbinding, and press-building, and the apprehensions of the uneasy were confirmed by proposals to start a paper-mill.

In 1550 Danner of Nuremberg made the first improvement to the press of Gutenberg when he substituted brass for wood in the screw. After another hundred years, Willem Janszoon Blaeu, astronomer, mathematician, and publisher of Amsterdam, passed this spindle-screw through a wooden block to guide the platen as it was lowered and lifted to and from the type-bed which he had arranged to slide easily in and out on iron gutters. A wood-engraving by Galle pictures a Dutch shop, probably that of Blaeu, showing a scholarly man with a long beard and clad in a long furred robe, reading from a manuscript to compositors, in doublets and hose and wearing swords and dirks, who work seated on benches. Freedom to display the blade was an honor conferred upon the printers of Paris also by royal ordinance.

At a date forgotten an unremembered genius contributed to the press the tympan and frisket; these hinged fabric-covered frames extending from type-beds folded inwards to protect paper from unwanted ink or impression. Nine separate steps went into the printing of each side of one page, and the mechanical progress of another century produced only the substitution of metal for some wooden press parts, although stone was early used in type-beds. The heavy black-letter type faces, careful imitations of the work of monastic scribes, soon gave way to lighter and more easily read characters. Time and experience added beauty to the fonts and slightly improved casting-mixtures and methods.

In England where books were turned off presses for salaries from royal purses, provender from royal larders, or promises of sport in royal preserves, Queen Mary Tudor, on ascending the throne, deprived Richard Grafton of his royal office for printing the Proclamation of Lady Jane Grey. Later she shut John Day in the Tower for "prynting of Noythy Bookes," and granted the ancient Brotherhood of Stationers a Charter of Incorporation in a gesture neatly calculated to secure control of all the kingdom's presses.

But "free" printing lingered to plague the peace of good Queen Bess, and a special court, appointed to deal with its offenses, met in the star-shaped chamber of Westminster Palace to devise the notorious Act to which Elizabeth, Regina, affixed her signature on June 29, 1568. Penalties for printing or importing printing without license from a Special Commission of Ecclesiastical Authorities were left to the discretion of these servants of the crown, and provision was made for officers charged with its protection against the press. Twenty years later a "Newe Decree" approved by a press-distrusting Parliament granted this Star Chamber Court the combined powers of accusers, prosecutors, judges, and executioners.

But news suppressed erupted in London's streets in a rash of "ballets" printed on small broadsides and offered by hawkers who sang the sensationally newsy themes of anonymous printers.

News was smuggled from Amsterdam for surreptitious English translation, printing, and sale. On sheets scarcely larger than a man's open hand the curious could buy uncaptioned news of the world, until titles such as *Coranto Out of Italie* began to appear. The prototype of all today's newspapers was called the *Corante, or, Weekly Newes from Italy, Germany, Hungaria, Polonia, Bohemia, France and the Low-Countries!* Its imprint: *London. Printed for N.B. October 11, 1621. Out of the Low-Dutch Coppy.* N.B. was either Nathaniel Butter or Nicholas Bourne—probably the latter.

Single sheet *corantes* were followed by the "newes-books." These were pamphlets printed and sold by license of "Authority." Their frequent mention of England and English affairs alarmed both church and crown, whose loyal defenders against the terrors of the printed word were supported by a third Star Chamber Act in 1637. Now, in thirty-three clauses of must-nots, the number of printers was limited to twenty, each under bond of three hundred pounds, and each permitted not more than three presses or three apprentices. No presses were to be built, no premises let to printers, and no printing to be done, or imported without Authority. Civil War, execution of the king, the political disturbances of the rule of Cromwell, and an epidemic of plague combined not only to prevent enforcement of the Act but also to increase the need for the news.

Within fifty years after Columbus proved the earth was round, a printing press came to the New World. Only twenty years after Hernando Cortez glimpsed the wealth of the Montezumas, Juan Pablos, employee of a Seville shop, arrived in Mexico City to produce many elegant books for missionary inspiration and ecclesiastical enjoyment. In 1594 Antonio Ricardi from Turin was printing in Lima, Peru, by Spanish Authority for the spiritual needs of the Incas whose gold made piracy an almost honorable profession.

Thirty years after the settlement of Jamestown, and almost twenty years after the one hundred and two emaciated passengers of the *Mayflower* stepped ashore on Plymouth Rock, New England heard the cheerful groans and creakings of its first press.

The Puritans led by John Winthrop to Massachusetts Bay Colony (chartered by the press-detesting Charles I) were thoughtful people who, "Dreading to leave an illiterate ministry to the Churches when our present Ministers shall lie in Dust," regarded the education of their children as their immediate responsibility. The Colony's General Court granted four hundred pounds towards a "schole, or college" in fortified New-Towne, and when John Harvard died and left to it his library of two hundred volumes and half his estate of seven hundred and eighty pounds, the new school was named in his honor and its site, in honor of his alma mater, was called Cambridge.

As visitor to the Colony came the Reverend Jose Glover, a wealthy Non-Conformist idling away the year he was suspended from his County Surry parish, on the *Planter*, a ship of which he was part owner. Impressed and enthused he sailed back to England to resign from his church and arrange his business affairs so as to make his permanent home in America.

While in Europe Mr. Glover bought a printing press for the new school for which he accepted gifts and money, especially acknowledging

"Forty-nine pounds & Something more" donated by "Some Gentlemen of Amsterdam" towards the purchase of an outfit of types. In England he engaged the services of Stephen Daye, a locksmith and with two sons, of which one, Matthew, was either a printer or a printer's apprentice. The Reverend Mr. Glover, according to John Winthrop's Journal, died "on the sea hitherward," but the press that arrived late in the autumn of 1638 was first used early in the following year, and was undoubtedly operated by Matthew Daye.

The first printing to come from the press was an issue of several hundred copies of the *Freeman's Oath*, a pledge of deep significance to the Colonists. Next was printed an almanac compiled by Captain William Pierce, Mariner. In 1640 went to press the first English-language book of the Western hemisphere: *The Whole Booke of Psalms, Faithfully Translated Into the English Metre*. An almanac by Samuel Danforth of Harvard College, Philomathemat, for the Year of Our Lord, 1647, bears the imprint of Matthew Day.

Matthew Day died in 1649 and the Cambridge press was silent until Court or College appointed Samuel Green as printer. The new incumbent was without experience and had to learn to print; but he became a capable craftsman and proved to be an able manager of both press and shop for forty years. In 1651 he published the famous *Bay Psalm Booke*, so freely pirated abroad, and three years later printed the *Primer*, or *Catechism* of the Reverend John Eliot of Roxbury. The Apostle to the Indians had labored long among the "Pequot, Pawtackett, Pawkunnawkut and Massachusett" Indians, all Algonquians whose dialects were similar to the Natick, in which he composed his *Milk for Babes*. From the *Primer* the missionary taught his converts to read, and for them he translated the *Book of Genesis* and the *Gospel of Matthew*, both of which were also printed on the Cambridge press.

But Samuel Green was driven to protest when Mr. Eliot announced that his Bible was ready for printing; he told the Court he would have to have another press, the help of another printer, new types, and more paper.

The missionary wrote to the Society for the Promoting of the Gospel of Jesus-Christ in New-England, whose London headquarters solicited funds for the salvation of this continent's aborigines, and, reminding them that he was now deep in years, prayed he might see the Indians supplied with the Scriptures. His appeal was supplemented by a letter from the Court, and, presently, a second press joined the first in the crusade to bring the light to darkest America. Over the joint imprint of Samuel Green and Marmaduke Johnson was published in 1661 the *New Testament*. The *Old Testament* was completed two years later with the assistance of our first native-born printer, an Indian taught to read and write by Mr. Eliot and apprenticed to Samuel Green. According to his tutor, James Printer was "able to compose the sheets and correct the press with understanding," and excepting for a year off when he donned the paint and feathers of the warpath under King Philip, his was a life devoted to the type-cases. Marmaduke Johnson, unsuccessful suitor of Samuel Green's daughter, after his contract with the Society expired, secured a press from England and opened a Boston shop where his career as independent printer was brought to an early end by death.

The Cambridge printer (Samuel Green) was a man of ready wit and easy laughter; his sons, Samuel Jr., Bartholemew, and Timothy, worked with him, and together they made the press famous throughout the Colonies. With him, Colonel Richard Nicolls, first English Governor of New York, in 1665 was obliged to dicker when he wanted some broadsides printed to advertise "Conditions for New-Planters" to induce settlers of the Bay and Plymouth Colonies to remove to his own, and superior, bailiwick.

In Jamestown, Virginia, William Nuthead in 1682 set up the first American press outside Cambridge and Boston. In obedience to the King's order that "Noe Person Bee permitted to use any press for printing upon any occasion whatsoever" the authorities ousted him. But in St. Mary's, Maryland, Nuthead found a slightly more liberal administration, occasionally agreeable to dispensing with the required license. But at his death William Nuthead's meager goods included, besides the press he willed to his wife, Dinah, only six pounds, a few shillings, a pile of lumber, and a weary old horse.

The order of King James II to Thomas Dongan, early colonial governor and capable agent of the Royal Proprietor, was short and to the point: "And for as much as great inconvenience may arise from the liberty of printing within our Province of Newyorke; you are to provide by all necessary orders that noe Person shall keep any press for Printing, nor that any book, pamphlet, or other material whatsoever bee printed without your special leave & lycence first obtained." Governor Sir William Berkeley of Virginia supported the theory of happy innocence as companion to ignorance with the words: "I thank God there are no free schools or printing, and I hope we shall not have these hundred years. For learning has brought disobedience and heresey and sects into the world; and printing has divulged them, and libels against the Government. God keep us from them both."

With William Penn came a William Bradford who had composed types for pamphlets in England. Setting up his press in the little Quaker village of Philadelphia, Bradford, whose types had become pied in bringing "that great Art and Mystery of Printing into this part of America," got to work on his *Kalendarium Pennsilvanienne, or America's Messenger, being an Almanack for the Year of Grace, 1686.*

For referring to the great Quaker as "ye Lord Penn" in the second issue of an almanac compiled by Samuel Atkins, Bradford was haled into court and warned to print nothing "but what shall have lycence from ye Council." Unintimidated, he printed, in 1692, *The Truth Advanced* of George Keith, celebrated Quaker storm-center then in Philadelphia. This was printed on paper made in this country's first mill, built in Germantown by William Rittenhouse, the printer, and two others. The Authority that disapproved of George Keith and all his works had Bradford arrested and his press and types confiscated. At the trial Bradford's type-forms, presented as evidence, were pied by a juryman who used his cane as an aid to its examination. William Bradford was found guilty, but before he was sentenced an extraordinary series of events led not only to his relief and release, but to a complete change in his life, outlook, and circumstances.

History was made by Captain-General Benjamin Fletcher, Governor of New York and Pennsylvania, when he led one hundred and fifty members of the militia up the Hudson River in little sloops to avert a threatened French-Indian attack on Schenectady. Of this exploit the Governor wanted a printed record, so, with a sweeping gesture of magnanimity the Assembly resolved, March 23, 1693: "That if a printer will come and settle in the City of Newyorke for the Printing of our Acts of Assembly & publick papers, he shall be allowed the Summe of forty pounds Current Money of Newyorke per annum for his Sallery & have besides the benefit of the printing that serves the publick." Governor Fletcher hastened to Philadelphia, heard Bradford's petition, dismissed the charges; press and types were restored to Bradford, who then removed them to New York, where he opened his shop sometime in May on Dock (now Pearl) Street, as the Royal Printer.

Manager of the Press of Boston was Samuel Sewall, publicly penitent judge of Salem witchcraft trials, and employer for the Colony of young Samuel Green who had purchased the shop of Marmaduke Johnson. John Allen and Richard Pierce, printers, arrived from England with their presses; a bindery was established to accommodate publishers, and many bookstores flourished in this already bookish hub of Colonial culture; but no printer could legally produce a paragraph of printed words not approved and licensed by diligent Authority.

Disaster crowded upon disaster in the Bay Colony; security was shattered when its Charter was annulled and Colonists were angered and appalled by the excesses of Governor Sir Edmund Andros. They were alarmed by continued Indian warfare, spiritually torn by endless church disputes, and disturbed by the rise of a Tory party. Men and women of the Colony needed news—news of Colonial affairs in the Houses of the British lawmakers, news of the Royal Disposition, news of policies and plans of Colonial Administrators, and news of the hopes and fears of fellow Colonists. They needed to know they were not forgotten by those at "home"; and they needed news of their own America to warm the hearts chilled by long isolation devoid of all news.

The only news to penetrate the almost unendurable silence came in occasional newsletters compiled by friends, relatives, business associates, or professional scriveners at home or abroad. These were shared by hand-to-hand circulation, posted near churches, read by ministers, and made available to customers of coffee house and tavern. The only journals they knew were the London *Gazette* and other English periodicals which were weeks and months old by the time they arrived. But these rarely carried news of the American Colonies or American Colonists.

In 1689 Samuel Green printed and sold a little broadside captioned *The Present State of New-English Affairs*. This faint foreshadowing of the American newspaper reported the progress of Increase Mather, then in England to "explain" the flare-up that had jailed the Royal Governor. It plead for "restoration of the Colony's ancient rights." It was remarkable not because it was "official," an almost forced response to the insistent demand for news, but for its subtitle, *This is Published to Prevent False Reports*, was a first and forthright acknowledgement of a primary responsibility of the free press of all times—To Prevent False Reports.

NEW-ENGLAND.   № 5.

THE
BoſtonGazette.

Publiſhed by Authority.

Nameplate. Boston, December 21, 1719. The first use of woodcuts in an American nameplate, a device made familiar in British Post-Boys. Courtesy of New York Public Library.

2

EARLY NEWSPAPERS

ENGLAND WAS RACKED AND TORN BY STRUGGLES BE-
tween Crown and Parliament, Romanists and Anglicans, Cavaliers and
Roundheads, and the Authorities were far too busy to deal with printers and publishers of the many weekly and semiweekly organs of opposing parties. Stout defenders of the Houses could read the *Kingdom's
Weekly Intelligencer* of Nathaniel Butter, or the *Mercurius Britannicus*
of Marchmont Needham; Royalists could peruse the *Mercurius Alicus*
of John Birkenhead, or the *Perfect Occurrences* of John Clowes. Cath-
olics and Protestants pressed upon each other "Infailable Newes, both

17

Domestick and Foreign," undisturbed by official oversight: a state of affairs welcomed as peace in the pressrooms.

The death of Oliver, the Lord Protector, was reported with a surprisingly modern news treatment by publishers of political tracts, now grown conscious of the tugging of the news; but with the Restoration of the Crown, powerful hands were again outstretched to limit, if not halt, the spreading wave of letters. Roger L'Estrange, slavishly Royalist printer and publisher of political pamphlets, recommended iron gloves and was rewarded with the authority to search for and to seize all unlicensed printing presses. Elevated to the newly created office of Surveyor of the Press, L'Estrange thus gave voice to the sentiments of the elect he so faithfully served: A newspaper "makes the *Multitude* too *Familiar* with the *Actions* and *Councils* of their *Superiors* and gives them not only an *Itch*, but a kind of *Colorable Right* and *Licence* to be meddling with the affairs of *Government*." This L'Estrange published on August 31, 1663, in the first issue of his *Public Intelligencer* which was, perhaps, the first general newspaper. It reflected the eminence of its publisher who was able to dispense death to its rivals. Two years later, in recognizable newspaper format, the London *Gazette* began, in Oxford, its seemingly endless usefulness as Royalty's Official Register.

With the Restoration the Star Chamber Act of 1637 was revived. One John Twyn was hanged on the gallows of Tyburn, convicted of printing a pamphlet in opposition to king and government. Almost all printers more than once suffered fines or jailings. Snipping off the ears of offending printers and "whypings at the Cart's Tayl" were common penalties. William Prynne who had previously been fined and had his ears publicly clipped, again was fined and then branded S.L. (Scurrilous Libeler) on the cheek. But the grasp of the Authority which was slowly forcing printers and publishers to their knees was once again loosened by catastrophe. Master printers, apprentices, and type-founders alike died in the sweep of the great plague, and printers' shops, their presses, types, and paper stocks were consumed in the Great Fire of London.

Of the twenty-odd newspapers launched in the new liberties of the reviving city, the most important was the *Domestick Intelligencer, or, Newes From Both Town and Country*, published "to Prevent False Reports." This was "printed for Benjamin Harris in the Piazza under the Royal Exchange in Cornhill," and not without forced suspensions, from July 1679 to April 1681. The publisher, who was also proprietor of a book-and-coffee shop, was fined, pilloried, and prisoned for pamphlets held seditious. He felt that London was "uneasy," and to evade another season of disquiet, fled to the New World.

In Boston Harris opened another bookshop, published John Tulley's *Almanach*, the classic *New-England Primer*, and other titles, before adding 'tea, coffee and chucaletto' to his wares. And the host who kept on hand files of English journals had ample opportunity to learn the depths of the great American hunger for news. Lacking official sanction, Benjamin Harris of the London Coffee House published the first and last number of the first American newspaper on September 25, 1690. It was printed by Richard Pierce.

Publick Occurrences, Both Foreign and Domestick occupied but three of four six-by-ten-inch pages of a folded half-sheet of paper. The journalist stated his publishing policies at once and with admirable clarity: he would issue the newspaper "once a moneth, or, if any Glut of Occurrences happen, oftener." He planned to expose, with the help of subscribers, the Malicious Raisers of False Reports; and his was the notion that newspapers should help readers understand "the circumstances of Publick Affairs . . . direct their thoughts . . . and affect their Businesses and Negotiations." Benjamin Harris's news was real news and the first and last offered to America for many years. *Publick Occurrences* was brought to an end at once by an outraged administration claiming that it contained "reflections of a very high order." It was printed without Authority, and Authority could not afford to harbor and indulge a fugitive from penalties imposed for similar offenses in the ruling country. An aroused bureaucracy issued a broadside warning against future publications of any kind without "licence first obtained from those appointed by the Government to grant the same." Five years later Harris returned to England, opened another bookshop, and, discovering that English Authority was now less rigorous, began another newspaper, the *London-Post*.

Fourteen years elapsed between the appearance of America's first and second newspapers. John Campbell, a bookseller appointed Postmaster of Boston, was burdened with the chore of writing monthly newsletters to governors and others of importance in the Colonies. The labor of composing and copying these reports that were carried free by the post was shared by his brother, but was so tedious that the frugal and unimaginative Scot could see the advantages of the printing press. Campbell's Boston *News-Letter*, the first newspaper firmly established in the western hemisphere, was first dated From Monday April 17 to Monday April 24, 1704. Only a little larger in size than *Publick Occurrences*, it

was printed on the press of the saintly Bartholomew Green for a continuous twenty-eight years. In its format and style it set all early
American news in a rigid English mold. The first established American
publisher's concept of news was a chronological report of events, although the chill austerity of his "extractions" from back numbers of the
London *Gazette* were lightened by local items, with a few brilliant exceptions stodgily reported by the undertaker.

In the first issue of the *News-Letter* there was but one advertisement:
"This *News-Letter* is to be continued Weekly, and all persons who have
any lands, houses, tenements, farms, ships, vessels, goods, wares or
merchandise to be sold or lett; or servants runaway, or goods Stoll, or
lost, may have the same inserted at a reasonable rate; from Twelve
Pence to Five Shillings and not to exceed. Who may agree with Nicholas
Boone for the same, at his shop next door to Major Davis's apothecary,
in Boston, near the Old Meeting-House. All persons in Town and Country may have the same News-Letter, Weekly, upon reasonable tearms,
agreeing with John Campbell, Post-Master, for the same."

Business was soon represented by advertisements for "Two iron anvils,
weighing between 129 and 140 pounds each" carelessly lost, real estate
for sale in Oyster Bay on Long Island, and an offer of reward for the
capture of a thief.

This, the first newspaper in this country, was never very prosperous,
but the publisher, who complained in his columns of lack of income
and need of money, had enterprise as well as stamina. In 1707 he published America's first news picture, a woodcut, not very large, of the new
flag of the newly united Kingdom of England, Scotland, and Wales.

When John Campbell left his news-strategic situation in the post
office, his successor, William Brooker, harbored the quaint idea that the
News-Letter was a perquisite of title. Campbell refused to surrender,
however, and the new postmaster deemed it necessary to start a new
and "official" newspaper. His first number of the Boston *Gazette*, wearing the woodcuts of the sailing ship and post-rider long familiar to subscribers to England's many Post-Boys, made its appearance on December
21, 1719, twenty-nine years after the stunning explosion of *Publick
Occurrences* and fourteen after the more circumspect *News-Letter*. The
printing of the *Gazette* was given to young James Franklin, who had
recently returned from England with mastery of his craft, an old wooden
press, and some odds and ends of equipment.

Greetings from the country's second newspaper to its third were

scarcely cordial; an early issue of the *Gazette* brought forth this comment from the *News-Letter*:

I pity the readers of the new paper; it is not fit reading for the people.
(Shortly after the *Gazette* was well launched and squarely faced with the
prospect of competition, John Campbell made this very practical suggestion
to his subscribers) . . . and such as have a mind to Pleasure their Friends
with it (the newspaper) per Post may have it every Monday a whole sheet,
one half with the news and the other half good Paper to write their Letter
on, which will fully Obviate that insinuation of People's being prevented
having it that live remote from hence, by only paying a single Postage for
both the news and their Letter every Post.

Within seven months William Brooker could sympathize with his
predecessor; the position of Postmaster of Boston was awarded to Philip
Musgrave who also took over the *Gazette*, the printing of which he
withdrew from James Franklin to give to Samuel Kneeland.

Promptly the pugnacious James, deprived of his most profitable business, decided to start a newspaper of his own. And against the advice of
friends and relatives who warned him that there were already more
newspapers than the country could support, he got out the first number
of his *New-England Courant* on August 7, 1721. His advertised policy
was: "To expose the Vices and Follies of Persons of all Ranks and Degrees under feign'd names, is what no honest man will object against;
and this the Publisher (by the assistance of his Correspondents) is re-
solv'd to persue without Fear, or Affection to any man." Decorous
Boston must have been titillated by Franklin's: "The publisher earnestly
desires his friends may favor him from Time to time, with some short
Piece, Serious, Sarcastic, Ludicrous or otherways amusing; or sometimes
professedly dull (to accommodate some of his acquaintances) that the
Courant may be of the more Universal use. The Undertaker promiseth
that nothing shall be inserted reflecting on the Clergy (as such) of
whatever Denomination, nor relating to the affairs of Government, and
no trespass against Decency and good Manners."

The ever impartial *News-Letter* commented on the newest member
of the country's now dangerously overcrowded profession of newspaper
publishing with the sour: ". . . The New-England Courant . . . by Homo
Unius Negotii, or Jack of All Trades, and, it would seem, Good at
None, . . . giving some very, very frothy fulsome Account of himself . . ."

Plunging gleefully into the wrong side of the controversy between
the clergy, doctors, and laity on the value of inoculation against small-

pox, James Franklin (with the help of a group of correspondents dubbed the Hell-Fire Club by Cotton Mather) made the *Courant* lively reading. Mrs. Silence Dogood was one of the most popular contributors of Comical and Diverting Incidents of Humane Life and, with the Hell-Fire Club, earned for the *Courant* much admiration in London's literary journals.

The government, then undergoing the discomfort of political opposition, permitted the publisher to escape its attentions until the following summer, when Franklin was sent to jail for certain insinuations, some disguised as advertising, concerning the administration's lack of interest in pirates harassing shipping off the New England coast. But while James cultivated a prison pallor, his thirteen-year-old brother and apprentice, Benjamin, composed types, read proof, worked the press, and weekly delivered the *Courant* to Boston subscribers.

Six months later and again in trouble for publishing unseemly remarks, James Franklin was forbidden to print anything without approval of the Secretary of the Province. So young Benjamin's name was substituted for that of James in the imprint of the *Courant*. The lad thus unexpectedly relieved, legally, from his rank as apprentice, and who could not get along with James anyway, ran away to New York and then to Philadelphia. Subscribers to the *Courant* wrote plaintive letters, hopefully printed by James, to inquire with heavy wit: "When will Mrs. Dogood break her Silence?" James apparently never guessed that Mrs. Dogood was none other than little Benny.

Publication of the *Courant* over the name of Benjamin Franklin was continued until 1726. Later James, by invitation, removed to Newport. Here he set up his press to print cash, calico, books and *Poor Robin's Almanac*. His *Rhode Island Gazette*, started in 1732, lived but a few months.

And when after eight years printing orders for the Boston *Gazette* were canceled, Samuel Kneeland, distinguished descendent of Samuel Green, took a leaf from the experience of James Franklin and from his presses at the corner of Dorset's Alley and Prison Lane turned off the *New-England Weekly Journal* from March 20, 1727. Further following the lead of the *Courant*, the *Journal* featured the letters, essays, and verses of its readers, but to the entertainment originated for American newspapers by Franklin, Kneeland added the news that that impishly provocative "Undertaker" failed to appreciate.

The fourth American newspaper, the first outside of Boston, appeared in Philadelphia on the day following the first number of William

Brooker's *Gazette*. The *American Weekly Mercury* was printed and published by Andrew Bradford, son of William, and its news at first, like the news of its two Boston contemporaries, was almost entirely foreign. In an early number Bradford boldly ventured a mild comment on an action desired of the General Assembly and was summoned by Authority for a scolding. The *Mercury* then shortly went to press with the solemn, tongue-in-cheek:

This being a dead time for news, no Vessell having arrived here since our last, Our readers must not expect impossibilities, or that we can entertain them with fresher Advices from England, Spain, France, &c., than already published in our preceding numbers; We shall therefor beg leave to recapitulate on those Heads, with some modest Reflections on the present Mysterious conduct of the European powers.

Local news seeped into the *Mercury's* brief columns slowly but assiduously; shipping news and prices current were regular features and, advancing beyond the Boston concept of news, Andrew Bradford published the court records revealing that Philadelphians convicted of minor crimes were punished with the whip, stating the number of lashes or "lashes on the back" prescribed by stern judges. News could also be found in advertising columns; here gentlemen announced their wives' elopements from beds and boards together with refusals of responsibility for their erstwhile ladies' bills. Plantations and "parcils" of Negroes were offered for sale; instruction could be had in the Italian Method of Book-Keeping, and also lessons in music and dancing. And the offers of peruke makers and other caterers to vanity indicated worldly aspirations and colors under Quaker coats of sober gray.

In addition to his duties as Postmaster and printer of books and pamphlets as well as his newspaper, Andrew Bradford kept a shop in which he sold books, almanacs, whalebone, molasses in barrels, snuff, tobacco, chocolate, and Good Corks. He made and sold lampblack, had "Ready Money on Hand for the purchase of Bees-wax," and was forever distinguished among all Americans of his trade as first to print with inks of two colors, which he did in embellishing the title page of a pamphlet in 1718. It must have been a tense moment in the craft when the big red letters were discovered to read GOVEROVR'S SPCEEH.

The Annapolis *Maryland Gazette*, started by William Parks who came from England expressly to print for the Provincial Assembly, was, in 1727, America's sixth newspaper. In beautiful typography the publisher offered well-written news, knowingly selected "extractions," and well-chosen verses. Letters from readers and subscribers in any way dealing with the cultivation and marketing of tobacco were given front-page space, but this *Gazette* was none too successful in the thinly settled Colony.

When Mr. Parks opened a second shop in Williamsburg there were complaints that he was neglecting his official printing, and his salary was withheld. A man of spirit, Mr. Parks removed to the more hospitable town where in 1736 he established the more gratifying *Virginia Gazette*, the original bearer of the title to be applied to almost all newspapers of the Old Dominion for many years. At one time there were three in Williamsburg alone. In an early number of Mr. Parks' Williamsburg newspaper was the first American advertisement of advertising:

All persons who have occasion to buy or sell Houses, Lands, Goods or Cattle, or have Servants or Slaves Runaway, or have lost Horses, Cattle, &c., or want to give any Public Notice, may have it advertised in all these Gazettes, printed in one Week, for three Shillings, and for two Shillings per Week for as many Weeks afterward as they shall order by giving or sending their Direction to the Printer hereof. And as these Papers will circulate (as speedily as possible) not only in This but also the Neighboring Colonies, and probably will be read by some Thousands of People, it is very likely that they may have the desired effect; and it is certainly the cheapest and most efficient Method that can be taken for Publishing anything of this Nature.

When William Parks, Public Printer of Virginia and a man of importance in sustaining the germs of culture in American life-streams, established a paper-mill in 1744, that great event and the prominence of the publisher were celebrated in verses to compliment The Printer, the Poet's Friend who from poet's rags made possible the printing of their rimes and roundelays.

Back in Philadelphia from London, Benjamin Franklin, that expert young compositor with a flair for writing and genius for money-making, was planning a newspaper to be the second in that city. When this news reached Samuel Keimer, the printer known to his contemporaries for an unkempt beard of amazing length, and remembered by posterity as first to give employment to the runaway from Boston, he at once proposed to set up competition with his unbelievable *Universal Instructor in all the Arts and Sciences; and Pennsylvania Gazette.*

Andrew Bradford's lively weekly was brushed aside by Keimer as "the late Mercury . . . wretchedly perform'd . . . , a Reproach to the Province. . . ." Franklin also publicly professed a low opinion of the *Mercury*, but wisely refrained from wagers on its early demise.

"The Proposer" who "dwelt formerly at the Fountains of Intelligence in Europe" advertised that he had "taken Effectual Methods to be Furnish'd with the most useful, material, pleasant and remarkable Occurences . . ." in "Fair letter and well-corrected . . . to please all and offend none (and that at the reasonable expense of 10 S PER ANNUM)." Further, ". . . this News Paper will in a few Weeks Time after Publication exceed all others that ever were in America, and always being a whole sheet, it will contain at Times, the Theory of all the Arts, both Liberal and Mechanical, and the several Sciences, both human and divine, with Figures, Kinds, Properties, Production, Preparation of Things natural and Artificial; also the Rise, Progress and State of Things Ecclesiastical, Civil, Military and Commercial, and with the several Systems, Sects, Opinions among the Philosophers, Divines, Mathematicians, Antiquaries, &c., after the Alphabetical Order. The whole being the most compleat body of History and Philosophy yet published since Creation." In short, Keimer proposed to print Ephraim Chambers' *Cyclopædia* for the entertainment and edification of any subscribers who might live through the fifty years or more it was estimated its weekly publication would require.

The fall was hard; in the first issue of the *Instructor*, dated December 24, 1728, was: "We have but little news of Consequence at Present, the ENGLISH prints being generally stufft with Robberies, Cheats, Fires, Murders, Bankruptcies, Promotions for some and Hangings for others; nor can we expect much better until Vessells arrive in the Spring, when we hope to inform our readers what has been doing in the Court and Cabinet, in the Parliament-House as well as the Sessions-House, so that we wish, in our AMERICAN world, it may be said, as Dr. Wild so wittily express'd it, viz: 'We are all seiz'd with the Athenian itch, News and New Things do the whole world bewitch.' In the meantime we hope our readers will be content for the present with what we can give 'em, which if it does 'em no Good, shall do 'em no Hurt. 'Tis the best we have and so take it." The *Instructor* managed to survive for nine months and secured not more than ninety subscribers.

Thankfully Samuel Keimer sold his newspaper to Benjamin Franklin and his partner, Hugh Meredith, whose shares Franklin was soon able to purchase. The *Cyclopædia* that had progressed only to AIR was discarded and the long title shortened. In their first number of the *Pennsylvania Gazette*, "From Thursday September 25th to Thursday October

2nd, 1729," the Authors and Printers made their modest bow to the
public they hoped with all their hearts to win to subscription lists:

> . . . we are fully sensible, that to publish a good News-Paper is not so easy
> an Undertaking as many people imagine it to be. The Author of this Gazette
> (in the opinion of the learned) ought to be qualified with an extensive
> acquaintance of the languages, a great Easiness and Command of writing
> and Related Things clearly and intelligently and in a few words; He should
> be able to speak of War by Land and Sea; be well acquainted with Geog-
> raphy and History of the Time; with the several interests of the Princes and
> the States, the Secrets of the Courts and the Manners and Customs of all
> Nations. Men thus accomplished are very rare in this part of the World,
> and it would be well if the Writer of the Papers could make up among his
> Friends what is wanting in himself.

This epitome of good sense in the pressroom was the much-quoted
guide to aspiring publishers and ambitious printers long after the newspaper it initiated was forgotten.

The Pennsylvania Gazette, which came into the hands of Benjamin
Franklin when he was twenty-three years old, he made with his breadth
of vision, urbanity and political poise the leading newspaper of colonial America, as well as its most prosperous. Franklin's Germantown
Philadelphische Zeitung, started in 1732, and the first foreign-language
newspaper in this country, failed. Seven years later Der Hoch-Deutsch
Pennsylvanische Geschict-Schreiber (The High German Pennsylvania
History, or, Collection of Important News) came from the press of the
Dunkers settled in Ephrata, Lancaster County. The newspaper, printed
by German workmen on a press imported from Germany and on stock
from the mill set up on Cacalico Creek by Peter Miller and the brothers
Samuel and Charles Funk, Germany-trained papermakers, was published
under the management of Christopher Sower, also successful at farming, tailoring, and building stoves. Franklin was humiliated by Sower's
success in serving the "Pennsylvania Dutch." As calendars were turned
from 1741 to 1742 Franklin lost the honor of being first with a monthly
publication; his General Magazine and Historical Chronical, for all the
British Plantations in America followed by three days the American
Magazine, or a Monthly View of the Political State of the Colonies of
Andrew Bradford. Franklin's Gazette also had to compete for local favors with the Mercury until 1742 when Andrew Bradford died. And
the Weekly Advertiser, or Pennsylvania Journal almost immediately offered by William Bradford, trained and educated at his uncle's presses,

soon acquired great local popularity with both subscribers and advertisers.

But the shrewdest of businessmen in the pressroom had already started to extend his sources of income beyond his shop, his bookstore, and his publications. As a silent partner he assisted other printers (his apprentices, his relatives, the protégés of his friends, and his own foreign discoveries) to set up presses in promising localities, supplying them with presses, types, tools, and stock, and profiting by interest on money advanced, on a percentage of the earnings, and returns on the sale of further necessities of the trade.

One of Franklin's young men, Thomas Whitmarsh, applied for the advertised position of Printer to the Provincial Assembly of South-Carolina; but after prolonged consideration of three applicants, the Assembly awarded the office to Eleazer Philips from the Boston shop of Thomas Fleet. It was Philips who published the first newspaper south of Annapolis, starting in 1732 the Charleston *South-Carolina Weekly Journal* of which no known copy remains; its brief existence closed with his death. Already in Charleston, Whitmarsh had begun early in the same year his own *South-Carolina Gazette* which survived the *Journal* by about six months before also dying with its printer. Then the French-born and Holland-trained Huguenot, Louis Timothée, arrived to take charge of the Franklin-controlled partnership and two years later, over the Anglicized name of Lewis Timothy, revived the *South-Carolina Gazette*.

The entertainment offered to subscribers by Timothy was more sophisticated than that provided by other publishers from Boston to Annapolis, but the news in the *Gazette*, a small folio and expensive at 15 Shillings per Quarter-annum, was thin and lacking in vitality except in the reporting of the theater; even the advertising columns offered little of the news that would today contribute to a picture of life as it was lived in Charleston two centuries ago. Franklin considered Timothy a "man of learning, but ignorant in the matter of accounts." After his death the widow, Elizabeth Timothy, continued to print and to publish the newspaper to support herself and six children. Her excellent bookkeeping enabled her to buy the shares of her admiring silent partner at the end of the Charleston agreement.

Thomas Fleet, at whose type-cases Charleston's first publisher had mastered his craft, came from England, a Shropshire lad, in 1712, and three years later married another Elizabeth. This Elizabeth was the daughter of Elizabeth Goose, or Vergoose, the Mother Goose who is said to have sung the famous nursery rimes to her children. Fleet is popularly credited with having printed these in 1719; but no copy has ever been found. Fleet was an accomplished printer and a capable businessman. The busy shop where presses worked by his apprentices and talented slaves thumped, creaked, and groaned from sun-up to sundown was in his Cornhill residence, where as an auctioneer he held evening sales of household furnishings, books and "other articles too numerous to mention" in his Commodious Front Chamber.

In 1733 Fleet bought the *Weekly Rehearsal* of distinct London literary flavor which had been established two years previously by Jeremiah Gridley, a young lawyer who had wearied of writing the essays and articles on politics, economics, and public morals that were the very substantial burden of Boston's sixth newspaper. Fleet, who had for a time been Gridley's printer, after two years changed the title to the *Evening-Post*.

Fleet's news had a new and refreshing sprightliness and charmed subscribers to those serious and plodding Boston newspapers whose "Undertakers" were inclined towards the sable. His news comments, like his news items, were often slyly malicious, sometimes nakedly sarcastic, and embarrassed the prissier of the Puritans. The more robust called them humorous. His opinions on public affairs brought him into disrepute with often ruffled Authority. He was hauled before the Council, but even that failed to discourage his talent. And when the preachers of the town publicly denounced the *Evening-Post* as a "dangerous engine, a sink of sedition, error and heresey," Fleet established a publishing precedent by printing a full account of the trial of John Peter Zenger. Thereafter Thomas Fleet, who made the *Evening-Post* Boston's best newspaper, felt free to regale his customers as he chose, and he frequently chose to make rude gestures in the general direction of his enemies, the clergy. Boston gossips could continue to clack with genteel sadistic joy as they read such delectable items as:

We hear for certain that the famous Mr. Gilbert Tennant has left his little Flock at Brunswick and is gone to preach at Philadelphia in the great House built there for Mr. Whitefield. It is reported one reason for his removal was want of success and 'tis said he is become a meer Beau since he married a rich wife.

But the *Evening-Post* was not very well supported by advertisers, and that the publisher found difficulty in collecting from his subscribers he made clear on October 24, 1743:

The season of the Year now approaching wherein MONEY will be in demand, the Publisher of the Paper desires his long-winded customers to consider whether 2,3,4,5 and 6 years credit (which they have taken by Force) is not more than is consistent with the strict rules of Justice, Honesty and the High Professions that many of them made.

Profitless though it may have been, Thomas Fleet, the successful businessman, continued to get out the *Evening-Post* until his death in 1758, and thereafter two of his sons issued it regularly until the crucial 1775.

Cartoon—the severed serpent—from Pennsyl-
vania Gazette, Philadelphia, May 19, 1754.
The first political cartoon to appear in an
American newspaper. Courtesy of New York
Public Library.

3

THE BRIGHT MORNING STAR
OF FREEDOM

'THE KING'S PRINTER FOR NEW YORK,' WILLIAM BRAD-
ford, climaxed forty years of press pioneering when, on November 8,
1725, he published New York's first newspaper, another weekly *Gazette*.

The New York *Gazette* was born tethered to the spurious respectability of caste. Extractions from its London namesake and other English
periodicals suffered, together with any domestic or local news the publisher might choose to admit, from poor editing and indifferent printing.
In spite of frequent pleas for support and threats to "cease from publishing the same," the newspaper continued, never quite a success.

From its first number the Gazette was the recognized mouthpiece of the government and it loyally and unhesitatingly assumed the role of defender of the grasping regime of the very ambitious and extravagant William Cosby.

On arriving in New York, Governor Cosby demanded of Rip Van Dam, last of the Dutch in the Council and Governor ex-officio for thirteen months, all the salary and revenues paid to him while in office. Cosby's intemperate claims were followed by a lawsuit conducted with such injustice that public resentment created a firm party in opposition to the administration. Leadership in this movement was both intelligent and articulate, and with its assistance John Peter Zenger, Bradford's one-time apprentice and former business partner, started on November 5, 1733 the city's second newspaper, the Weekly-Journal.

Zenger's Weekly-Journal published the letters of brash correspondents bent on airing unorthodox views on the rights of the people to trials by jury, to a voice in their government, and to a free press, therein drawing heavily on the Letters of Cato by John Trenchard and Thomas Gordon on these same themes. Already published in London newspapers, these Letters were known to be anathema to all transient colonial Authority. And in letters to the Gazette the faithful supported the administration, and damned Zenger with long quotations from England's Tory writers; but their platitudes were no match for the doggerel probably printed by Zenger and pushed under the doors of the important by night. A mocking advertisement for a redcoat-clad monkey of the larger sort LOST in Westchester was printed in Zenger's advertising columns with the audacity of fools or the inspired.

The infuriated Cosby stormed the House of Representatives commanding compliance to his order for the arrest and punishment of John Peter Zenger. He also wanted all copies of the "News-paper Printed and Published by the contrivance of some evil and disaffected Persons" destroyed. The legislators permitted the matter to Lye on the Table, and the Governor next demanded that Numbers 7,47,48 and 49 of the offending newspaper be "burned by the common Hangman or Whyper, near the Pillory." Again ignored, he called in the sheriff and "the sheets" were destroyed by that worthy's slave.

Zenger was arrested on November 17, 1734, charged with seditious libel. He was held in prison for nearly nine months during which time he had "only the Liberty of Speaking through the Hole in the Door" to his wife and servants, but from which, with their help, he continued the publication of the Weekly-Journal, missing only one number. His dignified and courageous conduct won admiration as well as sympathy from an interested country.

With the high hand of the petty tyrant, Governor Cosby removed the Chief Justice, Lewis Morris, from the bench to replace him with the more pliant James Delany. James Alexander and William Smith, Zenger's counsel, protested, attacking the validity of the appointment, and for this impertinence were disbarred, leaving the prisoner without legal defense.

The Zenger case, a matter of personal concern to all thinking men, was clearly a test of strength between an arbitrary executive and the people, and the administration intended the trial to provide a resounding triumph for the crown and a complete vindication of the Governor. So it was a thrilling surprise to the men who crowded into the hot, low-ceiled courtroom on the morning of August 4, 1735, when an elderly man—tall, thin, white-thatched, and distinguished—rose to permit court and spectators to discover that the humble printer would be defended by the celebrated Andrew Hamilton of Philadelphia, the most eminent lawyer in all the colonies, and whose presence had been secured secretly by Judge Morris, Alexander Smith, Rip Van Dam, and others well aware of the importance of the now impending contest.

A sharp "Order in the Court!" brought whispering to an end and set the stage for history. Hamilton astonished the court by readily admitting that his client had printed and published the evidence presented by the prosecution. But, contended Hamilton, the publication was truth and therefore Zenger could not be guilty of libel. The court ruled that printing alone was sufficient reason for conviction and refused to allow Hamilton to argue his interpretation of the law. Turning to the jury, in the most important appeal heard in American colonial courts, Hamilton charged perversion of the statute limited by its wording to the prosecution of the "false, scandalous or seditious" and asked that they "determine both the Law and the Fact, and where they do not doubt the Law they ought to do so"; . . . "it is in the Cause of Liberty . . . the Liberty of speaking and writing Truth."

The court held to the opinion that libel was libel even when it was the truth "and so much more provoking" to a government dependent on good opinion for security. Curtly it instructed the jury to "find Zenger printed and published those papers and leave it to the Court to judge whether or not they are libelous." Thomas Hunt, jury foreman, had the honor of reporting that twelve good men and true challenged Authority for all time with a verdict of Not Guilty. Three mighty Huzzahs rocked the hall; the court's gavel banged; officers shouted "Order, Order, Order in the Court." Thus the cornerstone of American freedom slid into its appointed place.

Andrew Hamilton was enthusiastically banqueted by John D'Honneur's Black Horse Tavern and given "the Seal of the Corporation in a Golden Box" as a "Public Testimony of the Glorious Defense he made in the Cause of Liberty." Zenger returned to his family, and his press got out the next Weekly-Journal with a full account of the trial; this was freely reprinted by newspapers of other colonies whose "authority" was without affection for other colonial governments and was also bound in a pamphlet for many reprintings in America and in England. The success won by Hamilton for the printer who defied the government was the first step towards free-flowing news and the essence of American rights to write, speak, print, hear, and read the truth.

From now on glimmerings of a free press were discernible; but early newspapers were cautious, for it was still fatally easy for a determined Authority to ignore, if not to suppress the voice of the people, to snuff out of existence any irritating publication. Yearly the colonists, whose eyes, ears, and minds were opened by the great debate of the letter writers, were less inclined to bare their heads and bend their knees when in the presence of representatives of Royal Government, and yearly the opposition to succeeding administrations assumed, with brightening clarity, the outline and form of the organized resistance whose ultimate goal was to be complete independence and freedom.

John Peter Zenger died in 1744 but the New-York Weekly-Journal continued: "Printed by the Widow, Catharine (sometimes spelled Catherine) Zenger at the 'Printing-Office on Stome-street' where advertisements are taken in" until she was succeeded by her stepson, John Zenger. Its mission accomplished, the first American crusader outlasted its stout-hearted founder only by about five years.

The next New York newspaper was the Weekly Post-Boy (1742) of James Parker, who, like John Peter Zenger, had been apprenticed to Bradford. Parker was a better printer than the pioneer and his the better newspaper. Press and types were supplied by Benjamin Franklin. The retiring Bradford turned over the Gazette, still dragging its "official" chains, to a partner, Henry DeForeest, who coldly abandoned it to begin the town's first Evening-Post. It was then that the suave and tactful silent member of James Parker and Company probably prompted the change of title to The New York Gazette, Revived in Weekly Post-Boy.

Signs of changes following the great "tryal" were first visible in Boston.

The *News-Letter* and the *Weekly Journal* that in the first of American newspaper mergers had embraced the old *Gazette*, continued in plodding dignity, but in the *Evening-Post* Thomas Fleet teased and tempted an administration determinedly blind. Ellis Huske, last of Boston's publishing postmasters, pleased all and offended none with his *Post-Boy* by bowing from a tightrope to the bureaucracy that employed him, while tossing to subscribers, however, a few nuggets of real news. Boston advertising offered real estate as far away as Danbury, Connecticut, and Newport, Rhode Island. Local appreciation was flagged by such notices as those of a Mr. Scott who was anxious to sell "some HAY over against Mrs. Payne's, near the Fortification," and Paul Revere, father of the noted excursionist, who offered to prospective consumers Choice, Good Blubber at his address Near the Red Cross.

The bright colors of the rebellious illuminated the columns of the Boston *Independent Advertiser* in a misadventure almost fatal to printers and publishers Gamaliel Rogers and Daniel Fowle. It was started on January 4, 1748, and was the quietly adopted organ of a group of young intellectuals organized by Samuel Adams in the Whipping-Post Club. Embarrassed when they discovered the cause of their popularity with subscribers and correspondents the owners, pushed into strange waters by the club members who met in an attic to smoke, drink "flip," and compose their letters to the *Advertiser*, retired from circulation with the issue of December 5, 1749. Slowly new newspapers, less cautious and less concerned with the whims and prejudices of colonial administrations, were firmly established on solid grounds of reader-service, and, like actors, waited in political wings for the cues that would summon them to undreamed subscriber usefulness.

Jonas Green, of America's First Family of Printers, went with his bride from New London to Annapolis by way of the Philadelphia presses of Thomas Bradford and Benjamin Franklin. And the "popular Postmaster, printer, and publisher," also "poet, purveyor and punchmaker" besides being an alderman, an auctioneer, a vestryman, secretary of the Masonic lodge, and clerk of the races, revived in 1745 the *Maryland Gazette* of William Parks. Green's *Gazette* lived almost a century, the seasoned patriot newspaper published after his death by the widowed Catharine, his sons, and his grandsons.

Repeating the publishing pattern farther down on the coast, James Davis, believed to be from Virginia and the printer of Virginia's first *Gazette*, came to New-Bern, North Carolina, in 1740 to assume the responsibilities of Official Printer to the Province, and on August 9,

1751, was born the *North-Carolina Gazette*. Its four small pages, two columns to each page, carried little news from any source, little correspondence from subscribers, and not much advertising beyond that of the owner who was, at different times, a member of the House of Burgesses, magistrate, and sheriff, as well as (steadily) job-printer, publisher, and bookbinder. Issue of this newspaper was irregular, and after a long suspension the printer and publisher gave it a fresh start as the *North-Carolina Magazine, or, Universal Intelligencer*. It could be distinguished from its predecessor only by its somewhat unconventional "entertainment," the serialized Account of the Life of Mohammed as Contained in the Koran. But this acorn among newspaper oaks of patriotism had the rugged pioneer virtue of durability; it outlasted the provincial government indirectly responsible for its institution.

Probably drawn and cut into a wood block for printing by Benjamin Franklin himself, the first political cartoon to appear in any American newspaper was published in the *Pennsylvania Gazette* on May 8, 1754. A sensational serpent, carved into eight sections, one part named for all New England and one part for each of the seven other colonies, urged all to "Unite, Fit and Conquer" the warring French and their Indian allies. Speedily and effectively reproduced in other newspapers the severed serpent was later the accepted symbol of the need for colonists to "Unite, or Die," in defense of their reasonable and self-respecting liberties of life, thought, and action threatened by another enemy.

Twenty years after the trial of John Peter Zenger and twenty years before blood was spilled on Lexington's Common, the first authentic newspaper spearhead of independence was delivered to its subscribers. Benjamin Eades and John Gill bought from Samuel Kneeland and Timothy Green the *New-England Journal* to which they had added, by purchase, the *Gazette* printed for a time by Kneeland for Philip Musgrave. They retitled it *Gazette, or, Country Journal* and made it into an utterly fearless and independent organ of American patriots on April 7, 1755. The publishers were unabashed when Governor Hutchinson bestowed upon them the epithet of Trumpeters of Sedition, and their hospitable columns were open as usual to the letters of Samuel Adams after he had been publicly branded as the Grand Incendiary. They also welcomed and published the white-hot epistles of John Adams, James Otis, Joseph Quigley, Joseph Warren, Samuel Cooper, and others.

Scarcely had the first copies of this rejuvenated *Gazette* been taken from the presses before the education of another famous patriot printer began in earnest. Benjamin Franklin and William Hunter, "Joint Deputy Post-Masters General of the British Colonies in North-America," appointed James Parker of the New York printing firm of which Franklin was a partner, to the postmastership of New Haven, Connecticut. Although it had been the seat of Yale for fifty years, the town was still without press or printer until, financed wholly or in part by the ubiquitous Franklin, Parker and Company acquired the old press of John Peter Zenger that was sold at auction and had it transported by sloop to the shop opened in charge of Hunter's brother-in-law, John Holt. Thus, Holt, printer from Williamsburg and the acting Master of the Posts between New Haven, New York, Hartford, and New London, entered a long and distinguished publishing career with the colony's first newspaper, the *Connecticut Gazette*, first issued on April 12, 1755.

It had been Benjamin Franklin's intention to provide in New Haven a comfortable berth for Benjamin Mecom, a son of his favorite sister, Jane. Mecom had gone reluctantly to St. John, Antigua, to manage another Franklin-controlled press and newspaper; but convinced that his talents were wasting away in this remote printing outpost and fearful that he had been forgotten by his uncle, Mecom packed up the press and crated the stock for shipment to Boston, his home town, to which he returned to publish his unsuccessful *New-England Magazine of Knowledge and Pleasure*. In Boston the young man earned his wide reputation as the country's best-dressed printer. Isaiah Thomas, then a small boy, might have been pardoned for staring at Mecom, elegant from ribbon-tied bob wig to silver shoebuckles. "I viewed Mecom with admiration," he wrote. "Mecom indeed put on an apron to save his clothes from blacking, and guarded his ruffles; but he wore his coat, his wig, his hat, and his gloves while working at press; and at case laid aside his apron."

From Boston Mecom went to New York, and on July 11, 1763, he started a newspaper, the *Paquette*, at "The Modern Printing-Office on Rotten Row." Well organized, well printed, interesting in content, and well supported by advertisers, the *Paquette* was for some mysterious reason permitted to expire after about six weeks. Not until the following year did Mecom arrive in New Haven where he found the *Gazette* suspended, John Holt in New York, and the printshop in charge of Thomas Green from New London. Appointed New Haven's new postmaster, Mecom also took charge of the printshop and revived the *Gazette* only to abandon it in 1767 for the uncertainties of Philadelphia, where he published a few numbers of the *Penny Post*, the country's first triweekly, before he also deserted this venture. Genius flared again a few years later when Benjamin Mecom, then an employee of another printer, made and printed from stereotype plates. In this, too, he lost interest at the moment success was certain.

A Franklin of a different caliber was James, the son of the printer and publisher of Boston and Newport. Ann Franklin had with the help of her two daughters, both very capable printers, served as Printer to the Colony of Rhode-Island and published over her own masthead "The Widow Franklin," while James learned his trade at Uncle Benjamin's Philadelphia presses. Returning to Newport a master printer, James worked with his mother at the Printing-house on Tillinghast's Wharf, near the Union Flag Tavern before establishing, on June 19, 1758, the *Mercury, or, Weekly Advertiser*. Under a nameplate showing Mercury guiding a sailing ship straight to Tillinghast's Wharf while the British flag billowed over an old stone tower in the background, the publisher set his price for the news of which ". . . Dearth . . . in this remote part of the World may reasonably be expected" at "One Dollar a Year as long as the present size of the Paper is Continu'd." He forestalled criticism by adding ". . . if it should be said, that the size is much smaller than those at present publish'd in Philadelphia, New York and Boston, let it be consider'd that the Price is also much smaller in Proportion." And the future of the still-living title was assured when copies of the weekly were bundled for the Proper Persons in their Respective Towns for delivery to subscribers in return for, each, ". . . one copy, Free and Gratis, for their Care and Trouble."

The too-independent publishers of the Boston *Independent Advertiser* parted company in 1750. Daniel Fowle, who went to work with his brother, Zachariah, was accused of printing a pamphlet called *The Monster of Monsters*, which was held to be an allegorical insult to the administration. He was arrested and although not proved guilty—all Boston knew that Zachariah was the culprit—he was jailed for five days. Vigorously Daniel Fowle protested his innocence; vigorously he tried to obtain redress and, failing, he vigorously expressed his disgust with the government he rejected to depart, by invitation, for one more discriminating. From Portsmouth, October 7, 1756, Daniel Fowle sent out the first *New-Hampshire Gazette*, the country's farthest-east newspaper, and his unusual nameplate included The Fox and the Crow from a series of small woodcuts brought along by the printer to illustrate *Æsop's Fables*. In his salutatory Fowle promised to refrain from the "abuse of the Liberty of the PRESS," a promise so faithfully kept that he was reckoned by patriots as "Too timid in the Cause."

The thin edge of the sharp blade that was to sever America from England slashed through newspapers "reporting" the war with the French and Indians. Letters from Acadia, Louisburg, Crown Point, Ticonderoga, and Quebec brought stale news made vaporous by the exalting of British officers and ignoring of the men who were meeting hardship and suffering as Americans. Adjoining advertisements revealed heavy desertions; titled commanders, comfortably billeted in American cities, offered rewards for information and delivery of His Majesty's "foot" departed, and threatened penalties of severest rigor to those suspected of feeding, sheltering, or clothing the same deserters.

To heavy taxes extracted for payment for this war had been added, in New York and Massachusetts, taxes on newspapers. The poverty of the press was obvious when publishers turned their newspapers to print late or continued news along narrow margins. Sharing advertising costs, Elizabeth Phaem, who sold all sorts of Dry Goods Cheap and who was short of Credit and needed Ready Money, permitted—under LIKEWISE in larger types—the announcement of Doctor Mulligan of the same Beaver-street address to tell the world of 1755 (via Parker's *Post-Boy*) that he sold Turlington's Balm of Life, Double Strength or Single, as well as Drugs and Medicines in General, Chymical and Galenical, neat, as imported. Yet in times as hard as these American newspapers multiplied and started their climb to a new usefulness to subscribers. The politics and policies of publishers began to lure letters from both foes and friends, and their newspapers became gradually the medium for the outpourings of a people just finding its voice. And new newspapers from old presses gave employment and education to a coming generation of printers and publishers.

Thomas Green, after Benjamin Mecom's full-dress assault on Yale, went to Hartford to circulate a prospectus for a newspaper for that colonial capital and, encouraged, set up his press over the shop of a barber to produce on November 19, 1764 the first *Connecticut Courant*. Three years later he left a thriving business in charge of a partner to return to New Haven where, with his brother, Samuel Green, he launched the *Connecticut Journal and New Haven Post-Boy*, and both newspapers, sturdy patriots, are, with changes wrought by time, still published.

Summoned by an ailing father, Timothy Green left the Boston shop he shared with his cousin, Samuel Kneeland, to return to New London where he started the *Summary* that came to an end with his death five years later. Then his nephew, Timothy Green, "the third," suspended its publication to bring out in November of 1763 the *New-London Gazette* which he later renamed the *Connecticut Gazette*. This latest of *Gazettes* was a small folio, each page printed to three columns. It was not very well printed and its "matereal" lacked organization, but Timothy Green, the third, was outstanding among colonial publishers for his sense of what makes news. He printed local obituaries and announcements of weddings other than those of important people, and was first to realize that customers sometimes enjoyed the thrills of a good scare. On August 10, 1764, he printed "An alarming report from Boston" to the effect that "We hear from Bristol, in the Colony of Rhode-Island, that a Tiger was seen in Town a few days ago, which killed several dogs." The *Gazette* of Timothy Green also always carried a little Poet's Corner, and advertisements "interesting to Mariners and Gentlemen in From the Sea" were plentiful: a full page unit not unusual in these days of modest "cards."

In defense of that popular song *Yankee Doodle* which affected the pulses and temperatures of patriots and Tories alike, he printed perhaps the original (and interesting, however far-fetched) letter to the newspapers on the subject: "A correspondent in Philadelphia has favored us with the following etymology of the word Yankee."

When the New-England Colonies were first settled, the inhabitants were obliged to fight their way against many Nations of Indians. They found little difficulty in subduing all except one tribe who were known by the name of Yankoos, which signifies *invincible*. After the waste of much blood and treasure, the Yankoos were at last subdued by the New-Englishmen. The remains of this Nation (agreeable to the Indian custom) transferred their name to their conquerors. For a while they were called Yankoos; but from a corruption, common to names in all languages, they got, through time, the name of Yankees, a name we hope will soon be equal to that of a Roman, or an ancient Englishman.

Another Green, Bartholomew, died in 1732 and the Boston *News-Letter* of which he was both printer and publisher became the property of his son-in-law, John Draper. Draper improved the venerable pioneer with the news solicited from the "Rev. Ministers and others"—his appeal in itself a news item of interest. Twenty-five years later John Green, a grandson of Bartholomew Green, with Joseph Russell started the Boston *Weekly Advertiser* to which they added the *Post-Boy*. They also published a supplement called the *Massachusetts Gazette*, which they shared with Richard Draper for insertion in the *News-Letter*. And Green and Russell, staunch Tories, were gratefully appointed Printers to the Governor, Council and House of Representatives, by an administration wishing to prove to publishers everywhere that loyalty to power paid.

Money was scarce and the comparatively few who could afford to subscribe to the newspapers shared their copies with an estimated five families each, and resentment aroused by the Stamp Act of 1765 outran and overshadowed the wrath of mere publishers. Prestamped paper taxed at a halfpenny to two shillings each sheet and taxes of two shillings on every advertisement printed would limit news to letters, imported newspapers and journals, and irresponsible broadsides.

Patrick Henry's protest against "Taxation without representation" was reported for Jonas Green's *Maryland Gazette* by Charles Carroll and was printed without reprimand, but when the Virginia Resolves were reprinted in the Newport *Mercury* that newspaper was suspended, but without discouragement to other publishers. And atop the *Constitutional Gazette* "Printed by Andrew Marvel, at the Sign of the Bribe Refused" on "Constitutional Hill, North-America," appeared another severed serpent with the words "Join, or Die," on September 21, 1765: a broadside manifesto against the Stamp Act. Two whole printings were hawked on New York's streets before the Authorities, who did not agree that it contained "news of matters interesting to LIBERTY and in no wise repugnant to LOYALTY," got the situation in hand and learned that printer William Goddard had produced this insult on the Woodbridge, New Jersey, press of James Parker.

By common consent November 1, 1765, the day the Stamp Act became effective, was a day of mourning; bells were tolled, flags half-masted, and Liberty buried to the muffled roll of drums. In Philadelphia William Bradford's newspaper was illustrated with cuts of skulls, crossbones, tombstones, black bands, and lugubrious legends completed with a cut of a coffin under the words: "The last Remains of the PENNSYL-VANIA JOURNAL, which departed this life on the 31st of October, 1765, of a Stamp in her vitals."

British agents were terrorized, their superiors hung in effigy; stamps were seized and destroyed; meetings and delegations listened to speeches of the Sons of Liberty, and the Act was repealed. Liberty, "showing signs of Life," was disinterred; newspapers returned to publication; and patriots discovered in their press a powerful partner ready and willing to help build the bulwarks of independence. New vigor swept into pressrooms to welcome correspondence full of new ideas and charged with new energy and confidence.

Newsy, well-organized, and well-printed was the *Massachusetts Spy*, started on July 17, 1770 by Isaiah Thomas. The printer and publisher who at the age of seven years had been apprenticed to Zachariah Fowle and, at eighteen after a serious fracas had run away to wander from adventure to adventure in romance and printing from Charleston to Halifax, now returned to Boston to work with his former master. The *Spy*, an effective medium for many of the most thoughtful of the letter writers, was soon branded by the administration as "incendiary," and any benefit of the doubt was dispelled by the publisher's own version of "Join, or Die" at his nameplate. Thomas's serpent was no longer severed and it weekly bared its angry fangs in defiance of a strange composite animal created from the armorial bearings of England, Scotland, and Wales: a lion, dragon-winged, with a griffon's head and clearly on the defensive.

The news found in subscribers' letters to the various "Undertakers" of their newspapers had a new firmness when the Mutiny Act, attempting to force colonists to shelter and feed the troops who would enforce payment of taxes on colonial necessities, stirred the wrath of patriots. Another broadside, this addressed to the Betrayed Inhabitants of New York, sent Authority scurrying to the press of the retired James Parker from whom they learned that the author was Alexander McDougall, who was arrested and clapped into jail. McDougall refused to give bail and in jail McDougall stayed. His visitors were so numerous that he had to have "cards" in local newspapers announcing that he would be at home to his friends "at the New Goal, from Three O'Clock in the Afternoon until Six." The action of the Assembly designating McDougall's protest as "rebellious" was recorded on page forty-five of that body's Journal, so Forty-Five was the password of local patriots who, on February 14, the forty-fifth day of 1770, took to the New Gaol forty-five pounds of beefsteaks cut from bullocks forty-five months old and other provender to give McDougall a dinner, complete with toasts, to provide news for circulation among the galleries of the irreverent.

American newspapers expanded to new latitudes of usefulness with the independent and peppery William Goddard, a consistent and constructive rebel against American as well as British gagging of the press.

The New London printer from the New Haven press of James Parker chose Providence as a "commercial city likely to appreciate the conveniences of a good Newspaper," but the *Gazette, and Country*

Journal that he started in 1762 was not very successful. After three years of trying the publisher turned over all his business to his mother, Sarah Goddard, and found employment with John Holt in New York. From New York it was but a step to Philadelphia by the Flying Machine which, roads and weather permitting, made the trip in two days, and in the City of Brotherly Love, Goddard rented a press from Benjamin Franklin, wrote his mother to send down some types from the shop under the Sign of Shakespeare's Head, and with two partners, Joseph Galloway, a lawyer, and Thomas Wharton, a merchant, issued, in 1767, the first number of the *Pennsylvania Chronical, and Universal Advertiser.*

Galloway insisted on admitting to the firm a fourth member, Benjamin Towne, and soon the newspaper was suspended, while printers Goddard and Towne confined their time and energy to the production of spiteful pamphlets vindicating neither of the bellowing contestants. Goddard also fought with Galloway who was of Tory convictions (Towne's politics depended on the wind) and in a temper departed for Baltimore. The press of Baltimore's first printer was purchased from the widow of Nicholas Hasselback and on it, on August 20, 1773, Goddard established the *Maryland Journal and Baltimore Advertiser.* Six months later this excellent and thriving newspaper was left in the capable hands of his sister, Mary Katherine Goddard, a compositor of talent, while Goddard himself was "to be absent on business interesting to the common Liberties of America."

Goddard's mysterious business was the organization of a postal system to compete with that under the control of the British. He traveled throughout the colonies and on his return announced that the necessary capital had been secured through sales of stock, and that postmasters and post-riders had been engaged for "Goddard's Post-Offices"—a private enterprise that flourished until taken over by an enactment of Congress on July 26, 1775. Not only was Goddard uncompensated and unrewarded for his system (today the Post Office Department) that forced the British from American roads, but, as noted by the always news-alert Timothy Green in his *Gazette* of the following August 18: "Philadelphia, . . . The Honorable Continental Congress has established a Continental Post-Office, and has appointed Dr. Benjamin Franklin to be Post-Master General of the United Colonies of America at a salary 1000 Dollars a year."

In the Boston *Gazette* of Eades and Gill, the most popular of newspapers in the bundles sent by the Committee on Correspondence to

patriots of all the colonies, there had been already circulated a letter
from Samuel Adams urging "an Independent American Commonwealth." Fittingly, on November 29, 1773, there was exciting news
well-displayed for the reading of all but the British, in this standard-
bearer:

Friends! Brethren! Countrymen! The work of Plagues, the detested
TEA shipped for the Port by the East India Company is now arrived in
this Harbor. The Hour of Destruction or Manly Opposition to the Machina-
tions of Tyranny Stares you in the Face; every Friend to his Country, to
himself, and to Posterity is now called on to meet at Faneuil Hall at Nine
O'Clock THIS DAY (for which Time the Bells will ring) to make a united
and forceful Resistance to this last, worst and most Destructive Measure
of the Administration.

And the men who met with the editor of the *Gazette* to don Indian
paint and feathers voted the Boston Tea Party an unqualified success.

Samuel Hall, son-in-law of Ann Franklin, publisher with his brother
Ebenezer of the *Essex Gazette* of Salem, sent a horseman into Boston
weekly for the latest news on the rebellion then beginning to seethe.
Thus new vistas of news while it was news were discovered by American newsmen.

Policy plainly labeled every pre-Revolution newspaper of America.
Publishers were too "fair and impartial" and in the worsening relations
were popular with neither patriot nor Tory. Loyalists looked for news
from "home" and wrote their condemnation of the "rise of the Spirit
of Mutiny" and its leaders; and patriots in patriot newspapers held forth
on themes rapidly contracting to Liberty, or Death. Currents deep and
strong beyond stopping were swirling through the country's pressrooms.

Silently by night Isaiah Thomas left Boston to meet Paul Revere
and warn the countryside of the nearing fracas. With press types and
"utensils" already sent to Worcester he could report the battle of Lexington from first-hand knowledge, in the first issue of the *Spy* from its
new address. Benjamin Eades hastily moved the press of the *Gazette*
to Watertown; John Gill delayed in Boston and was arrested. The *Evening-Post* of the brothers Fleet toppled from the lofty eminence from
which its publishers had hoped to please all and offend none. The *Post-
Boy and Advertiser*, sold by Green and Russell to Mills and Hicks, disappeared forever as its native-born Tory owners scurried to New York
to serve the British. The ultra-loyalist *Chronicle* of Mein and Flemming
had previously expired and the Boston *News-Letter*, wearing British

arms and published by Margaret Draper and John Boyle, was Boston's only source of printed news, vanishing as Washington chased the lion and the unicorn to the sea.

The Bright Morning Star of Freedom was high and clear. Eighty-six newspapers had been started in all the colonies since Benjamin Harris's *Publick Occurrences*, and of these not more than three dozen had survived officious Authority, lack of money and scant and thinly-spread populations. Of these at least twenty-eight staked their futures without reservation on a free country, a free people, and a free press.

Nameplate. Boston, January 12, 1776.
Courtesy of New York Public Library.

4

DRUMS OF REVOLUTION

SCOOPING THE WORLD, BENJAMIN TOWNE'S *PENNSYL-vania Evening-Post* reported on July 2, 1776: "The Continental Congress has declared the Colonies Free and Independent States."

And the strongly patriotic Heinrich Miller's *Der Wochentliche Staatsbote* beat all others with: "Philadelphia, the fifth of July. Yesterday the respected Congress of the Western Land declared the Colonies Free and Independent States. This Declaration, in English, is in the press; it is dated the Fourth of July, 1776, and will appear in print today or tomorrow." And on July 5th John Dunlop printed, from the manuscript of Thomas Jefferson, the Declaration of Independence on the press of the *Packet*, or *The General Advertiser*. These broadsides, to which were appended the flourishing signatures of John Hancock, President of the Congress, and Charles Thomson, Secretary ("the Sam Adams of Philadelphia, the life of the cause of Liberty, so they say") were sent to the assemblies of the thirteen colonies by horse, and by sail to England and the capital ports of Europe.

The *Pennsylvania Evening-Post* on the 9th also printed the text of the Declaration and reported: "Yesterday, at twelve o'clock INDE-PENDENCE was declared at the State-House in this City, in the presence of many thousand spectators who testified their appreciation of it by repeated acclaimations of Joy." And the bell hanging in the tower of the State House, so prophetically inscribed "Proclaim Liberty throughout the Land unto all the Inhabitants Thereof," pealed over the heads of applauding thousands and was answered by bells in every steeple. And Heinrich Miller hurried to get out his newspaper with a supplemental page to carry the Declaration in full, in big types, and for the first time in any language other than English.

Wounds of Lexington and Concord were bandaged; the acrid smokes of Bunker Hill cleared away and George Washington, before Boston, was keeping the British securely isolated while training his Continentals, when Samuel and Ebenezer Hall, at Congressional request, removed their press from Salem to Cambridge. And at Stoughton-Hall of Harvard College the *New-England Chronical and Essex Gazette* remembered their promises to support the Rights and Liberties of our Country. It also acted as official spokesman for the Congress, and printed important extracts from its Journal, army orders, and other communications for the people, which were relayed as fast as horses could cover the miles between newspaper presses.

There was a healthy respect for the engines that had started fires from uncertain embers and fanned the flames into Revolution. To British commanders a newspaper press, a newspaper publisher, or an author of inflammatory letters for newspaper publication were among the most desired prizes of war. Patriot-Printers, all heroes to their countrymen, had to be nimble fellows ready to scuttle with their presses when enemy fire came too close or too hot. All were aware of the need for the news they supplied.

John Holt, enthusiastic patriot, able writer, and fearless publisher, established in 1766 his New York *Journal, or, General Advertiser* and was, together with his editorial assistant, the stubborn Alexander Mc-

Dougall of New Gaol fame, and his son, John Hunter Holt, high on the list of printers "wanted."

As Admiral Howe's reinforcements joined the troops of General Howe on Long Island, Holt and his family with as many of their possessions as they could transport escaped to New Haven. From New Haven the "Printer to the State of New-York" went to Kingston (Esopus), and on the way his household goods were pillaged and burned by British soldiers. In Kingston he turned out the *Journal* in reduced format until Kingston too was burned almost at his heels as he again escaped, and he was left nearly destitute. "Happy to have saved the two best fonts of Printing-Letter belonging to the State," he again opened shop, and from Poughkeepsie issued his newspaper irregularly until the evacuation, when John Holt, home again, could set up a new nameplate: *The Independent Gazette, or, the New-York Journal Revived.*

A printer and a patriot and in business with his father, John Hunter Holt was publishing the caustic *Virginia Gazette; or, The Norfolk Intelligencer* when the *Pennsylvania Gazette* for October 15, 1775, reported this strange event: "Williamsburg. October 7. Yesterday came on shore about fifteen of the King's soldiers who marched up to the printing-office out of which they took all the types and part of the press, and carried them on board the new ship *Eilbeck*, in the presence of, I suppose, between two and three hundred spectators without meeting the slightest molestation; and upon the drums beating up and down the town, there were only about thirty-five men to arms. They say they want to print a few papers for themselves; but that they looked upon the press as not to be free, and had a mind to print something in vindication of their own characters. But as they have only part of the press and no ink yet, it is out of their power to do anything in the printing business. They got neither of the compositors, but I understand there is a press aboard the *Otter*. Mr. Cummings, the book-binder, was pressed on board, but is admitted on shore at times. He says Captain Squire was very angry that they did not get Mr. Holt."

The mayor, the aldermen and the common council of Norfolk jointly addressed a letter of protest to the Earl of Dunmore, then a refugee aboard the warship *Flowey*. The reply from the Royal Governor, then at such odds with his people that he dared appear on shore only when he was prepared to fight, was very bitter. He had, he said, only tried to save his subjects from contamination by a newspaper which he considered the "instigator of treason and rebellion."

Norfolk was destroyed by bombardment before Holt's newspaper could be revived, and the governor, then aboard the flagship bearing his name, himself set up to get out one more *Virginia Gazette*. Compiled by the governor's secretary and righthand man, Hector McAllister, this *Virginia Gazette* carried such exclusive news as the governor's order for martial law in the Old Dominion, a promise of freedom to slaves who would bear British arms, and an order forbidding the payment of taxes to the rebel government. Taken on shore under cover of darkness by small boats, copies were "distributed among His Majesty's faithful subjects like pious books among the poor and ignorant, to lead them into the true faith and understanding of the present unhappy dispute between Great Britain and the American Colonies," said John Anderson in his New-York *Constitutional Gazette* for May 22, 1776. The reply to the governor was the coiled rattlesnake on the flags of the Virginia Colony and Culpeper County Minute-Men. Another slithering serpent on the first American naval jack warned all callers by sea.

Fully as desirable to the British as military success was the conversion of American newspaper publishers to the British cause. Sympathetic news treatment in British-held American cities, gained by appeals to reason or sentiment, by bribe, subsidy, or force, were important objectives.

Famous among converts at the presses was James Rivington, an Englishman, who started in 1773 the modestly-titled *Rivington's New-York Gazette, or, the Connecticut, Hudson's River and Quebec Weekly Advertiser* and whose policy was: "Never to admit any performance calculated to injure Virtue, Religion or other Public Happiness, or to raise a blush in the face of Virgin Innocence." Rivington's "EVER OPEN and Uninfluenced Press, fronting on Hanover Square" was so conspicuous a fountain of pamphlets in favor of appeasement that it was condemned by patriots and twice suffered from angry mobs before the Sons of Liberty led by Isaac Sears rode in from Connecticut to destroy it and take the types for bullet-making.

From England Rivington acquired a new press and new type and an appointment as Printer to the King's Most Excellent Majesty. And at his new location, His Majesty's Printing-Office at Number One, the Corner of Queen street, he offered "Elegant Silk Stockings Excellent Boots and Neat Slippers. Hyson Tea, a Sure Cure for Warts and Corns and other Medicines, playingcards, tickets to the bathing machine in the North-River behind Mr. Harrison's brew house, lottery tickets and Exquisite Pigtail and Smoking Tobacco" as well as subscriptions to

Rivington's Gazetteer, or, the Connecticut, Hudson's River, New Jersey and Quebec Advertiser.

Shortened to *Rivington's Loyal Gazette*, it was known to patriots as Jemy Rivington's Lying Gazette. Rivington pleased his masters, who subsidized him with the purchase of many copies for distribution among soldiers and sailors and loyalists in Canada and the colonies and supplied him with frequent "news" of General Washington's death or capture; he reported "In every number more patriots killed in battle than there were white inhabitants in the Country."

A less spectacular but greater victory was the conversion of Hugh Gaine. From Belfast "without basket or burden" Gaine went to work for James Parker, and in 1752 set up his own business as a publisher of books, proprietor of a book store, and printer and publisher of a newspaper, the *New-York Mercury*. By 1776 Gaine's Queen street shop was crammed to the rafters with a wonderful miscellany of merchandise including, as well as books, a stock of brass-mounted broadswords that, he advertised "would come in handy in case of a war with the French." As General Howe bore down on New York, Gaine took a press and fled to Newark, New Jersey. In Newark he continued to get out his newspaper, while in New York, Ambrose Searle, on orders of Lord Howe, also got out the paper, using Gaine's presses, his title, and his correct serial numbers. Beaten, Gaine returned to New York and regained his property, and then regularly published the *Mercury* as an unqualified Loyalist organ until the evacuation, when this long favorite butt of American publishing humor quietly expired.

In 1769 Loyalists James and Alexander Robertson in New York started the *Chronicle*, but abandoned it to go to Albany where in 1771 they began that town's first newspaper, another *Gazette*. When the British took New York they buried their press on the farm of a friend and hurriedly returned to engage in a more profitable enterprise, the *Royal American Gazette*. Then as Philadelphia and Charleston were occupied by luxury-loving redcoats, Alexander obliged them with the *Royal Pennsylvania Gazette* and James, in partnership with two other Scotsmen, supplied Charleston with British-biased news in the *Royal South-Carolina Gazette*. But before the war was ended, both brothers found a hasty retreat to Halifax expedient.

The four newspapers of British-held New York—two Gazettes (Rivington's and that of Robertson, Mills, and Hicks) and two Mercurys (Hugh Gaine's and that of William Lewis) had more than a superficial family resemblance. All wore big cuts of the British arms and the lions and the unicorns wore identical expressions of astonishment as they presided over neat boxes enclosing news of the Assiz of Bread, High Water, and Prices Current. All shamelessly bid for American pledges of loyalty to the British crown, and all dwelt on patriot losses and weaknesses rather than on British might or British victories. All had the tone of hurt surprise at frustrated hopes rather than righteous anger.

The advertising in New York's captive newspapers excited British friends and foes alike, who could see in New York harbor the rotting prison-ships into which were crowded ill, wounded, and dying patriots. Offers of goods and services indicated that those able to subscribe to the newspapers lived not only well but, for the times, luxuriously, and other news more than intimated that the plight of the poor caught in the British military net was desperate. Royal proclamation permitted the indigent to cut firewood from confiscated land; lotteries and benefits were arranged for the needy, and printers employed on these same newspapers complained that with the rising cost of living, they could not afford to work for five dollars a week. They got the salary increase they demanded, and were then able to command six dollars for six long days' work at the typecases.

Written on a drumhead and straight from his heart came the first of the "appeals"—*The Crisis* by Tom Paine. "These are the times that try men's souls" was first published in the *Pennsylvania Journal*, December 19, 1776, and was read from this newspaper on General Washington's orders to every little corporal's division at Valley Forge. This piece of writing is credited with having lifted the spirits of the ragged and hungry Continentals who crossed the ice-filled Delaware to surprise the enemy rollicking in Trenton on Christmas night.

Washington, busy scratching up an army, training men and officers, campaigning for tents, blankets, food, medicine, and shoes, planning the war and fighting it, took time to write an occasional letter to just one newspaper, and these morale-building communications, published and republished, reached the most remote of newspaper readers in the record time of about three weeks. The rank and file of writers of letters to patriot newspapers quoted unidentified "eye-witnesses" and "authentic sources" and letters from Army officers to their wives and best girls. "A Genuine Letter from an Officer of High Rank to Miss F . . . of Philadelphia" vied with "A Letter From One American Officer to Another" as the acme of war news. Newspaper publishers could ride— and sometimes walk—to see the battles, but they were yet to discover the worth of first-hand war reporting.

Patriot newspapers printed lists of war casualties and also lists with names and addresses of army deserters, for whose discovery their commanding officers offered rewards of sometimes as much as eight dollars. They gave conspicuous space to the pleas of the Army for needed spades, shovels, and axes, "new or second hand," and other tools, scarce in a country where the manufacture of such necessities to pioneer life was the jealously guarded prerogative of the politically favored and favoring of the powers at "home."

Late in 1777 Isaac Collins, a Quaker printer in Burlington, started his *New-Jersey Gazette*, and two years later Lieutenant Shepherd Kollock resigned his army commission to establish at Chatham his *New Jersey Journal*. Both of these newspapers featured army news and orders and the letters of the famous, as well as letters from subscribers concerning the prospects and progress of war. Circulations were more than local; these papers were for the men behind the cannons, mortars, and muskets of the wavering lines between New York and Philadelphia. To assist these first of army newspapers the government directed its quartermaster to contribute worn-out tents for the making of paper.

The novelty of news for soldiers was both for publishers and their subscribers still undimmed when a friendly sea press aboard the *Neptune* of Rochambeau's convoy sailed into Newport. The press was set up on land to resume publication of the *Gazette Française; À Newport, De l'Imprimerie Royal de L'Escadra, Rue de la Pointe* with Number 611, dated November 17, 1780.

The lion and the unicorn which smiled smugly from atop the New-York *Mercury* was one day omitted from that paper of William Lewis's. The date was April 6, 1783, a Sunday. This in itself—a Sunday extra—was an event in early publishing history. Across the *Mercury's* first page, in large type, appeared the following: "The Printer presents the following to the Public, and declares, upon his Honor, without intention to give offense to a single individual, but at the request of a number of Gentlemen, in order to show the pains the inveterate *Rebels* (a term he will use at the risk of his Ears) are already taking to excite the people at large to continue the prosecution of the Loyalists which has marked their conduct from the commencement of the Revolution." And starting from the column-caption: "From the Rebel New Jersey Journal, printed at Chatham by Shepherd Kollock, April 2nd, 1783" was reprinted an allegorical dialog, some news letters and Articles of Intelligence, all discussing the disposal of Loyalists and their properties with vindictiveness. Reprisals were demanded from the Loyalists accused of living in luxury while patriots fought, bled, and starved.

Change in the political weather was marked by an EXTRAOR- DINARY of Rivington's *Royal Gazette* of the following July 12th. Under the British arms was printed the news of George Washington congratulating William Green, Governor of Rhode Island, on the successful conclusion of the war! And in this same newspaper for November 6th, under the expanded title *The American Royal Gazette* was a touch of pathos: "Mr. Rivington entreats those Gentlemen who are in Arrears for this Gazette to favor him with payment before their Embarkation. This is suggested with great diffidence on the Presump- tion that some perfectly willing to satisfy him may leave the City with- out recollecting Trifles."

General Washington's Farewell Orders to the Armies of the United States was front-page news for Rivington on November 13, 1783; and on December 6 the again converted *Rivington's New-York Gazette, and General Advertiser*, without a trace of British bias, reported the farewell of the Commander-in-Chief to his officers at Fraunces Tavern and his departure for Mount Vernon and well-earned retirement. Men wept as the great American stepped aboard his barge and oarsmen pulled for the Jersey shore. And on an inside page in small type is found a still poignant news item: "We are informed that the last divisions of British troops have left Staten Island on their passage to England." This was the publisher's only obit to former friends, companions, and patrons. The British drums of war, once so cockily assured, were no longer muffled by disbelief, uncertainty, or confusion; they were silent.

When the Revolution began there were scarcely fifty printing presses in all that is now these United States, and of these few were much superior to the press used by Gutenberg. The need for news and printed documents was far beyond their combined capacity to meet, and the building of presses and their improvement was started in Hartford and more effectively continued in Philadelphia.

All printers' types were being imported from England when, in 1767, Abel Buell, a jeweler of Killingworth, Connecticut, in letters of his own make memorialized the colony's General Assembly for assistance in establishing a foundry. A loan was granted and advanced but Buell's further accomplishments were negligible.

In 1770 Christopher Sower of the enterprising Ephrata press, im- ported the essentials for punching matrices and casting the Gothic char- acters he used in printing for the Pennsylvania Dutch. After his death his tools were purchased by the talented Jacob Bay, a former employee, who with them cut and cast the English-letter types used on April 7, 1775, for printing the first number of the Philadelphia *Pennsylvania Mercury*. Publishers Enoch Story and Daniel Humphreys respectfully noted: "We are sensible, that, in point of elegance, they are somewhat inferior to those imported from England, but we flatter ourselves that the rustic manufacturer of America will prove more grateful to the patriot eyes, than the most finished productions of Europe." When these same tools came into the hands of Francis Bailey, also from Ephrata, he made the types with which he started in Philadelphia, in 1781, the *Freeman's Journal; or, the North-American Intelligencer*, a paper that was truly "Open to All Parties; Influenced by None" and, besides, typographically beautiful.

Inks were another source of grief for patriot publishers and printers; only Rogers and Fowle in this country had made "weak and strong" mixtures for presses. But the process of trial and error over a few war years, produced home-made inks solemnly pronounced by printers "Superior to those of London."

It was the high cost of paper that kept printers and publishers awake nights. So great was the need for paper that the poverty-ridden Continental Congress, and also several states not much richer, subsidized the erection of mills. And as prices for raw material soared, men in horse-drawn belled carts began their ambling, rambling, endless, and melodious journeys up and down highways and byways seeking to buy RAGS! RAGS! for the presses.

The Dutch Engine was the one improvement in paper-making. One Massachusetts mill had two of these mechanical beaters driven by water-power, but the industry generally followed its primitive course. Rags, preferably clean, white, and part linen were shredded or torn and the bits thrown into vats to be beaten with heavy hammers or pounded with stones. The pulp, bleached when necessary, was steamed and stirred to the right consistency; sizing was added and the mixture lifted from the vats on sheet-sized strainer-molds, shaken of excess pulp, and set to drain and dry. To hasten the process the sheets were lifted from the screens and alternated with layers of felt to be squeezed under the weight of heavy presses, and as a final concession to hurry, the sheets were separated from the felts and hung to age in drying-sheds. They were then tied in bundles for delivery to presses by oxen, horses, or sail. Thus newsprint rose to new value and was first recognized for what it is—a commodity essential to civilized life.

Cartoon, "Federal Edifice," in The Massachusetts Sentinel. Boston, June 25, 1788. One of a series advocating the adoption of the American Constitution. Courtesy of New York Public Library.

5

THE DAILIES

IT WAS A WOMAN WHO PUBLISHED THE FIRST ENGLISH-language daily newspaper. Elizabeth Mallett, right "next door to the King's Arms TAVERN at Fleet-bridge," started her *Daily Courant* in London in 1702. In the salutatory of that small sheet printed only on one side was her plan and policy:

It will be found from Foreign Prints which from time to time as the Occasion offers will be mentioned in this Paper, that the Author has taken care to be daily furnished with all that comes from abroad in any language. And for assurances that he will not, under Pretense of having Private Intel-

57

ligence impose any additions of feign'd circumstances to an Action, but will give his Extracts fairly and Impartially; at the beginning of each article he will quote the Foreign Paper from whence 'tis taken, that the Publick seeing from what Country a Piece of News with the allowance of the Government, may better be able to judge the Credibility and Fairness of the Relation; Nor will he take upon him to give any Comments or Conjectures of his own, but will relate only Matter of Fact; supposing other People have Sense enough to make the Reflections for themselves. This Courant (as the title shows) will be published daily, being design'd to give all the Material News as soon as every Post arrives; and is confin'd to half the compass to save the Publick at least half the impertinences of the ordinary newspaper.

But the time-saving and temper-saving *Daily Courant* was abandoned within two weeks, although it was later revived and published for several months by Sam Buckley of the Dolphin in Little Britain.

Three quarters of a century and more after the demise of the enterprising Elizabeth's *Courant,* British-occupied New York City had its newspapers almost daily. Under arrangements of the clever Jemy Rivington, his own *Gazette,* the town's only semiweekly, was issued on Wednesdays and Saturdays. Alexander Robertson, Nathaniel Mills, and John Hicks' newspaper of the same name was published on Thursdays, and the *Mercurys* of Hugh Gaine and William Lewis appeared weekly on Mondays and Fridays.

With the Revolution had come imperious calls for more news and news more often. Subscribers wanted news of relatives and friends in the ranks as well as news of the commanders. The country needed news of the Continental Congress, its difficulties, its seeming futility and surprising progress; and they were anxious to hear of the successes and failures of emissaries sent abroad to win friends, money, and fighting men. They wanted news of the enemy, news of Loyalists in their midst, and of the Indians never far away. And to supply what news they could obtain, the country's newspapers became more regular of issue, increased the frequency of publication, and new titles were added to the young American newspaper press as fast as printers and would-be publishers could secure capital, presses, types, paper, and ink.

Din and dismay marched into Philadelphia with the red-coated troops of Britain, and the *Gazette* of Benjamin Franklin, together with the Continental Congress, retreated to York. The press of the *Packette* of John Dunlop was removed to Lancaster; Heinrich Miller, a little late in leaving the city, was forced to leave his press behind, and His Majesty's forces a good six months later carted it away. The *Journal* of William

Bradford had previously suspended for the duration; its publisher was away at the wars. But the busy Benjamin Towne, the "patriot" who had so righteously done his share towards driving loyalist James Humphreys and his *Ledger* out of business, remained to continue his *Evening-Post*, to the satisfaction of a more prosperous circulation for whose favors he abused the rebels in competition with Sower's *Staats Courier*, Robertson's *Gazette*, and the new *Market Day Advertiser* of the same James Humphreys.

Returning to the evacuated city Philadelphians accepted with scepticism Towne's protestations of faith, but he was permitted to remain at his press unmolested. So strained were the bonds of confidence, however, that Towne's subscription list dwindled; his correspondents were decidedly hostile, and advertisers frankly uninterested. Towne had established the *Evening-Post* as a weekly early in 1775, and news demands made it successively and successfully a semiweekly and a triweekly. In each copy a half-sheet of paper was used to make four almost square pages and each small page was printed to two wide columns. The *Evening-Post* was only Two Coppers a Copy (for a short time, Three Coppers) when other Philadelphia newspapers, if sold by the single number, were sixpence and more each. There was publishing vision in Towne's advertisement, unique for many years to come: "A news-hawker will meet with good encouragement upon application to the Printer hereof."

But the fortunes of the *Evening-Post* steadily waned; Towne removed from Front-street, near the London Coffee-House, to cheaper quarters in Pewter-Platter Alley and gradually himself assumed the work of collecting and writing news, selecting extractions from other newspapers, soliciting subscriptions and advertising, composing types, and working the press; he also sometimes sold the finished paper on Philadelphia streets. In a desperate attempt to regain his former position he issued his newspaper as the *Pennsylvania Evening-Post and Daily Advertiser* on June 17, 1783, using sometimes two half-sheets to make eight pages, and publication was continued with fair regularity until at least October 28, 1784.

From these unhappy circumstances emerged the first American daily newspaper—its end unknown, vanished into that black obscurity the world reserves for failures long afterwards discovered to have been in advance of their times.

Only a few weeks before Benjamin Towne's doomed newspaper expired, the first American daily to become firmly established had its origin also in Philadelphia. John Dunlop, who learned to print at the cases of his uncle, William Dunlop, himself once an apprentice to William Bradford and later one of Benjamin Franklin's many partners, and Lieutenant David C. Claypoole, a former apprentice, issued on September 24, 1784, without warning, celebration, or explanation the old *Packette* under the new title of *Pennsylvania Packett; and Daily Advertiser.*

The new *Packett* was strikingly superior to the *Evening-Post*; its pages were larger, each well-organized and printed to four columns. Foreign intelligence at first dominated its news, but increasing domestic and local items, newsletters on topics of the day, and anecdotes obviously selected for the enjoyment of ladies as well as their gentlemen gave genuine interest to the scanty space held for this text. The rest of the newspaper was crowded with the cards and squares of advertisers, and this was the news and intelligence that the publishers "served subscribers at their houses every morning; those at a distance by quickest conveyance." To accommodate the nearby or impatient, copies could be had at the print-shop counter for sixpence each.

After John Dunlop's death the *Packett*, guide and companion to many eminent Philadelphians, was known as *Claypoole's American Daily Advertiser*, and was finally lost together with seven other titles in the expanding *North-American*, which started in 1839 and in 1925 vanished under the cloak of C. H. K. Curtis's *Public Ledger.*

The third American daily and the first outside of Philadelphia was a native of Charleston. On November 30, 1784, the *South-Carolina Gazette* of John Miller, added *and Daily Advertiser* to its title, and survived less than a year.

The New York *Evening-Post*, a weekly newspaper established in 1782, two years later blossomed as the *Morning-Post and Daily Advertiser*,— "Printed and Published by MORTON and HORNER, at their office at No. 22 Water-street, opposite the Coffee-House." New York's first daily catered to New York's commercial interests, well supported by "merchants, importers and underwriters" from February 23, 1785, until early 1792, when William Morton, left alone by his partner's death, omitted *and Daily Advertiser* to continue the paper as a semiweekly for a few months before ceasing publication altogether.

Number One of Volume One of the famous, and more enduring, New York *Daily Advertiser* was published March, 1785, just five days after the *Morning-Post* made its first daily appearance. Francis Childs, its publisher, as an orphan had been apprenticed to William Dunlop, and for him John Jay asked Benjamin Franklin's advice, interest, and assistance, and although Franklin was then in France, he generously arranged to have the printer supplied with an outfit of types and other equipment on long-term credit. The first address of the newspaper was "17 Duke-street, the first door from the corner of Old-Slip and Smith-street"; its next was "No. 189 Water-street, at the New-Printing Office, mid-way between the Coffee-House and the Fly-Market"; and it progressed within the same year to "No. 22 Hanover Square, next door to the corner of Wall-street."

The contents of the *Daily Advertiser*—its title soon "improved" to the *Daily Advertiser, Political, Historical and Commercial*—were not, beyond the advertisements, particularly interesting until Philip Freneau's sophisticated contributions and editorial assistance made this newspaper a must for all smart men-about-town. With changes of owners, editors, publishers, and policies the New York *Daily Advertiser* was continuously "useful" to its faithful subscribers until 1836, when it was merged with the New York *Morning Express*.

Three established newspapers bid for daily circulation in 1786. Revived by Nathan Childs, the *South-Carolina Weekly Gazette* became a daily publication, and shortly also did the well-known Charleston *City Gazette and Daily Advertiser*. The experienced Shepherd Kollock made his semiweekly New York *Gazetteer, and Country Journal* into the *Gazetteer, or Daily Advertiser*, which returned to former publication dates within three months. In Philadelphia Colonel Eleazer Oswald on October 7 got out his *Independent Gazetteer, or, the Chronicle of Freedom* as a daily newspaper and returned to semiweekly publication on October 7, 1790.

"They skipped town," was whispered of Murphy and Brown who started Baltimore's first daily newspaper in 1787; it was published only a few days. Of sterner stuff, the *Daily Repository* of David Graham, William Yundt, and Leonard Patterson, from 1791, under the changing titles and owners, supplied excellent commercial and financial news. Philip Edwards made his *Evening-Post* a daily publication in 1793, and two years later it was merged with the newspaper of Katherine and William Goddard. And, also in Baltimore, in 1795, and fifty years before the Morse invention, Thomas E. Clayland and Thomas Dobbin made their *Telegraphe* a daily newspaper.

The famous newspaper of Patriot-Printer John Holt was Thomas Greenleaf's New York *Journal and Daily Patriotic Register* for less than a year, but the *American Minerva, Patroness of Peace, Commerce and the Liberal Arts* established by George Bunce and Company in 1795 lived long in the same city. French refugees in Philadelphia daily had their *Courier Française* from 1794 to 1798. And a stormy petrel of the press, James Carey, had his brief flings with the *Virginia Gazette, and Richmond Daily Advertiser* in 1792, and in 1793 with the Charleston *Daily Evening Advertiser and Tea Table Gazette,* testimony to his enterprise for only a few weeks. In 1796 the *Polar Star, Boston Daily Advertiser* made its appearance with the radical John D. Burke at its helm and was lost from view within six months.

Thomas Bradford, great-grandson of William Bradford, started his *Merchants' Daily Advertiser* in Philadelphia in 1797; within the year its public-spirited publisher changed its title to the more appropriate *True American.* It was the first newspaper in this country to offer a now familiar weekly feature, a literary supplement. The *Desert* that first went to subscribers on July 14, 1798, was—with its title-spelling amended—published for a little longer than a year. A folio with pages about ten by fifteen inches, a typical *Dessert* dated February 23, 1799, gave first-page place to a romance set in Spain; this was followed by a shorter tale called "The Death-Bed of a Deist," and completed with a fashionably funereal cut of a silent lyre and weeping willows atop the tear-inducings: "Monody: In Memory of an Only Daughter Who Died at the Age of Eleven Years," by Her Father.

The century's last daily newspaper, John Lang's *New York Gazette, and General Advertiser Daily,* from 1795 provided its patrons with excellent news of shipping and the police courts under the title launched by the McLeans in 1793. But of the perhaps two dozen daily newspapers hopefully started since the success of the *Packett,* only about a third lived to use 1800 at their datelines. The failures, however, were to be soon solaced by the arrivals of other and distinguished company.

In anticipation of prosperity presumed as a natural accompaniment to the removal of the seat of government from Philadelphia to the mud flats on the Potomac, no less than three newspapers gambled for success as Washington dailies. Charles D. Green and David English on November 18, 1800, renamed their *Centinel of Liberty,* established four years previously, to the *Museum and Washington and Georgetown Daily Advertiser,* which shortly faded from existence. The *Advertiser,* started as a daily by Samuel Snowden and Matthew Brown on November 20, 1800, came to an end after one lone issue; but the *Federalist* of William Alexander Rind and John Stuart, a weekly only a few weeks old, became a daily on November 24, 1800, and with various changes lived about ten years.

Snowden and Brown moved across the river and in Alexandria, Virginia, on December 8, 1800, started the weekly *Advertiser and Commercial Intelligencer*. Three years later this newspaper started daily publication and it is still published, oldest of its class in this country, as the *Alexandria Gazette, and Daily Advertiser*, the name it has worn since 1813.

The history of America's pioneering daily newspapers is an open book to those with the meagerest of hindsight. Populations of the country's proud centers of culture, commerce, finance, shipping, and industry were not large enough to support daily newspapers in addition to the already-established weekly and other publications. With but few exceptions the publishers of dailies sought as patrons only business and professional men, and further restricted their potential circulations by high subscription prices. But the most baffling barrier to the success of the daily newspaper was the coffee house and the time-honored meetings of men to transact business. Only the daily newspapers whose news was really news, especially in the advertising columns, had a chance for survival in rivalry with the charms of these regular news centers.

In this country impoverished by war and its government without credit, the need for news after the signing of the Treaty of Peace in Paris was acute. Unpaid soldiers of the Revolution were bitter; taxes were high and the high-handed methods of collectors trying to wring money from the penniless (whose losses were reckoned by the dead and maimed, pillaged and burned homes, depleted stocks and stores) brought ominous threats bordering on insurrection.

News was as necessary as food and drink to men and women who had risked their possessions, their lives, and their futures for freedom and independence, and who were now fearful that chaos would erase their gains. Publishers and printers responded with more news and new newspapers.

But news was still largely confined to the letters of correspondents anxious to add their own words of gloom or hope to the spectacle of conditions deteriorating to the intolerable. Inexperienced publishers followed the traditional custom of featuring foreign news "extracted" from domestic or foreign publications. To news of England's politicians and lawmakers they added dreary paragraphs of "intelligence" from faraway courts of kings, tsars, and emperors, and the more outlandish the dateline the more valuable they considered the news. "Extraordinaries" were issued upon receipt of "latest advices" from the Honorable Continental Congress, and these publishing sensations secured from broadsides sent by Congress to the state legislatures, or from public-spirited members who "posted" publishers, did not necessarily convey much real news.

The publishing of any general American news was a real event. Local news was usually considered too well-known to justify the labor of printing. It was a remarkable publisher who first saw news in these most important of local events, the town meetings. Local deaths and weddings were not always news for printers, and births, except those of royalty, were never mentioned. These events were regarded either as unimportant accidents, or else considered not quite nice to mention such intimate happenings in public print. Only a few of the postwar newspapers succeeded in keeping pace with new reader demands. There were more failures than successes among newspaper ventures which still followed the patterns fixed by the country's first newspapers. There was a certain inelasticity among the publishers, who were, first and foremost and for all their days printers, and blind and deaf to what constituted the kind of news that was so sorely missed by the most easily pleased of customers.

Many of the best newspapers of post-Revolution America were interesting, but unprofitable, sidelines to the main business of job-printing, and "getting out the paper" had to wait while printers otherwise earned their bread and butter. Newspaper finances were as mysterious to publishers as to subscribers, who usually felt little responsibility to pay rates per annum at any time, much less in advance. Subscriptions exchanged for promises to pay in commodities of equal value were a total loss when crops were bad, and sometimes in whole districts there were neither cash nor commodities. These risks every publisher knew. They knew, too, the awe—if not reverence—for the printed word that gave to the fraternity a moral and social standing almost equal to that of the clergy. Publishers were important men who, if they lived long enough, became personages of more than local fame; they were no longer Undertakers or Printers Hereof, but the Authors and Conductors whose comments on current affairs often appeared in news columns in advance of editorials.

"Taken in" or "thankfully received" advertising was also subject to barter. Publishers were happy to accept pork, flour, firewood, or medicines in exchange for space; tonics, liniment, and salves were sold at the print-shop or exchanged for luxuries from the "chymist's." And rags were as good, if not better, than currency at every print-shop counter.

Ships, horses, houses, and running men, cut in wood for printing, directed eyes to sailings, real estate for sale or rent, slaves or runaway servants, or lost, strayed, or stolen horses. A cut of a fish was a sign that supplies of that staple of diet, the salt cod, had just arrived. Men of affairs, presumably prosperous, could in their daily newspaper's advertising, locate rare pomades for perukes at apothecaries, to be found behind their big red and green jars. Sedan chairs were to be had by the weary or gouty; there were imported classics for the bookish, lotteries for gamblers; for gormandizers there were marvelous cheeses; wines and rums by the hogshead (together with good corks) were advertised as "just unloaded."

But in small type in the cramped space of daily and weekly newspaper advertising columns appeared news worth volumes. "Parcils" of Negroes —men and women, old and young—were offered to any buyer who had money. To the highest bidders went the time and labor of poor immigrants prepared to work out their passages from England and Europe; buyers were requested to apply to the Captain, the agent for ship-owners, at once. Interest stirred by Joseph's "Whereas: My wife Susan . . ." flamed to the sensational when Susan advertised right back with: "Whereas: My husband, Joseph, has advertised me as having left his bed and board, but as he has turned me out of doors with two infant children and nailed up the windows and doors without any just cause or provocation, and left me to shift for myself and them, this is to forwarn all persons harboring him until he provides for our maintainance, or gives security for that and his good behavior." And through the advertising columns, especially in the dailies, threaded the first chapters of early American success stories whose heroes boasted of their swelling affluence by giving notice of new addresses, new services, and new honors.

The heart of every American newspaper was kept at its work by its public. Newspapers were the free and open channels of communication of common men, and here they blissfully blasted the post office at home, the Parliament of England, and the Pope of Rome with a fine impartiality. Letters from subscribers, letters received by readers, and letters lifted from other newspapers diagnosed the diseases consuming America, and offered infallible remedies and inflexible opposition to all other prescriptions.

News letters describing big storms, floods, earthquakes, epidemics, and other catastrophes, like letters describing conditions on western frontiers, circulated over the entire country in a mere six or eight weeks and were recognized as news by a public and press inclined to consider that news was not news until it was printed.

In those simpler days of newspaper publishing, when the title of editor was only an affectation, a clever publisher could, when the spirit or quantity of news letters sagged, write to himself for publication regarding something intriguing, signed with a name or quotation from the Greek or Latin, letters that would bring interesting response on publication. These artificial discussions made stimulating reading until time and conditions started another flurry among the goose-quills. Unfailing literary bait was a letter for or against the Order of the Cincinnati. Letter writers always hurried to denounce these ex-officers of the Revolution as ambitious to set themselves up as American royalty; eagerly they demanded that they be rooted out of public office at once. With equal fervor others urged that experience had given these men the fortitude and firmness essential to restoring order to a depressed and confused America.

But suddenly the need for the manufacture and fanning of newspaper-driven enthusiasms vanished. The Convention called for 1787 in Philadelphia had secretly planned and prepared a proposed Federal Constitution. It was printed on the press of Dunlop and Claypoole and copies were dispatched to the governments of the thirteen states. The full text of the Constitution was published for the first time on September 19, 1789, in the *Packett, and Daily Advertiser.*

Here was something everyone, and especially newspaper publishers, felt with a whole-souled conviction to be a conception of government either entirely right or utterly wrong, a frame to be accepted or rejected by the nation. Immediately the country's newspapers became not only carriers of public opinions but the *only* vehicles for concerted, organized propaganda for or against ratification and adoption of this yet untried form of government.

In New York Samuel Louden's weekly *Packet*, the McLeans' semi-weekly *Independent Journal*, and the *Daily Advertiser* published the eighty-five famous Federalist essays of which fifty were written by Alexander Hamilton and the others by John Jay and James Madison. Addressed To the People of New York, and still regarded as the major exposition of the American political ideal; the essays were quickly reprinted in the country's newspapers to provide foundation for intelligent understanding. The peace-loving John Dickenson, whose Letters Of a Farmer in Pennsylvania had angered various less resilient pre-Revolution patriots, and a member of the framing Convention also contributed a series of newspaper-circulated opinions signed Fabious.

These letters clearly explained the merits and advantages of a "Federation of the States."

Energetic support for the proposals of the Founding Fathers came from Major Benjamin Russell, publisher of Boston's *Massachusetts Centinel; and Republican Journal*. This important newspaper not only supplied its home city with better-than-average marine news, news of town meetings, and local deaths and marriages, but its foreign intelligence was of superior range and understanding and won for it an enviable subscription list that was almost national.

The, "Federal Edifice," a series of cartoons, the country' first, and as important in politics as Franklin's severed serpent, was Major Russell's great gift to the crystallization of sentiment in favor of the Constitution. In the *Centinel's* little pictures (each not more than an inch tall, only the width of one narrow column and buried in the middle of the third page) a row of star-strung pillars increased and lengthened out over the months, as ratification and adoption was voted by state legislatures. Each rising pillar was named for a state; South Carolina hesitated and its pillar hesitated at the half-way point. "It must go up," read the caption, and at last it stood even with the others. Rhode Island's pillar, broken at its base, was titled: "The foundation is good, it must go up." And when the Massachusetts legislature showed signs of balking at adoption, the enthusiasm of New England's first journalist, a printer trained by Isaiah Thomas who proudly called himself a mechanic, organized meetings to demonstrate the weight of public approval.

News—exciting news—of Great Federal Processions held in the capitals of states adopting the Constitution was printed and reprinted; the parades were news from the very first orders to inhabitants to sweep, water, and garnish their streets. Guns and bells greeted the dawn; miles of floating stages passed reviewing stands for the salutes of Continental soldiers. And histories of the winning of freedom honored the nation's printers and the Federal Press. In New York after the parade, printers, bookbinders, and booksellers met at the home of another William Bradford to toast the "patriot-printers" and publishers from whose presses had poured the news that was the strength for this new freedom.

In the columns of the influential Providence *Gazette, and Country Journal* of March 20, 1790, in the tiny meticulously corrected types that distinguished this newspaper published by Sarah Goddard's successor, John Carter, Sr., was the following and quite different estimate of the Federal Roof already ratified by twelve of the thirteen original states: "People of the State must be very happy in their present Circumstances, as they are disinclined to alter them. If happiness lies in absolute sovereignty and Independence, no People on earth have a better claim to it. The State is as free from Congress as it is free from the King of Great Britain or France. In short, the State is as free as an Individual in a State of Nature. And there is no more Reason for an adoption of the new Constitution than there is for such an Individual to enter into a State of Government."

Equally remarkable was a little news item modestly tucked away on an inside page of John Fenno's New York *Gazette of the United States* of May 15, 1790:

We are informed that the following is now pending before the Senate of the United States: An Act to prevent Goods, Wares and Merchandise from the State of Rhode Island and the Providence Plantations entering the United States, and authorizing a demand of Money from said State; the demand for payment of money and goods for expenses raised for discharging engagements before March 4th, 1788.

The last pillar was whole and erect on the 29th; Rhode Island was the thirteenth state of the Federal Union.

Mathew Carey came from Dublin in 1785 to become one of the great American printers, publishers, and booksellers. His most outstanding contribution to the land of his adoption lay in the training he gave to countless young men who worked at his presses and who carried their experience and ambitions to the outermost and expanding American frontiers.

Some seventy years after the youthful Franklin's rebellious declaration of independence against his employer-brother James, who induced his fellow master printers in Boston to boycott the aspiring apprentice, the idea of cooperation on the local level first found concrete expression. Encouraged, perhaps, by reading between the provocative lines of the precious type they picked and sorted from ink-stained cases, the first strike of printers occurred in Philadelphia in 1776. Successful in sustaining its objective, the "association" fomenting the act dissolved. Again, on June 7, 1786, twenty-six determined workmen defied their employers by agreeing among themselves not to work for less than six dollars a week. This was done in protest against a decision of Philadelphia employing printers to reduce wages. As before, this organization of employees failed to survive the emergency, but the seed was planted, and another thread added to the warp and woof of the country's growth.

Associations of printers and publishers had begun to take shape; in

1788 many important men of the printing and allied interests and crafts met at Philadelphia to discuss trade practices and regulations. Isaiah Thomas attended these meetings and on at least one occasion the fabulous old Doctor Franklin was their host. Two years later, April 7, 1790, America's first Gentleman of the Press died, and the epitaph, written by himself, and so fitting runs: "The body of Benjamin Franklin, printer (like the covers of an old book, its contents torn out and stript of its lettering and its gilding) lies here, food for worms. But the work shall not be lost, for it will (as, he believes) appear once more in a new and more elegant edition, revised and corrected by the Author."

THE

New Hampſhire

AND

GENERAL

PORTSMOUTH

By ROBERT GERRISH,

THE LIBERTY OF THE PRESS IS ESSENTIAL TO THE SECURITY OF FREEDOM IN A STATE—IT OUGH

Nameplate. Portsmouth, August 9, 1799.
Courtesy of New York Public Library.

MERCURY,

T H E

ADVERTISER.

PRINTED **AND** *PUBLISHED*

IN CONGRESS-STREET.

THEREFORE TO BE INVIOLABLY PRESERVED. *Conft. N. H.*

6

THE PIONEERS

HARBORS OF BOSTON, PHILADELPHIA, CHARLESTON, AND
New York gave to America its first printed news; from these ports enterprising printers and supporting citizens sent out the newspapers that
helped to end government without representation, and spread visions
of the beginning of a world new in more than geography.

Looking beyond the narrow rim of settlement, that thin fringe of
humanity clinging to the crescent of the Atlantic's shore already served
with newspapers from Savannah to Portsmouth, another generation of
young printers from the shops of the Greens and the Bradfords and the

Benjamin Franklin and Isaiah Thomas partnerships, surveyed new fields from East to West and North to South.

Postal services had been resumed after the war with inspiring plans and promises. The great Post Road from Maine to Georgia was improved and cross post roads were already growing inland from the sea.

Transportation was the all-important problem confronting every ambitious journeyman considering an independent future. Printers, moving, had to take with them their heavy presses, their types so easily pied, and a reasonable store of stock; in addition they had to explore possibilities of delivery of the supplies on which the use of a press relied. Printers seeking new locations chose the seacoast and river banks, where sloops linked the towns to main ports of entry and the craft that plied shallower waters, giving promise of permanence and prosperity.

But when the mountain trails, lowland traces, buffalo tracks, tobacco roads, and water highways leading to the unknown interior exercised their irresistible allure on footloose America, pioneering printers took the gamble that lone horsemen, wagon trains, or rafts could survive Indians, wild animals, and the elements.

There were numerous complaints that those postmasters who were also publishers, as many were, failed to forward any newspapers but their own, and that post-riders not only commonly refused to tie news-bundles to their saddles when the weather was bad but also sold for a little cash in pocket the newspapers carried by the "Kind Indulgence" of postmasters and as a "curtesy" for subscribers. So printers and publishers everywhere were immensely heartened by the Postal Act of February 2, 1792. This Act decreed that ". . . every printer of a newspaper may send one paper to every other printer of a newspaper within the United States, free of postage, under such regulations as the Post-Master General may devise." This was sensational news to be shared with subscribers. The "exchanges" were bottomless grab-bags from which "advices," "intelligence," "anecdotes" and "entertainment" were "extracted" to swell scant news rations. And now carried free by the United States mails they proved to be standard publishing life-savers. The regulations for this exchange, eagerly awaited, demanded not much more than that printer's ink be dry and newspapers well wrapped before delivery to post offices. And printers were also notified that newspapers would be delivered as regular mail to subscribers at their post offices, or left at taverns, inns, or other convenient stops upon "postage being paid or promised."

James Franklin expected his apprentice, his brother Benjamin, to deliver the *Courant* to Boston subscribers; his son, James, offered a weekly copy of the Newport *Mercury* "Free & Gratis" in return for out-of-town delivery; but his son-in-law, Samuel Hall, businessman that he was, encouraged riders whose payment would be shared by subscribers. The Salem *Essex Gazette* advertised: "John Church, News Carrier &c., begs to inform his customers that the time of his last engagement ends on the 12th of April, next, when he earnestly hopes for punctual payment at the usual places receiving their newspaper. He likewise earnestly desires to hereby give public notice, that he proposes, on further encouragement, to ride weekly on his usual roads, for the term of six months next ensuing the said April 12th, and to supply each customer with one of the Public News papers. Dumbarton, March 16th, 1769."

Once their presses were set up in new shops and a few subscriptions to their proposed newspaper secured, the next task for every pioneer publisher was organization of routes for delivery. Apprentices, devils, small boys, even total strangers were pressed into local service, but for delivery to country subscribers riders, men owning horses, had to be encouraged by pledges to shares in subscription returns, and hope for eventual small retainers regularly paid by the government. Then to the Postmaster General went pleas and demands for more post offices, and pioneer publishers kept right on pleading, demanding, arguing, and debating until they obtained post-office service for the little settlements of which they themselves were often the first postmasters. Their riders then delivered newspapers and other mail to other post offices and convenient stops for postage: paid, or promised.

Straining to reach frontiers that passed them by and still swept on, the publishing postmasters next demanded coaches to carry more mail and to carry it farther; then—logically—they lifted their voices for roads, more roads, and better roads for the coaches and wagons to travel on. The pioneer newspaper press, always abreast of immigration and sometimes ahead of it, created the first American highway network.

Judah-Paddock Spooner, brother-in-law of Timothy Green of New London, and his brother, Alden Spooner, arrived in the hamlet of Dresden, Vermont, (now Hanover, New Hampshire) in 1778 with some worn types and tools and the press believed to be the one brought to Cambridge by the widow of Jose Glover some one hundred and sixty years previously. The following summer the Official Printers to the General Assembly started a newspaper. The Dresden *Mercury and Universal Advertiser*, a small folio, bore at its nameplate a crude woodcut of the winged messenger and the lovely and unusual motto: "Free as the Savage roams his native wood . . . or the finny nations cleave the flood." The shop of the *Mercury* was in the South End of Dartmouth College, and its salutatory was addressed: "To the People of the New-Hampshire Grants, East and West of the Connecticut River; My friends and Fellow Countrymen . . ." Well patronized by advertisers and crammed with news, the lively little *Mercury* in one number (August 9th, 1779) combined public service with patriotism in a story of the serious depredations among local herds and henhouses by wolves, and endorsed a meeting for considering their extermination by "hunting, trapping, bounty, or any other way that may be thought best, and to wage an open War, not only on the Wolves of Britain, but on the wolves of the wilderness also." This first press is now in the possession of the Vermont Historical Society at Montpelier.

From the *Mercury's* own advertising it is plain that there was little money in Dresden; the print-shop was also a general store and the whole venture profitless. In the issue for September 27, 1779, and probably the last (as the newspaper certainly expired before the first fall of snow) the publishers had for sale ". . . cheap for cash: West India Rum, Tea, Loaf Sugar, Brown do., Indigo, Tobacco, Nails, Rock Salt, Pepper, Allspice, Copperas, Pins, Yarns, Stockings, Chalk Lines, Twist &c.," also "A few pairs of men's shoes will be exchanged for wheat."

In 1780 in Westminister, Vermont, Judah-Paddock Spooner and a nephew, Timothy Green, began the *Vermont Gazette and Green Mountain Post-Boy* that did a little better than the *Mercury*, living for a year. But the *Vermont Journal and Universal Advertiser* established in Windsor in 1783 by Alden Spooner and George Hough, a printer from Connecticut, was of sturdier stuff. It still lives. This *Journal* was packed with news and "entertainment" from the start, and its well-filled advertising columns were distinguished by woodcuts of good size and unusual variety. In one number an advertisement for a runaway boy, "wanted (one penny reward)" was illustrated by a cut of a running boy; the sheriff's notice for one Alariah Snow, a jailbreaker, was illustrated by a cut of an old man with a walking-stick; and a wife eloping from her husband's bed and board could read the details of her latest misbehavior, together with her husband's usual refusal of responsibility for her debts, alongside a cut of a fat baggage in a pork-pie hat leaning heavily on a long staff.

In June of 1783 Anthony Haswell, from the shop of Isaiah Thomas and David Russell, first issued the influential *Vermont Gazette, or, Freeman's Depository* in Bennington. Well-printed and organized, this newspaper featured political news from Philadelphia. Its local news was generous, its "entertainment" was "extracted" from domestic and foreign newspapers with a news-sense not often found in offices of country weeklies, and its advertising columns were always well larded with the legal notices which were ever profitable business. Anthony Haswell, a nationally known publisher, was the General Postmaster of Vermont before that colony was admitted to the Union; his riders delivered his newspaper and the mail to Brandon, seventy miles north of Bennington, for the high price of four bushels of wheat a year.

Georgia, last of the colonies, had a newspaper from 1763 when James Johnson, the colony's first printer, established the Georgia Gazette in Savannah. This was a dignified little sheet with wonderfully little news but filled with advertising; with interruptions it was published for forty years. The Georgia State Gazette, or Independent Register, established in Augusta in 1786 by John E. Smith, three years later was retitled the Augusta Chronicle, and Gazette of the State; and in 1804 when sold to Dennis Driscoll, its name was abbreviated to today's Augusta Chronicle.

Savannah lost its distinction as the southern outpost of printed news when John Wells, Jr., and Doctor William C. Wells turned up in St. Augustine in 1783 to entertain refugees in British-held territory with the East-Florida Gazette. These brothers had inherited from Robert Wells the South-Carolina and American General Gazette and transformed it into the Royal South-Carolina Gazette during the British occupation of Charleston. For years a mystery to scholarly printers, the East-Florida Gazette, often mentioned in Southern exchanges, was lost. It was thought probably that the owners, who had taken their press to the Bahamas, had removed it to Florida. Only recently a few copies were found in London, last haven of these native-born loyalists.

The early pioneer newspaper press, in its slow spread from the ports of its origin, reached Falmouth, now Portland, Maine, with the Falmouth Gazette, and Weekly Advertiser on January 1, 1785. This offering of Benjamin Titcomb and Thomas Baker Wait, under the nameplate of delicate copperplate flourishes, printed the following as its first news item in the first column of the first number: "Messers Titcomb and Wait: As you intend to publish a weekly newspaper in this place, the following extract upon the Rise and Advantages of Newspapers may not be an improper introduction. . . . An Intended Customer." The long article concluded with a homespun note of wisdom ". . . newspapers, which were at first of a very singular nature . . . have given us a taste for reading, this occasions all useful knowledge, to be cultivated and encouraged." The *Falmouth Gazette*, renamed the *Cumberland Gazette* and again the *Eastern Herald*, was merged with the *Gazette of Maine* (started by Benjamin Titcomb, Jr., in 1796) and expired in 1804.

Delaware, kept informed by news published in Philadelphia and Baltimore, had a newspaper of its own when Jacob A. Killen started the *Delaware Gazette, or the Faithful Centinel* in 1785 in Wilmington. This paper was particularly strong in items of interest for a farming state. A year later Samuel and John Adams, sons of James Adams, the colony's first printer, got out their *Delaware Courant and Weekly Advertiser* from their Market Street, Wilmington, shop, but its life was short.

The course of American history was altered when inquisitive Americans set out to see for themselves the prospects of a new life beyond the mountains and took with them the printing presses that turned off newspapers to underscore with solid type metal the unity, individuality, and independence that built America. And American printing history was made when newspaper presses crossed the Appalachians and traveled so far from easy supplies of paper, types, ink, and news.

The trail-blazer was Thomas Davis, son of the first printer and publisher of North Carolina. Returning to New Bern after he was mustered out of the Continental Army, Davis worked in the home shop until his father died and then moved press and business to Halifax, where he is believed to have published a newspaper; he also engaged in printing and publishing in Fayetteville and Hillsborough in the same state.

The Hillsborough *North-Carolina Gazette* that was "Printed by Robert Ferguson for Thomas Davis" had an undiluted pioneer flavor; its tang, color, and verve reflecting the vim and vigor of far-from-simple native-born adventurers also marked the change from traditional to a new American kind of news evaluation. The molds set in Boston, Philadelphia, Charleston, and New York by compulsions of poverty, defenselessness, and a nagging Authority, were damaged beyond repair by a few feckless pioneers. Oddly the Hillsborough newspaper was rarely, if ever, quoted in the "exchanges" whose dallying Undertakers, Authors, and Conductors must have found in it a new zest they dared not imitate for more sedate constituencies.

In the Hillsborough *Gazette* for February 16, 1786, there were "extractions" amazingly different from the usual innocuous generalities which attracted the scissors of most early American publishers. Here under a London date line was red meat for red-blooded men in a long "Commination" beginning: "Britianica: Cursed is the man that heavily oppresseth the poor by burdensome taxes, and that worshipeth the image of himself above the interests of the people . . . And the people shall answer and say 'Amen.' " There appeared also a political creed that patriots were urged to repeat each night and morning, which started with: "I believe that a Kingdom divided against itself cannot stand. . . . I believe that a Kingdom can never prosper in which lawyers are paid for the perverting of the sentiments of the people."

And here also was news about the weather with a unique touch of drama. In Quebec on October 16, a mere four months before this printing, the sun had disappeared at midday. It was Sunday and the blackness deepened to that of night and even the Protestant churches had to be lighted with candles; high gales, rain, and thunder persisted throughout the day, and the rain that fell was almost black.

Although social events were omitted from the news columns of its *Gazette*, Hillsborough undoubtedly had its full share of fun. There were house-raisings, huskings, and bees, and on the Fourth of July after the parade and speeches, men met to "throw the log," the only sport considered worthy of mention by early publishers. But St. Patrick's Day was something special, and an advertising card notified "Such Hibernian Gentlemen as intend celebrating the Anniversary of their titular Saint on Friday the 17th of March Next, are requested to leave their names at the bar of John Tyler, Esq." In the same columns appears:

Joseph Stubbins, Currier and Furrier, late from Connecticut, takes this means to inform the public that he intends carrying on the Tanning and Currying Business in Hillsborough; he will allow the highest prices for hides and calf-skins. He likewise carries on the boot and shoe making business. Those Gentlemen who please to favor him with their Custom may depend on having their work done in the best manner and on the most reasonable terms for cash or country produce. . . . N.B. Those who have hides they want tanned on shares may have them done at the above mentioned place.

Contemporary sanitation and science are made open books with: "Any persons that will dispose of their FRONT TEETH (slaves excepted) may receive up to two Guineas for each by calling on Doctor Laymeur. For further particulars inquire of the printer."

Over roads scarcely more than badly marked trails, John Scull and John Hall, each twenty-one years old, sent press, types, paper, and ink to the Manor of Pittsburgh at the junction of the Monongahela and Allegheny Rivers, where a real-estate boom had attracted almost three hundred settlers to unplowed acres held by the descendants of William Penn. Setting up shop on Water Street, at the Corner of Chancery-

Lane, the partners printed the first number of the Pittsburgh *Gazette* on July 29, 1786. "Subscriptions at 17s 6d, plus costs of delivery." ". . . Essays, advertisements, &c., thankfully received and Printing in general performed with accuracy and dispatch."

The early death of John Hall left John Scull to print and publish under difficulties that multiplied with his success. He at once started a campaign for a post office and was obliged to find horsemen who could be "encouraged" to make deliveries to a growing subscription list. In 1790 his persistence was rewarded; John Scull was appointed postmaster of Pittsburgh and John Scull's riders became post-riders. With wondrous faith Scull continued to advertise that riders were "authorized to accept and receipt arrearages." Newsprint was delivered to the pressroom door by nose-to-tail pack-horse trains; when trails were impassable to these freighters and supplies exhausted, the publisher went to press on cartridge paper borrowed from Fort Pitt. A paper-mill erected on Redstone Creek in 1797 provided some relief from this anxiety, but its dependability was limited by the scarcity of rags.

The early Pittsburgh *Gazette* was notable for its interesting articles describing the New Settlements of Pennsylvania. Written by H. H. Breckenridge, these were widely reprinted in the country's newspapers whose subscribers were avid for the information they offered, and many of the adventurous started West for Pittsburgh almost at once—just what publisher and author both were angling for. Their intelligent use of the newspapers was largely responsible for the town's early start towards the great industrial city whose first smoking stacks John Scull lived to see. In this, America's first "boomer," the "latest from Europe," morbid "entertainment" and moss-grown anecdotes were often pushed into total eclipse by local news and the letters that shed light on local politics and politicians. And John Scull's columns sizzled with scorn for the effete East and the general sappiness of a people who permitted members of the United States Senate to vote themselves a lordly three dollars a day "in order to convince unbelievers of their importance." The Whisky Rebellion of 1794 and other national and domestic sensations of the times occasioned other outbursts of letter-writing to reveal the best and the worst of pioneer minds.

The newspaper press made its third great assault on the wilderness west of Philadelphia when John Bradford, Indian-fighting surveyor, agreed to provide an "organ" for settlers advocating that Kentucke become a state separate and independent of Virginia. In return for his commitments Bradford was given a town lot in Lexington, on which

he immediately started the erection of a log cabin to house his family
and also to house the printing press he dispatched his brother, Fielding,
to purchase in Philadelphia. Family and press traveled by horse and
wagon to Pittsburgh; flatboats carried them down the Ohio to Lime-
stone—now Maysville—where horses and wagons were waiting to haul
passengers and freight over the last sixty miles to Lexington.

The first number of the *Kentucke Gazette* came from the new press
on August 11, 1787, printed from type that had become pied in transit
and had been patiently reassembled into cases. And although the new
publisher was inexperienced, with the help of his brother the new
newspaper was well organized and printed. For many years the *Kentucke Gazette* was the only newspaper in that vast, sparsely settled area.

From its earliest numbers the *Kentucke Gazette* caught and held the
glamour and romance of the Old Kentucke of song and story. Its
generously filled news columns often quite casually reported encounters
with Indians. Among the local news items on September 8, 1787, were:
"On Monday night last, a Mr. Schooler at Harrison's Station on Licking
Creek, hearing something in his garden which he supposed to be horses,
he went out to see, and an Indian fired at him and missed him; he
immediately flew in with the Indian and laid hold on his gun, which the
Indian let go and made his escape, leaving the gun with Mr. Schooler."
And "On Wednesday last George Mason with . . . Gluscock came over
Licking from the Salt-Works in order to cut and draw some wood; two
Indians crawled within ten steps and fired on Mason, both shots
wounded him, of which he died that night. They got some horses in
the neighborhood and went off." Some of Bradford's Indian stories were
called sheerest moonshine, but they are interesting reading even today.

The pioneer love for "lawing," the waspish legal bickering which relieved the monotony of peace, often reached a furious boil in the
Gazette's advertising columns. The classic "personal" of Charles Bland
who "would not pay a note given to W. Turner for three second-rate
cows until he returns a rifle, blanket and Tomahawk I loanded him," is
matched by:

The public should be cautious how they deal with a certain Capt. John
Martin of Lincoln County, as that man has lately taken advantage of the law
in pleading the Limitation Act and that only because he has been indulged
nearly three years. This I hope will be sufficient warning to all citizens of
Kentucke, particularly those in business. M. Nagle, Danville, Dec. 11, 1787.
N.B. He says I owe him, let him produce his accounts, proved, and then I
will give him credit on the execution I have against him. M.N.

In early numbers of the *Kentucke Gazette*, sometimes on front pages and in little boxes appropriately made of printers' stars, was: "NOTICE. A large Company will meet at the Crab Orchard on the 19th of November, in order to start early the next day through the wilderness. As it is very dangerous on account of Indians, it is hoped that each person will go well armed." And in advertising columns always filled with horses, horses, horses—for sale, stolen, strayed, lost, found, or wanted— were little notices of the new classes being started by Captain Thomas Young, Dancing-Master.

Pioneering printers and their presses almost anticipated prospective subscribers arriving with whetstones and axes to tame the wilds of western Virginia, Tennessee, and Ohio. Although Georgetown, now in the District of Columbia, was old enough to have a cemetery when Charles Fierer started his *Times, and Patowmack Packet* in 1789, it had, it seemed, no need for a newspaper. But at Shepherd's-town, at the mountain-mirroring confluence of the Potomac and the Shenandoah, the *Patowmack Guardian, and Berkeley Advertiser* established by Nathaniel Willis, printer and publisher from Boston, not only lived but survived a removal to Martinsburg, where it was continued until he sold out ten years later.

In Tennessee, George Roulstone, Boston-born printer with experience in Salem and Fayetteville, and Robert Ferguson from Hillsborough introduced the printing press and got out the initial number of the Knoxville *Gazette* from Hawkins Court-House, now Rogersville, on November 5, 1791. When Knoxville was made Territorial Capital, the newspaper, though none too successful, went along and was continued by Roulstone alone irregularly, for a few years before it disappeared.

"The Printer . . . to the Public: Having arrived at Cincinnati, he has applied himself to that which has been the principle object of his removal to this Country: the Publication of a *Newspaper*."; William Maxwell, veteran of the war, whose press was newly set up in a brand-new log cabin, went on and on with his high-falutin' salutation in the first number of his *Centinel of the North-Western Territory* of November 9, 1793, only to confess, on page three of the folio, that he had mislaid the list of subscribers obtained in advance of publication—would they kindly call at the printing office? He had but little local news, but the story of an attack by Indians near St. Clair made the newspaper important reading for pioneers. After three years, when he was appointed postmaster, Maxwell sold the *Centinel* to Edmund Freeman.

Publishers and idle paper-mills called for more and more "old clothes, old bedding and old wagon covers." Eastern presses depended on Europe's rag-bags; and mills both east and west used more and more cotton in paper, which came out strangely mottled as the washed blues, tans, and grays favored by pioneers were thrown into vats to be under-bleached or over-blued. High prices for rags made for high-priced news-print and the business of newspaper publishing became, if possible, more hazardous than ever. Serious experiments seeking "pulp-extenders" were undertaken by the ingenious.

Press builders were unable to build presses fast enough to supply demands. Platens and type-beds of the newer presses made common newspapers almost twice the size of those still regularly printed on ancient importations from Europe, but the newest, exactly like the oldest, were operated by the strong arms of pressmen who, with feet well braced, gave mighty horizontal pulls to levers that turned the screws forcing platens down—hard—on the prepared type-beds to make just one impression on one side of each news sheet.

Adam Ramage, a talented Scotsman in Philadelphia, made the first major improvement to the press of Gutenberg in 1796 when he replaced the ancient spindle-screw with one of "triple thread, rapid action"; two men, working at a Ramage, a small wooden press in which, later, platen and type-bed were of iron, could turn off the unprecedented volume of seventy-five impressions an hour. In the same year and in the same city, Archibald Binney and James Ronaldson, friends of Ramage and also immigrants from Scotland, opened their famous type-foundry. Two years later the Earl of Stanhope in England patented a press made entirely of cast iron and operated by a series of compound levers. The Stanhope had a platen double the size of the largest known to press-men; it had greater speed and was easily operated, but its many fine qualities were offset by its great weight and the numbers of pressmen its operation required.

The Ramage press was beloved by the American pioneer printers who, with the first westward expansion of America, carried it by horse and wagon, ox-cart, prairie-schooner, flatboat, bull-boat, canoe, and dug-out to remote frontiers to set up the newspapers that were the thin lines of communication between raw wilderness and "home." It was the Ramage, representing the entire worldly goods and chattels of printers arriving in tiny settlements, depots, and stations to "strike off" new newspapers, that comprised the only articulate links binding individual pioneers to territorial, state, and federal governments.

Greenleaf's Nea

Nameplate. New York, January 5, 1797. The first appearance
of an anti-administration newspaper. Courtesy of New York
Public Library.

Daily Advertiser

7

COCKADES TO COCKED HATS

FREEDOM OF THE PRESS WAS MORE THAN AN EMPTY
phrase from some politician's store of shop-worn oratory to early America. It was more than the meaningless words of some too-familiar refrain to printers and publishers and to the mechanics and inventors
whose skill was to lead, step by step, to today's high-speed printing
presses and processes.

Freedom of the Press to every thinking American meant freedom to
print the truth: freedom to oppose, publicly, views, opinions, or events
affecting personal or public welfare; freedom to criticize publicly the

conduct of any elected officer or appointed official of any administration; freedom to complain of abuses by persons, parties, or corporations in newspapers themselves as free from control and censorship as every American.

And Freedom of the Press, before the end of the century in which it was won, was a cloak for the mischievous who would bend the young Republic to compliment one European country or insult another, a protection found lacking in warmth for the delicate, and a shabby garment whose ownership was denied by a government claiming it had never been legally ordered.

Under the bold motto of "Here truth UNLICENC'D reigns, and dares accost e'en Kings themselves, or Rulers of the Free," the New York *Journal and Patriotic Register* achieved, by accident rather than design, the dubious distinction of being the first of the still-notorious "party-prints." The *Journal* had its origin in the old *Independent Gazette;* or *the New-York Journal Revived* of John Holt. After the death of that patriot-printer, it was published by his widow, Elizabeth Hunter Holt and her son-in-law, Colonel Eleazer Oswald, who changed the title to *Journal, or Weekly Recorder,* before selling out in 1786 to their employee, a Bostonian, Thomas Greenleaf. A new career for the old campaigner began with Greenleaf's support of a faction fearful that adulation of George Washington would lead the people back into a monarchy of which the great commander-in-chief would be the first American king. With the emergence of opposing political philosophies, the *Journal* swung its considerable influence to the aid of the anti-Federalists.

To offset advantages conferred by the sympathetic *Journal* upon the party of its choice, and to inoculate and extend the dogma of the Federalists, the *Gazette of the United States* was started in New York on April 15, 1789. Alexander Hamilton financed it—this first newspaper of the "party press," of which many were to come and go without either public cheers or private weeping.

John Fenno, a schoolmaster without printing or publishing experience, was given the reins of the *Gazette,* and in the first number announced that his would be a "National paper, published at the seat of Government." Further, he proposed to supply "Early and Authentic Accounts of the Proceedings of Congress—its Laws, Acts and Resolutions; communicated so as to form an history of the Transactions of the Federal Legislature under the new Constitution." This should have held a potent appeal for prospective subscribers at only three dollars a year at this time when an acute, intelligent, and not always approving interest in the First Federal Administration, yet to be inaugurated, was revealed in letters of the public to the country's publishers.

Hamilton made Fenno's *Gazette* the medium for attack on Thomas Jefferson, with such success that anti-Federalists were convinced that they must also set up an exclusive organ. And as party members met to ponder the all-important question of who might "conduct" such a newspaper, Philip Morin Freneau, sea captain, adventurer, journalist, and poet, sailed into New York Harbor in command of the schooner *Columbia* eight days out of Charleston. As reported in the *Daily Advertiser* the *Columbia*, dressed and decorated in the most superb manner, next day welcomed General Washington and led the gaily garlanded and streamered aquatic parade escorting that old soldier from Elizabethtown Point to the first "Capital City" where, a week later in a simple ceremony on the balcony of Federal Hall, he became the first President of these United States.

Freneau found many friends in the town humming with an excitement far more exhilarating than the tang of the sea he had deserted for the *Daily Advertiser*. His sparkling verses, lampooning the pompous, pretentious, and self-important, were widely reprinted in newspapers, and made Philip Freneau a national as well as a local celebrity.

When the seat of government moved from New York to Philadelphia, Fenno and the *Gazette of the United States* went along with the Federal offices. And, shortly, James Madison, the classmate of Freneau at the College of New-Jersey, now Princeton, with the help of Thomas Jefferson, persuaded the ex-seaman to join them at the capital where, with their assistance, he started the *National Gazette* on October 31, 1791. In the *Gazette* Freneau campaigned against Fenno, his *Gazette*, his Federalists friends, and all they stood for with energy, ability, and an agile and sometimes comic irony.

The newspaper war grew shrill and bitter; both *Gazettes* printed letters from not unknown correspondents containing acidulous attacks on leaders of opposing parties whose policies became more irreconcilable with every issue. The grateful Jefferson, patron saint of the anti-Federalists, got Freneau a job as translator in the State Department at two hundred and fifty dollars a year "and little to do," and Hamilton remained financially faithful to the bumbling Fenno. In vain the humiliated Washington suggested to his Secretaries of State and Treasury that the squabblings of journalistic henchmen be hushed.

That Freneau's *Gazette* "saved the Constitution that was fast galloping into a monarchy" was Jefferson's firm conviction. Other anti-Federalists, now Republicans, dubbed Fenno's paper the "Court Journal" and accused it of "making way for a King, Lords and Commons." Fenno was clearly obsessed with the resonance of titles and enjoyed writing of "Our Illustrious President and His Suite" and of "His Excellency, the Vice-President." Once, to that gentleman's undeserved embarrassment, Fenno wrote (March 22nd of 1792) of Washington as The Protector, and Freneau in response promptly dreamed up a Royal Levee over which would preside Her Highness, the Protectoress. Many of Fenno's correspondents wrote him at length deploring the sad plight of American ambassadors to foreign courts who were looked down on because they had no titles. The opposition came right back with: "If plain Mister isn't good enough for any American in any foreign court—let 'em stay home." John Fenno, to his credit, published the protests of both sides.

Fenno's *Gazette of the United States* had somewhat exclusive access to the news of the administration besides the paid advertising of the Treasury Department; and Freneau, although the recipient of many favors from the State Department, considered his right to the news as valid as that of his rival publisher. There was neither precedent nor claim for recognition of the people's rights to news of their government when the Constitution was devised. The Journal of the Continental Congress, now by evolution the *Congressional Record*, was thought all that was necessary for the curious—an opinion heartily endorsed by representatives of that same people.

The doors of the House of Representatives were open to newsmen from April of 1789. A year later the Senate, filled with old men to whom the country wished to do honor and callow youths just cutting political eyeteeth (according to the letter-writers who thought the House the more important arm of government), rejected a resolution to admit representatives of the press. Wrote Freneau in February of 1792:

A motion to open the Senate Chamber has again been lost by a considerable majority . . . in defiance of intention, in defiance of your opinion, in defiance of every principle which gives security to free men. What means this condition? What expression does it carry with it? Contempt for you or tyranny? Are you free men who ought to know the individual conduct of your legislators, or are you an inferior order of beings, incapable of comprehending the sublimity of senatorial functions and unworthy to be entrusted with their opinions? How are you to know the just from the unjust steward when they are covered with the mantle of concealment? Can there be any question of legislative import which freemen cannot be acquainted with?

What are you to expect when stewards of your household refuse to give an account of their stewardship?

Secrecy is necessary to design and a masque to treachery; honesty shrinks not from the public eye. The Peers of America disdain to be seen by vulgar eyes, the music of their voices is in harmony only for themselves and must not vibrate in the ravished ear of the ungrateful and unworthy multitude. . . . Remember, my fellow citizens, that you are still free men, let it be impressed upon your minds that you depend not on your representatives, but that they depend on you, and let this truth be ever present to you; that secrecy in your representatives is a worm that will prey and fatten upon the vitals of liberty.

This was the kind of pressure, wielded unremittingly and with the force of a crowbar in the hands of an angry man, that in 1794 persuaded the Senate to reverse its motion. The doors that had been open only during the debates on the seating of Albert Gallatin were grudgingly conceded open to the country's newspapers. In some quarters, however, senatorial objection to reporters was adamant; Republican and Federalist members of both Houses distrusted the innovation and denounced it as dangerous. The shorthand of the times, not easy of mastery, was unknown to American newspaper publishers, and the English and Irish practitioners sometimes employed were constantly accused of bias and misrepresentation. That there was much bungling in the transcribing of their notes could not be denied. It was years before provision was made for more than one newsman to attend sessions of either House or Senate. The reporter assigned to the House was seated at the speaker's table where he could see and hear all that was going on; and the reporter for the Senate sat in the box with the Vice President.

Freedom to report the doings of the government, instead of news government-doled to favorites, was won by Philip Freneau. The new freedom, however, found newsmen inexperienced to handle news-in-the-making; and they failed to appraise or appreciate the news behind the forces then shaping American politics. News had hitherto consisted of unvarnished presentation of matters political, printed by friends and omitted by enemies. Now there was a sudden epidemic of professional propagandists who, for cash, or in an honest crusading spirit, burst into print with endless letters to sympathetic and scornful publishers alike.

Both political parties in process of clarifying disagreements on Federal powers were profoundly moved by the Revolution of the French. The shocked Federalists, leaning towards English ideas of aristocracy, looked to England to act as Europe's stabilizer; but the Republicans, their fears sharpened by this attitude towards a recent enemy, glorified the upheaval that marked the end of European feudalism as a local party victory.

Party leaders, whose animosities were already dramatized in party-subsidized newspapers, were fortified by the independent "party prints" that hurried to their support, and they were heartened by the fighting words of partisan letter-writers who, on missions of mischief, filled their columns with praise or slander. "Now was the time" for the evil to influence war-weakened America in the alliance with the country it was expected to make prosperous by a protective treaty.

The only really important newspaper to give its full and independent support to the Washington administration was Major Benjamin Russell's *Columbian Centinel*, which had been renamed in honor of the adoption of the Constitution. Fenno was unswerving in upholding Federalists principles, but Fenno was known to be Hamilton's man and Hamilton had many enemies even in his own party. The subsidized Freneau was enthusiastically aided by the independent Greenleaf, and around this quartette other newspapers aligned their space and talents for coming battles in whose ink-slinging frenzies few newspapers were to remain unsullied.

Into the speeding spiral of the political cyclone swung the young Benjamin Franklin Bache with his *Aurora*, established in 1790 as the *General Advertiser, and Political, Agricultural Literary Journal*. The title under which the newspaper rode to notoriety was an afterthought. Bache was the favorite Benny of the illustrious grandfather who took him to Paris when he was but seven years old. Franklin had the lad taught the art of printing by the Pierres of Versailles, the Didots, and other masters. And although Bache had been in this country for five years and was only twenty-five when he started his newspaper, it was immediately outstanding for its fine foreign coverage. When contentions of party lines brought everything French into American prominence, Benjamin Franklin Bache was revealed as more French than American, and the possessor of a deep and festering hatred for England and everything English.

The first signal of coming storm was the arrival of Doctor Joseph Priestley, the eminent scholar, theologian, and chemist, who had been so staunch in his support of the French Revolutionists that irritated English neighbors had burned his Birmingham home, including his library, on Bastille Day of 1791. Public interest in this distinguished refugee to the Land of Freedom was wide-spread; news of his landing from the *Samson* on June 3, 1794, quickly circulated throughout the newspapers that also gave much space to the flowery addresses of welcome by New York's many Societys and Orders and also to the responses in kind.

Citizens and visitors turned out to meet the traveler arriving in the capital city with greetings so spontaneously warm that Republicans were jubilant—and Federalists appalled. Before the excitement subsided there appeared for sale in windows of Philadelphia's bookshops an anonymous pamphlet called "Observations on the Emigration of Doctor Priestley." This pleased the Federalists, infuriated the Republicans, and amused the amiable scientist. The author of this tract, William Cobbett, was so enchanted with the commotion he had stirred up that after further pamphleteering (which earned him the name of Peter Porcupine) he started another Philadelphia newspaper on March 4, 1797. This was, of course, *Porcupine's Gazette.*

The provocative, perverse, pugnacious, and unpredictable Porcupine was an extremely personal journalist who used the first person singular without hesitation or restraint. In an early issue of the *Gazette* he remarked: "Of professions of impartiality I shall make none. They are always useless and are besides perfect nonsense." The Porcupine was an unabashed possessor of an unrivaled command of billingsgate, and, accustomed as he was to threats of tar and feathers, often engaged in newspaper battles for the sheer love of fighting and the display of his very special talent for stirring up other editors.

The Porcupine and Lightning Rod, Junior, as Bache was known to his contemporaries, seized upon an opportunity not delivered by Heaven to lead in the debasing of American newspapers. Bache took ambush behind the editorial We, and as he increased his attacks on the Federalists, the administration, and the President, the Porcupine became Washington's defender. Although a political refugee from England himself, Cobbett advocated an American alliance with that country against France.

While Fenno, Bache, and Cobbett in Philadelphia, Greenleaf in New York, and Major Russell in Boston struggled to coax, cajole, threaten, or shame the country into acceptance of opposing creeds, other publishers whose newspapers—sedate and assured, pompous or pedantic, reckless or racy—tugged frantically to push or pull the slow pendulum of time to favor impatient Republicans or cautious Federalists.

Republicans were irked and Federalists pleased by David Carlisle's

Tory sheet. The *Farmer's Weekly Museum*, that began in Walpole, New Hampshire, in 1793 was so popular that on publication days two post-riders were on duty to forward its phenomenal two thousand copies to every state and territory in the Union. The grandfathers of all American columnists made their debuts in this newspaper. Of the more famous features were the pithy paragraphs From the Shop of Messrs. Colon and Spondee (Royall Tyler), the verses of Simon Spunky (Thomas Fessendon), and the widely quoted and reprinted Little Sermons of the Lay Preacher (Joseph Dennie) still regarded as among the best of American newspaper essays.

The dignified *American Minerva* whose "conductor," and also instigator, was the distinguished lexicographer, Noah Webster, came to the support of President Washington. This newspaper was frankly of the Federalist persuasion but independent of party control. It was Webster's conviction "that newspapers should be placed on a respectable footing; they should be the Heralds of Truth and the protectors of Peace and Good Order." A semiweekly, the *Herald* was made up of texts from the daily *Minerva* and reprinted for rural circulation without recomposition of types. The success of the *Herald* revealed more than an untapped source of revenue to newspaper publishers; it set the pattern for coming Country Editions in which great American editors became powerful in shaping national thinking.

The party prints grew more international with every number and each issue carried less local and general domestic news, but advertising columns were crowded with evidence that life went along merrily enough for the politically sane. Editors and publishers whose eyes pried political keyholes of London, Paris, Rome, and Hamburg may have disapproved of the frivolous interests of fellow citizens, but they accepted their cash, produce, or promises to pay in exchange for space to advertise theatrical performances, lotteries, fireworks, horse races, exhibitions of apes, monkeys, lions, and elephants, and the new sensational, and fascinating patent-medicine testimonials.

News followed the party lines of the Republicans when it was necessary to explain the arrogance of Citizen Charles Edouard Edmond Genet, who calmly assumed that propaganda had already made the United States a subject country of France. And news followed the party lines of Federalists, conscious of coming criticism when the articles of the Jay Treaty with England were known. And the public, reading between the lines as it always does, sensed the difficulties of the administration trying to preserve neutrality and chose its ally, or its enemy, in the current dispute between England and France.

The Jay Treaty was ratified by Special Session of the Senate. On June 26, 1795, Benjamin Franklin Bache wrote in the *Aurora*: "This imp of darkness illegitimately begotten, commanded the bare Constitutional numbers required." And in his very next number he could print:

Dear Mr. Bache:—I have been daily hoping to see in the public prints a copy of the late treaty with Britain, but as such a publication has not been made, I transmit the heads of that instrument, after an attentive perusal. There necessarily must be deficiencies in an account of this kind which depends entirely on memory, and for the same reason there must be inaccuracies, but I trust the latter are few. A Citizen."

"The fountains of the deep are broken up—halleluiah"—wrote Mr. Bache as he published the essentials of the treaty in advance of its release by the President and Senate. A few days later he offered the complete text in a pamphlet. "A Citizen," the country was startled to learn, was Stevens Thomson Mason, United States Senator from Virginia, who was praised by some and denounced by others for his embarrassing disclosure.

Republican newspapers, underscoring the disappointments of the Jay Treaty, used news to stir public anger to the pitch of stoning Alexander Hamilton and burning John Jay in effigy. Newspapers of Federal sympathies fought with the long series of "Camillus" articles by Alexander Hamilton, the greatest political writer of the times, and with the "Curtius" series by Noah Webster that had many reprintings and aided in winning for the Treaty public understanding and approval.

"Truth, Decency, Utility" in the original motto of the *Aurora* were lost when Bache printed a number of scandalous letters, (proved forgeries) and attributed them to Washington. "A Calm Observer" (probably Bache himself) made the charge that the President had overdrawn his salary and was "no better than a common defaulter"; and a burlesque poem, Bache's contribution to February 22, 1796, made thinking people wonder if there were no limits to newspaper freedom.

Abuse of the President and his Administration was continuous and not confined to the opposition. It must have been with relief that President Washington sent for Lieutenant David C. Claypoole to give him the manuscript of the famous Farewell Address that appeared in the *American Daily Advertiser* on Monday, September 19, 1796. With modesty shocking to the modern eye it was printed in tiny types on pages two and three of the folio. The heading, "To the PEOPLE of the United States; Friends and Fellow-Citizens," occupied but two lines atop the first of the five narrow columns it filled, and the tallest types were only a quarter-inch. Page one was covered as usual with little advertisements. There was no indication of its somewhat special contents, nor was the Address mentioned editorially in this or in any immediately succeeding numbers.

The Aurora became openly the organ of the French Executive Directory. Two decrees of that body were communicated by Adet, the French Minister, to this newspaper and to Timothy Pickering simultaneously, and the American Secretary of State answered in the same fashion including an acid comment on its singularity. Again Adet used the Aurora for an impolitic harangue urging all Frenchmen in America and all sympathizers with the French Revolutionists always to identify themselves by wearing the tricolor in a cockade. And in the Aurora for March 5, 1797, Benjamin Franklin Bache climaxed his career as exponent of political opposition by journalistic violence with his Valedictory: ". . . now if ever there was a period for rejoicing, this is the moment, and every heart in unison with the freedom and the happiness of the people ought to beat high with exultation, that the name Washington from this day ceases to give a political currency to political inequity and to legalize corruption." His call for a Jubilee was answered almost at once by a mob led by veterans who had fought under Washington: they beat the publisher soundly and wrecked his office.

After the inauguration of John Adams, the Republican press that had considered Washington and his political household the only barriers to eviction of the "American aristocracy rooted in the Federal Government" sat back to await the tides of the new Revolution, anticipating recognition, assistance, and favors. But disappointment, disillusion, and irritation bred new recklessness. The presses of both parties were newly responsive to goadings of recently arrived editors and writers, who cared only to continue the wars of Europe from the safety of American shores. Dignity was thrown to the winds as editors and publishers, native and alien, turned upon each other: "Noah is patronized by old Tories and British Agents," screamed the Aurora. "Bache is only a splinter from the old lightning-rod," sneered the Porcupine. "Cobbett literally hadn't a second shirt to his back, a broken-down school-teacher when he started the Gazette," confided Major Russell to his subscribers.

To the Republican press had rallied the Boston Independent Chron-

icle owned by Isaac Larkin; another of its new members was the *Bee*, published in New London, Connecticut, by Charles Holt. (Price one dollar and a half per annum, payable in anything. A dollar in advance will not be refused.) These newspapers earned great party prestige and the letters from subscribers and propagandists who freely used their columns (reprinted with "extracts" from Freneau's writings and quotations from Greenleaf's newspaper) furnished the bulk of the news dispensed to their publics by party small-fry.

The *Argus*, under a larger-than-life human eye and a new motto, "We Guard the Rights of Man," was enlivened by letters addressed in all seriousness to "Citizen Greenleaf, Dear Sir:—" John Lang, in his New York *Gazette* remarked: "Censure from the *Aurora* or the *Argus* is preferable to praise when applied to the principles of this *Gazette*"— and added, "In our leisure moments we shall continue to counteract the policies of these two newspapers." And Cobbett, looking for a fight, ran headlong into James Carey, whose Philadelphia *United States Recorder* was then advertising its publisher's tract: A NOSEGAY for YOUNG MEN dedicated without love or affection to The SKUNK Porcupine. Carey wrote and published this little bedtime story called "Porcupinade":

"Peter Porcupine has at last length discovered that cookery is his forte; and still desirous of serving a ROYAL MASTER, has volunteered to supply the table of his Infernal Majesty with delicacies from this sublunary world of ours. His generous offer was made yesterday in language polite, elegant and classical. But let the Porcupine speak for himself: 'Send me a file of your papers, you trimming rascals, and you shall see what pretty creatures I'll make of you. I'll cook you up a dish fit for the DEVIL. Wm. Cobbett.' We are yet to learn whether or not Beelzebub will accept this eleemosynary from his good friend COBBETT, but on Porcupine's qualifications for superintending the infernal kitchen, not the least doubt can be entertained; for every man of good taste will readily admit that the OLIOS and OLLA PODRIDAS which the arch cook has hitherto served up to the sovereign people of America, were calculated for a HELLISH APPETITE."

The X.Y.Z. Affair exploded and in the face of wrath echoing Pinckney's "No, bo, not one sixpence" with "Millions for defense; not one cent for tribute," Republican newspapers hysterically tried to whitewash Tallyrand and the Directory. Bache's supreme efforts brought upon him the charge that he was in the pay of France, and although this he denied, the *Aurora* suffered a loss in circulation. It remained for the

Independent Chronicle to shame the shameless with its unasked advice that the government purchase from France "16,000,000 Dutch subscriptions at par"; then France could be expected to "reimburse the equitable demands of America rising from prizes" and to give "Free Navigation to other ships in the future." Before public anger at this suggestion that America buy the freedom of the seas lessened, "Major Ben" hoisted his party into another row by asking all true Americans to "Mount the Cockade," and the editor could soon report that the ribbons were "now generally worn," in spite of Adet's instantly revived "Order."

The newspapers of both parties, grown venomous, drove outraged Federalists into sponsoring the Alien and Sedition Laws in order to confine, if not control, the press. First arrested was Benjamin Franklin Bache, charged with libel of the President. He was released on parole and died before trial. The *Aurora* was then continued by William Duane, American-born publisher of the *Indian World* of Calcutta, whose persecution had made him even more anti-British than Bache. Federal newspapers gossiped happily about the niggardly salary the Bache heirs were supposed to be paying Duane, until they were silenced by news of his marriage to Mrs. Bache.

Federal fireworks began to burn Federal fingers when, after much pious searching, they found "actionable matter" in Anthony Haswell's Bennington *Gazette* of June 29, 1796, and were able to make their most important arrest. Congressman Matthew Lyon, Republican member of the House of Representatives from Federalist Vermont, and notorious for his floor fight with Roger Griswold, was charged with writing and causing to be published:

As to the Executive, when I shall see the efforts of that power bent on the promotion of the comfort, the happiness and accomodation of the people, that Executive shall have my zealous and uniform support. But when I shall, on the part of that Executive, see every consideration of public welfare swallowed up in a continuous grasp for power, in unbounded thirst for ridiculous pomp, foolish adulation and selfish avarice . . . I shall not be his humble advocate.

Matthew Lyon's trial was sensational and the repercussions infinite. The veteran of the Revolution was fined one thousand dollars and sentenced to four months in prison. Anthony Haswell tried to raise money for Lyon by lottery, and was himself arrested and convicted of sedition, but friends and admirers paid the fine and reelected Lyon while he was in jail. In the Scourge of Aristocracy and Repository of Political Truths, Colonel Lyon, a printer and once a publisher, told his whole story with types he cut and cast himself and on paper he made of basswood pulp.

Federal and Republican newspapers agreed, for once, in upholding Colonel Lyon. "Pomp" was an accusation which always aroused suspicion. But for James T. Callendar, Republican writer and scandal-monger of industry and imagination, there were no evidences of honesty. This patentee of the technique of smearing fled to Richmond for safety and employment by Merriwether Jones on the *Examiner*, and here he published the "Prospect Before Us." He was found guilty of slandering President Adams and fined two hundred dollars. While in jail for nine months, he got out two more offensive pamphlets with money supplied by Thomas Jefferson. After his inauguration Jefferson freed Callendar and remitted his fine, but not quickly enough, nor was the demanded postmastership of Richmond at once forthcoming. The journalist abused his most recent employer, Henry Pace of the *Recorder*, and in letters addressed to the "respectable" Federal newspapers accused Jefferson of immorality, cowardice, dishonesty, and ingratitude. The President's lame "explanation" was that he had thought Callendar "a misunderstood genius" finding support in letters to the newspapers defending the "man who does not wear powder on his hair, a martyr to the English because he is a gifted Irishman." Callendar was born in Scotland.

Greenleaf was a victim of yellow fever, and his wife continued his newspaper. Fenno, too, was a victim of yellow fever; and his son got out the *Gazette of the United States* for a few years. Freneau had suspended his publication in an earlier epidemic, partly because of lack of money. The *American Minerva* in 1797 became the *Commercial Advertiser*, merged in 1905 with the New York *Globe*, was purchased by Frank Munsey, and disappeared with the New York *Sun*, and the *Herald* became the *Spectator* to vanish with its ilk.

The Porcupine who came into American journalism on a pamphlet made his exit by the same conveyance. Cobbett had savagely attacked Doctor Benjamin Rush, Philadelphia physician, practically accusing him of murdering his yellow-fever patients with bleedings and purges. Charged with libel and sued for five thousand dollars, the publisher who had fled the stricken capital for nearby Bustleton, abandoned his newspaper, and in New York published a whole series of pamphlets called *The Rush Light*, and also in pamphlet form a farewell number (778) of *Porcupine's Gazette* on February 15, 1800. He then returned to England. In the tone and temper of the times Major Russell, in the *Colum-*

bian *Centinel*, administered this polishing-off: "Cobbett never was encouraged and supported by the Federalists as a solid, judicious writer for their cause; but was merely kept to hunt Jacobinic foxes, skunks and serpents. The Federalists found the Jacobins had the *Aurora, Argus* and *Chronicle*, through which they ejected their mud, filth and venom and attacked and blackened the best characters the world has ever boasted; and they perceived that these vermin were not to be operated on by reason or decency. It was therefore thought necessary that the opposite party should keep and feed a suitable beast to hunt these skunks and foxes, and the 'fretful Porcupine' was selected for this business. This imported, or transported, beast has been kept as a gentleman keeps a fierce *bull Dog*, to guard his house and his property against thieves, Jacobins and Frenchman, and as such he has been a good and faithful *Dog*, and has been fed and caressed accordingly."

Last of the avowed "organs" of Federalists and the Republicans, who were just beginning to be called Democrats, were the Washington *National Intelligencer* and the New York *Evening-Post*. Both were comparatively sane; the first lived to hear the guns of Fort Sumter and the other, with ownership, politics, policies, and editors many times changed, after a century and a half, still survives.

Mr. Silky, Milky Smith's National Soothing-Plane, the *National Intelligencer*, was originally the *Independent Gazetteer* of Colonel Eleazer Oswald. He sold it to Joseph Gales, Sr., an English refugee printer, who made the first verbatim report of Congress for the *American Daily Advertiser*. Gales sold the newspaper to William Harrison Smith, a protégé of Jefferson, at whose request he moved to Washington. Four days late, due to a storm at sea, the first number of the first newspaper actually printed in Washington came from the press on November 17, 1800. And in the hands of Joseph Gales, Jr., and Colonel William W. Seaton, both also experts at shorthand, the *Court Journal* faithfully and profitably served the administrations of Jefferson, Madison, Monroe, and John Quincy Adams. Its power declined with the inauguration of Jackson.

Organ of the opposition, the New York *Evening-Post*, sponsored by Alexander Hamilton and under the able guidance of William Coleman, in its salutatory on November 16, 1801, flatly stated: "We openly profess our attachment to that arm of politics denominated as Federal"—but—"this newspaper shall be free to all parties." And the *Evening-Post's* columns were free to the discredited Callendar for his letters of attack on Jefferson, and they were free to James Cheetham, publishing Greenleaf's old newspaper as the excellent *American Citizen* and writing to defend the leader of his party. And when the correspondence of Coleman and Cheetham led to a challenge in the grand manner, the planned duel was prevented by arrests of both men, who promised to cancel their engagement. Accused of cowardice by Captain Thompson, New York Harbor Master, Coleman sent his card, and early in January of 1803, in an open space between Sixth and Eighth Avenues, at about Twenty-first Street, then known to New Yorkers as Love Lane, honor was sustained in the eery stillness of gently falling snow of a late afternoon. Captain Thompson was left dying of his wounds, while Coleman hurried back to his office where "he got out the paper in good style, although half an hour late."

After a battle lost in the court it was, curiously, Alexander Hamilton, admitting a distrust of democracy, who won for the people the war against threatened curtailment of their free press. And, also curiously, this almost successful attempt to bring the country's news under the control of politics was made in the name of the aristocrat whose faith in the ability of the people to govern themselves was, even then, a glamorous political legend and the foundation of his party.

Felled by the Sedition Act, Charles Holt, once publisher of the New London Bee, in Hudson, New York, was made editor of another Bee, this one for solidly Republican Columbia County. The Bee was soon challenged by an angry little Wasp that, so read its masthead, was "published by Robert Rusticoat, Esquire," and "Printed for the Editor in Defiance of the Devil and a Whole Host of Democrats." Under a motto dear to the hearts of publishers—"To Lash the Rascals Naked Through the World"—the Wasp conjectured whether Holt was purchased or hired; it accused Jefferson of paying Callendar to defame the characters of Washington and Adams, and dared the Bee "To tell the truth and shame the Devil."

Here was opportunity on a golden salver. Quiet conviction of an obscure publisher would secure legal precedent for the humiliation of other, more important, independent publishers. Harry Croswell of the Hudson Balance, on whose press the Wasp was printed, never denied that he was Robert Rusticoat. Charged with libel of Thomas Jefferson, Croswell was arrested and the fate of the real victim, the free press, moved ponderously through the courts to its carefully rigged climax.

Instructing the Jury, July 11, 1803, Chief Justice Morgan Lewis ruled that the old law of libel (obsolete in England for fifty years) was still the law in the United States, and they were, legally, "judges only of the facts of printing and publishing, and not of the truth or intent of the publication." The verdict was Guilty. Croswell and the Wasp were no longer obscure. An appeal was made to the Court of Errors; and in Albany, on February 13, 1804, Alexander Hamilton held court and spectators spellbound for nearly six hours with his plea for a "free—not unchecked—press." And the judges, evenly balanced in party affiliations, permitted the verdict to stand by a tied vote on a motion for retrial.

But Hamilton's conception of the American press "free to publish, with impunity, Truth, though reflecting on government, magistracy, or individual" was, eventually, written into the laws of the states to make truth the essence of that free speech guaranteed by the Constitution to every American. And every American, basely attacked through the newspapers or by them, is guaranteed redress by juries charged with hearing and weighing the intent and truth of libelous publications before finding the extent of injury subject to legal penalty or punishment.

Politics and politicians increased the country's newspapers, if not their quality, to untold numbers. Some ornamented a single session of some territorial or state legislature; others had a short and merry few months immediately preceding the elections they were expected to influence. Only a few politically inspired newspapers managed to overcome the handicaps of the frail human beings they had to make into heroes, slates that had to have votes, or parties that, whatever their shortcomings, had to be installed in public office.

New newspapers were promoted to promote political aspirations, to promote presidential candidates, and to promote presidential dicta contrary to simple economic sanity and political sense. New newspapers were promoted to promote new and bizarre political movements, as when, in the 1830's, in New York and Pennsylvania alone, no less than a hundred came from nowhere to uphold the banners of the Anti-Masons rising high from the fantastic disappearance of the shadowy William Morgan.

In quality the political newspapers ranged downwards from Johnston Verplank's excellent New York American, organ of the Tammany Bucktails, to the New York Transcript, whose versatile editor was on the city payrolls as Stenographer to the Superior Court for $3,000 a year, as Stenographer of the Bureau of Elections, $3,000 a year, as Examiner of Public Accounts for $3,500 a year, and whose newspaper was primarily the vehicle for municipal advertising, at further expense to taxpayers.

Newspapers, the organs of politics, again flourished in the bitter aftermath of the War Between the States, when circulations danced to editorial tunes in measures called by party leaders. Then the magic waned until the political power of the press was permanently muted by the power of news. Party deserters—the "mugwumps"—gave their influential support to news-favored candidates sponsored by political enemies, and party "regulars" noisily rooting for mayoralty and presidential hopefuls less fortunate suffered from politically devastating landslides.

Experience, example, and public pressure at last impressed on the country's politicians the futility of politically conducted newspapers. Those of today may be classified as Republican, Democratic, or Socialist in sympathies, according to the political leanings of editors, publishers, and owners, but, and almost without exception, American newspapers of today are basically independent of party or political control. News, accepted as honest reporting, is the criterion by which candidates, platforms, and policies are admitted to the columns of every newspaper and to the respect of the intelligent newspaper-reading public.

Second U. S. Regiment

OF

LIGHT DRAGOONS.

EVERY able bodied Man from the age of 18 to 45 years, who shall be recruited for the army of the United States, for the term of five years, or during the war, will be paid a bounty of

SIXTEEN DOLLARS,

An Advance Pay of

TWENTY-FOUR DOLLARS,

AND

EIGHT DOLLARS PER MONTH,

And whenever he has served the term for which he enlisted, and obtained an honorable discharge, he will be allowed and paid in addition to the above bounty, an advance of three months pay, and

160 Acres of LAND.

And in case he should be killed in action, or die in the service, his heirs or representatives will be entitled to the said 3 months pay and 160 acres of Land. For further particulars, please to call at the Rendezvous, No 12. Elm-street, Boston.

ABEL WHEELOCK,

Lieut. Light Dragoons, Second Regiment.

☞ The Men will be completely equipped with implements immediately.   Feb 18

Advertisement for soldiers, in Independent Chronical. Boston, February 23, 1813. Courtesy of New York Public Library.

8

TO THE TERRAPIN WAR

SWIFTLY ROLLED THE YEARS OF PEACE. PROUD POS-
sessors of the new presses of Adam Ramage, as well as the owners of
antique presses, types, paper, ink, and an irrepressible itch to publish,
were able to choose between setting up in cities with more presses than
populations could support, in towns without press or printer, or the
beckoning West, that Promised Land for every man needing elbow
room and freedom to breathe.

Newspapers printed with hand-composed types on hand-made paper
were sustained by the hope, faith, and courage of printers, most of whom

were badly equipped for the business of publishing. Newspapers were still luxuries in the towns, and scarce and scattered country subscribers were, like their city cousins, lacking in ready cash.

The advertising that steadily gained in variety and volume, like the subscriptions "payable in advance," was only too rarely represented by cash paid into print-shop tills. Publishers whose presses were in their homes (often log cabins of two rooms) and who employed only one apprentice, whose corn-husk bed in a cold and comfortless loft and his food and washing comprised the major share of a meager wage, had to depend on job-printing to pay for the few necessities of life. Those popular centers of masculine conviviality, the warm and cheerful coffee houses where wayfarers, travelers, and local citizenry met to read the newspapers and discuss the news, were the most valued subscribers of every publisher, for theirs was the aristocracy of the paying customers.

News evaluations began to improve in the early 1800's. Foreign intelligence was still most important to publishers, who were then beginning to measure "extractions" by other values than oddity of date line or specifications for filling blank space. Laws, resolutions, and appointments of federal, state, and territorial administrations provided subscribers with solid reading. But local news, still "too well-known to print" lagged. And news for the nation's weeklies had to be selected with an eye to its wearing qualities; every publisher knew that every copy of his newspaper had an independent circulation of its own, and many, many readings.

"Awful murders" and "horrible suicides" liberally peppered the newspapers and stirred up storms of protest; but any news that was either a detriment to calamity or an encouragement to crime, in the opinion of Fisher Ames, was "properly news, and mentionable in the newspaper— but casually, and without morbidity." So the bald facts of butchery and the indecencies of self-inflicted death—unheadlined, briefly and brutally told—continued to be printed and reprinted.

And as the press continued its assaults on the tenants of the wilderness, newspaper history was star-studded with tales of riders who urged wearied nags on and on through miles of mud or choking dust, through dusky forest traces, or up and over mountain trails to lonely settlements, where entire populations—sometimes less than a dozen families—summoned by the blasts of a horn, waited around a tree-stump which was promptly mounted by someone who would read to them every line of the news.

Over more roads more riders carried eastern-shore newspapers redolent of "home," and new newspapers, in swelling numbers, returned compliments that but dimly reflected the lives of adventuring home-folk. Publishers, east and west, freely "extracted" from each others' columns; and this exchange gave to the nation its most cherished, most important, and most powerful news.

When letter-writers of inland forests and prairies took their quills in hand to complain of the difficulties, indignities, and expense experienced at the Spanish Port of New Orleans, their letters (culled by unpressured, unpropagandized, and inexperienced publishers) made the Mississippi Question a matter of country-wide interest and paved the way for satisfactory settlement by President Thomas Jefferson's "illegal" Louisiana Purchase. The West generally followed the time-hallowed formula to give first place to the Latest From Europe; but gradually this news was displaced by reports of British and French humiliation of American claims to equal freedom of the seas and to hints that hostile forces were supplying Indians with firewater and ammunition. And news of politics and politicians, of statesmen and lawmakers not only intrigued, inspired, and educated young westerners with inquiring minds, but led them back over the mountains to useful careers that won undying fame.

It was the American newspaper, scant in the news it so stiffly presented, that held the United States intact and prevented its early disintegration into isolated groups separated by the walls of sectionalism. It was news supplied by early newspapers that weakened the trend towards the concentration of settlers of similar origins, languages, interests, and religions. And it was often only the exuberant confidence of a come-early publisher that held together discouraged settlements visited by illness, Indians, crop failures, and extremes of climate.

New settlements stemmed from new settlements scarcely rooted, and the fast-growing newspaper press of western Pennsylvania, Kentucky, Ohio, and beyond was the product of native as well as of immigrant talent and enterprise. Settlements grown to towns and towns grown to cities hummed with the zest of their second and sometimes third newspapers, which usually were the outgrowth of blistering political differences.

It was less than twenty-five years after eastern newspapers could (thanks to "correspondents" and publishers with discriminating scissors) warn prospective pioneers that the "Indians at Fort Pitt are very troublesome," that Pittsburgh enjoyed three newspapers. In addition to John Scull's newspaper, today the *Post-Gazette*, John Israel's *Tree of*

Liberty, started in 1800 with the "encouragement" of Republican Hugh H. Brackenridge, was published for ten years. Ephrim Pentland's *Commonwealth* ran from 1805 to 1818, when John Scull, retired, saw westbound traffic arrive by the magnificent National Road and depart by keel boats, packets, and steam-driven paddles.

Kentucky's second newspaper, the *Guardian of Freedom*, was a Bradford enterprise begun in Frankfort in 1798; and its third, the Lexington *Stewart's Kentucky Herald*, after seven years, in 1802, became a Bradford property.

Cincinnati's *Western Spy, and Hamilton Gazette* was started May 1, 1799, by Joseph Carpenter, a printer from Massachusetts. Towards the end of 1804, the Reverend John W. Brown, "successful at preaching, patent-medicine peddling, and publishing," started his *Liberty Hall, and Cincinnati Mercury.*

To Chillicothe, new capital of the Northwest Territory, went Ohio's first newspaper, William Maxwell's Cincinnati *Centinel*, to die as *Freeman's Journal*. And to Chillicothe went Nathaniel Willis, veteran newsman and publisher, who had pulled up stakes in Martinsburg to join the exciting snowball of men, women, and children rolling west. On the heading of the *Scotio Gazette*, started by Willis and his partner Winn Winship in 1800, they describe themselves as "Printers to the Honorable Legislature." In an early number news sounded a new note of horror with the story of the murder of Mrs. Sara Crawford by Negro Jack, a slave who was "condemned by the Court to be burned on the Common of Knoxville": a story whose few words, other than details of the dismemberment of that unhappy lady, conspicuously lacks facts— and the ring of truth.

Elihu Stout, a compositor in Bradford's Lexington shop, afflicted by western fever, acquired a press, types, and equipment and lashed it all on board a peroque to float down the Ohio to the Wabash, up which he traveled by hard labor with paddle and pole to Vincennes. This printing pioneer of energy turned off his press on the last day of July 1804, the first number of Indiana Territory's first newspaper—another *Gazette*. Early numbers followed the well-worn format. Ancient foreign news held first position, a few items of domestic news already worn and dispirited were interspersed with anecdotes of exceptional gloom, extracts from the essays of Goldsmith, and poems, preferably sad, to entertain the more lachrymose of subscribers.

News of the duel between Hamilton and Burr, and news of the "heart-rendering death of Colonel Hamilton" gave a touch of life and liveliness to the little newspaper that soon included a short biography of Albert Gallatin, by "A Gentleman from Geneva." This was a fine example of the "intelligence" so highly valued by publishers and their readers. But local news also found its way to Stout's office, and news of local trials, begun on the *Gazette's* last page, if too long, was "continued on our first" without complaint of readers deprived of foreign date lines. Abraham Lincoln marveled at the world as he read by the light of burning logs the newspaper renamed the *Western Sun* after a disastrous fire in 1806.

That famous, time-honored, and bewhiskered hot-weather perennial of American newspapers, the sea-serpent story, made its debut in the thirteenth number of the first volume of Elihu Stout's *Gazette*. "An old gentleman of venerable appearance passed through this Country a few days since, and gave a number of our citizens the following information. That he was from the neighborhood of Cayuga Lake and just as he started on his journey he saw two men who were fishing on the Lake, when they beheld at a distance a monster in the shape of a snake rise from out of the water. That his appearance was (and in smallest italic types for emphasis) *Fierce as ten furies, Terrible as Hell.* And that the fishermen, with more than ordinary courage, ventured near enough to reach him with a rifle ball, and both firing at once, fortunately, dispatched him. On admeasurement he was found to be one hundred and three feet, four and a half inches & his size proportionately great. From his head projected a horn of considerable size."

This was a good fifty years before Henry W. Faxon, in the Buffalo *Republic*, reported the famous Silver Lake Varmit, a "disgusting-looking creature" with a fan-tail and a head like a calf. "Fifty-nine feet and nine inches long, six feet in girth," this sea-serpent harpooned by a whaler-man was held captive until all rocking-chairs of local summer boarding-houses were filled. Phineas T. Barnum, "notified by telegraph," let a great opportunity pass.

From the Mississippi River to Maine to Michigan, from the Great Lakes to the Gulf of Mexico, new newspapers remarkable only for their sameness of format, typography, and news evaluation, sameness of style of writing, and sameness of prose, poetry, and anecdotes extracted from the same sources, continued to burst upon gratified Americans. The appearance of every little newspaper was an occasion for civic celebration lasting only until the novelty wore thin, or until the publishers found they were obliged to supply "useful" news and information in return for cash, commodities, or promises, if they were to remain in business.

To be useful was the ambition of every new newspaper. The *Gazette* and other familiar titles that had bridged the miles from "home," preserved in new surroundings the traditional in format, but news letters and "articles of intelligence" of local and regional use and interest were the final measures of success. New publishers with newer ideas ignored local claims and bestowed on their readers exclusively European diets. New newspaper titles also improved somewhat upon the trite with names of colorful individuality.

A Supplicant missionary to the traders, trappers, and Indians who made Detroit their headquarters, stationed a crier outside his church, Ste. Anne's, to acquaint his parishioners with the news. After the great fire that left but one building standing in the snow, Father Richard went east for funds, and returning had with him a press and a printer, one James M. Miller from Utica. Together they produced on August 31, 1809, the first and probably the last number of the *Michigan Essay; or, the Impartial Observer*. The little folio was of a literary tone, and one and one-half columns were printed in French. But there were not enough literate adults in all Detroit to support a newspaper, not even a weekly "to be handed to City subscribers at 5 dollars per Ann."

Experience and the luck of the Irish (given health, strength, faith, inquisitiveness, and single-minded perseverance) enabled Joseph Charless to establish the *Missouri Gazette* of St. Louis, Louisiana Territory Gateway to the West on July 12, 1808.

Charless, a political refugee arriving in New York in 1796, added an extra 's' to his name to insure hearing its ould sod sibilance, and set out for Philadelphia and employment in the bookshop of the great printer, Mathew Carey. Advised by Henry Clay to "go West," Charless printed and published in Lexington and also in Louisville, Kentucky, before taking his assistant, Joseph Hinkle, and his belongings by keel boat to St. Louis, then a thriving trading post of over a thousand souls.

With the prospectus that he had probably printed in Louisville, Charless secured one hundred and seventy subscribers to the newspaper that he "pledged his reputation to begin without unnecessary delay," the "types being already in Louisville and the press expected from Philadelphia in the course of a month." The new newspaper was promised to be in "handsome types and paper," a weekly, the day of publication depending on the arrival of the post. The price of subscriptions, including an occasional page supplement during sessions of Congress, was three dollars a year, cash in advance, or four dollars in pledged country produce. His all-important editorial policy was: "To advocate the extinction of party animosities and to further a cordial union among the people on the basis of tolerance and understanding."

Six months after producing the first issue of the *Gazette*, Charless was obliged to jog the memories of his subscribers who had contracted to pay him in pork, beef, corn, or flour. It cost money, he told them, to publish a newspaper, his expenses being upwards of twenty dollars a week. Charless sometimes had difficulty in getting supplies of paper for the *Missouri Gazette*, and was forced to reduce his pages and go to press on foolscap. Finally he had to suspend publication. When Congress created the Missouri Territory in 1812 and the newspaper's original name was restored, "tolerance and understanding" had flown the editorial coop with the nameplate used since 1809.

A little political opposition with large ideas advertised in the Lexington, Kentucky, *Reporter* for a printer of "correct Republican principles and even moderate abilities." In answer Joshua Norwell came from Nashville, Tennessee, to start in May of 1815 the *Western Journal*. It was later retitled the *Western Emigrant* and again the *Enquirer*, was made famous by Thomas Hart Benton, and was later the property of another publisher of political prowess, General Duff Green. Charles Keemle, who started to the west and an interesting career by walking all the way from Baltimore to Pittsburgh, in 1827 acquired the *Enquirer* and renamed it the *Beacon*.

In compliment to Thomas Jefferson, Edward Charless, son of its founder, renamed the *Missouri Gazette* the *Missouri Republican*, and twelve years later, in 1835, it was a daily. In 1887 the old *Gazette* had become the *Republic* that in 1919 was absorbed by the *Globe-Democrat*. The *Working Man's Advocate*, born in St. Louis in 1831, became in turn the *Argus* (a daily) in 1838, the *Missouri Reporter* of Shadrock Penn in 1841. As the *Union* it merged with the *Signal*, became the *Missouri Democrat* that in 1875 was added to the *Globe*, then three years old. To complete the confusion, the *Republic* that lost its last name in its last merger was ever the support of the Democrats, and the *Globe-Democrat*, still published, was actually Republican in political sympathies.

The press usually moved speedily into new country to the seat of the Territorial Government where the printing of laws would employ the publisher until the advance guard of new settlers arrived to demand news. It was slow, however, in reaching any town where printing in

French, Spanish, and English were necessary. Winthrop Sargent, Governor of the Territory of Mississippi, had to write to Timothy Pickering and ask for press and printer. The Secretary of State sent Lieutenant Andrew Marschalk from nearby Fort Sargent. He took with him his own little mahogany press and a small assortment of types, and was warmly welcomed in Natchez. The enthused and clever official printer built a larger press which he sold to Benjamin M. Stokes. Stokes, with R. T. Sackette, began the *Mississippi Gazette* in the autumn of 1800, which survived little more than a year, although it was up against only the ineffectual competition of the even more momentary *Intelligencer* of Darius Moffatt.

In 1802 Andrew Marschalk began weekly publication of his own *Mississippi Herald*, and this small folio, its news almost entirely foreign, expired after six years. A Valedictory following the last number of this newspaper quoted with cold fury other publishers obliged to dun non-paying customers.

In French for the French and under the flag of France, the *Moniteur de la Louisiane* of Louis Duclot served important news to New Orleans from 1794. Soon taken over by J. B. L. S. Fontaine, it was, in 1803, the duty of this newspaper to print in French, Spanish, and English the stunning announcement of the forthcoming transfer of the Colony and Province of Louisiana to the United States.

And right on hand for the flag-raising was James Lyon, son of Colonel Matthew Lyon of Fairhaven, Vermont. A week in advance this old settler published the first number of his *Union: New Orleans Advertiser and Prices Current*. Native talent (Beleurgey et Renard) on the following day, December 14, 1803, produced in French, *Le Telegraphe, et le Commercial Advertiser*, later partly in English.

A late straggler to New Orleans was James M. Bradford from Lexington, Kentucky. He started the *Orleans Gazette: and Commercial Advertiser* in 1804 and also purchased the *Union* from Lyon. In 1811, in territory between the Mississippi and Pearl Rivers, at St. Francisville, "West Florida," Bradford started the *Time-Piece*, which he continued to publish until he joined Andrew Jackson in writing history with bullets and blood. And for subscribers also in the Spanish domain, Samuel Miller and John H. Hood provided the *Mobile Gazette*, which was probably printed at Fort Stoddert in 1811. In 1813 James M. Lyon gave Mobile its second newspaper of the same name; the third was published by Godwin Brown Cotton and Isaac Miller four years later.

In another climate far from New Orleans Calvin Day and Nathaniel

Willis, Jr., established in Portland the *Eastern Argus* in 1803. "Democratic" when the party of their choice was still the hyphenated Democratic-Republican, the *Argus* became a pivot of political storm and the bulwark of eastern party members.

From Canandaigua the Salisbury brothers, Hezekiah and Smith W., went to Buffalo with their press. Their *Gazette* was the first newspaper in that hustling frontier town. Started in 1811 their subscription lists soon reached a sensational thousand, and "took two full days for printing, even with two men at the press to strike off." Rain or shine, summer and winter, weekly copies were delivered as far away as "the head of Lake Ontario" by Paul Drinkwater, post-walker, whose only conveyance was shanks' mare.

In Baltimore Hezekiah Niles in 1811 established the *Weekly Register* that for almost a half century published the concise details of all legislation proposed or enacted, and other national news, important or interesting. The well-indexed Niles was relied on for facts by careful editors and publishers; his bound volumes were the original morgues.

Newspapers found their headlines in "extractions" from the seaboard. Angry frontiersmen had no patience with the frivolous niceties of diplomacy while American seamen were being impressed aboard British ships, American ships were being detained in foreign ports as prizes of war, and American ships were being boarded under fire when scarcely out of home harbors.

Newspapers were, even then, the eyes and ears of America, and, in spite of differences between publishers and subscribers, lines of fine type and incredibly stilted writing held a hint of authority. As the voice of the people, newspapers were still unaware of their range and power; they were, as ever, confused by emotion, and they were still handicapped by the convention of regarding Federal news as a boon granted by the government.

Subscribers to almost all newspapers could read the text of the peace-loving Jefferson's Embargo Act. For some this was followed by an uncredited accounting of American naval might. When France and England were disputing the privilege of clipping the eaglet's wings, the American navy consisted of two frigates, one brig, and one schooner. The good news was that ships were being built and newly purchased ships were being overhauled. "Cannon, mortar and brass" were being augmented and even the sword-makers were showing great forwardness in turning out weapons necessary to both navy and army.

Letter-writers as far from the heat of politics as the cooling breezes of the sea, and whose trade and commerce were no more than a negligible amount of barter, were as sharply outspoken in criticism of the government as were newspaper subscribers immediately affected by the ordered paralysis of shipping. There were no protests when the administration charged that a news leak sent a horseman from Washington to Boston in a record seventy-nine hours, and countless New England vessels, warned, up-anchored, and put out to sea just before the ports were closed.

Letters on conditions in the West circulating through the newspapers sharply changed their tone. No longer did they dwell on tantalizing descriptions of rich, well-watered lands, of grass-blanketed prairies stretching beyond human vision, of plentiful game for the pioneers' pots, and fur-bearing animals whose pelts were as gold to fortune-seekers. Now writers stressed danger, hardship, and sudden death against which no man could relax vigilance. Massacres were described in awful detail; it was more than hinted that Indians were being excited and armed by enemies of the Republic.

And while the war clouds massed to the solid intensity that cast a shadow on every American life, the country suffered from control of news at its source. The *National Intelligencer*, favored organ of the administration, dispensed through its columns, free to all other publishers, news "Authentic From Washington." But publishers and their subscribers had grown sceptical; the suspicion of political pollution numbed the country's nerves, and war drifted in upon an unready and unprepared people from whom its probability and possible seriousness were concealed.

"In the box" with the Vice President, chummily sharing the august snuffbox, sat Joseph Gales, Jr., to report the Senate. His partner in ownership of the *National Intelligencer*, Colonel W. W. Seaton, reported the House. Only the more acute publishers commented on the pliancy of Gales and Seaton to the administrations they were obliged to please if they were to retain fat contracts for government printing. Beyond Washington they were mildly accused of "glossing over" the weaknesses and shortcomings of the office-holders, bureaucrats, party leaders, and politicians they so lavishly wined and dined. From 1807 to 1820 Gales and Seaton commanded a handsomely paid monopoly in government news. Doors of the Senate and House were open, each to one newspaper reporter guaranteed to be "useful"—not to the public but to executives and their appointees.

The newspapers of the Ohio Valley were shrill in support of the

War Hawks anxious to get on with the business of annexing Canada. Newspapers of New England sullenly muttered of seceding from the Union. And newspapers in the borderlands of public opinion, exercising their Constitutional rights to free speech on the cause, justification, or excuse for war, sometimes met with violence.

Printing the important news of the Declaration of War against England made by Congress on June 19, 1812, the *Federal Republican and Commercial Advertiser* of Baltimore expressed objections to the war as "unnecessary and inexpedient." It was their belief, wrote the editors, that "Mr. Madison was in heart and judgment" against this war, but had been "led and persuaded" by the young hotheads who made use of the Court Journal to convince the President that the country was unanimous in its demands for this drastic action.

Next day a drunken mob led by "the French apothecary" stormed the *Republican's* shop, broke its windows, destroyed the press, hurled types, type-cases, and papers into the street, and then threw wrecked window-frames, doors wrenched from hinges, and all movable furniture after them to burn in a bonfire, to warm and whip the savage orgy of destruction that held the city in a two-day grip of terror.

After suspending publication of the newspaper for five weeks a press and print-shop was reestablished in the home of one of the newspaper's owners, and publication was resumed under the voluntary guard of twenty veterans of the Revolution armed, in defense of the freedom of the American press, with six or eight muskets.

The first number of the *Republican* issued from its new quarters brought a volley of stones crashing through the windows; a beating of drums summoned the town's super-patriots lounging on the waterfront swapping tales with sailors or bending congenial elbows in the grog-shops. The men gathered in the street; angry muttering was stilled by shots fired into the building. The shots were returned and then the swarming, swearing, whooping, screeching gang, bent on blood and destruction, battered down the door. The constabulary was strangely missing, but at last the militia came to march away the gallant little band, escorting them to the jail "for their safety" and leaving them there without even a key turned in a lock. Without hindrance maddened men poured into the sanctuary provided by the law to drag out the publishers and old soldiers to beat them all, clubbing them without mercy, before hurling their limp bodies down the stone steps. General Lingan was killed, General Henry Lee, father of the great Confederate leader, left for dead, and all were maimed and bleeding.

Again the *Republican* was forced to retreat. When it was revived in Georgetown, wide mourning bands on its margins reminded subscribers of its losses. But its editors were unintimidated and continued to air their convictions in regard to men, affairs, and newspapers. A lengthy legal investigation placed the blame for the disgraceful riots, arson, malicious mischief, destruction of property, personal injuries, and murder squarely at the doors of the publishers, Alexander Countee Hanson and Jacob Wagner. And to the chagrin of all who upheld freedom of the press as long as it did not oppose their policies, Alexander Hanson was elected to Congress.

For Hartford the *Connecticut Courant* printed an extra with news of war declared, a state that newspaper regarded with "dissatisfaction, disquiet, and apprehension of an alarming nature." "Wicked, foolish, unnecessary and in no interest to America, but in subservience to France" was the tone and temper of honest editors whose war reports and letters were gloomy. The *Courant's* news bore the novel credit line, "From Our Washington Correspondent," and a commentary on "official" war news, offered free, by the *Intelligencer*.

In support of the war then going so slowly that the condescending called it "Mr. Madison's terrapin war," the *Argus* was established early in 1813 in Albany with Jesse Buellaas as editor. News in the *Argus* was as cheerful as the *Courant's* was dolorous. Father Thomas Ritchie of the Richmond *Enquirer*, which, given the wherewithal by Thomas Jefferson's pledge of political dole, had been erected on the bones of the old *Examiner*, loyally sustained the administration that benefited by his standing with other newspapers of the Republican-Democrats. And Henry Wheaton, the greatest editor the war produced, analyzed with legal knowledge and clarity implications of victories and defeats in the New York *National Advocate*.

And when untrained and unequipped government clerks in a hastily organized militia were startled by the fire of dread Congreve rockets and scampered away to leave Washington to the British, the enemy after setting fire to public buildings paid special attention to the *National Intelligencer*. In August of 1814 Admiral Cockburn ordered all books and papers removed to the banks of the canal and burned and "destroyed the types, presses and other printing paraphernalia." The rains that saved the President's Palace completed the ruin of the newspaper.

Victorious, confident, and a little complacent, the redcoats of England stepped smartly. The capital of the rag-tag and bobtail calling themselves the United States was going up in flame and smoke and they were on their way to Baltimore.

British Major General Robert Ross was shot by a sniper and British timetables were destroyed by a Maryland militia. The assault on Baltimore by land and sea went awry. Off Fort McHenry Admiral Cockburn was preparing to shell his way into the city known as a Rebels' Nest when, aboard the American cartel ship, the *Minden*, came Government Agent John S. Skinner and Francis Scott Key to arrange the release of a civilian, Doctor William Bean. Detained at the rear of attacking ships the men paced the deck all the night of September 13-14, and in the flash of Congreve's rockets and the crash of bursting bombs, Key composed "The Star-Spangled Banner," which he perfected next day at the Fountain Inn. Printed on handbills by the presses of the Baltimore *American*, it was distributed on the streets before British ships had left the Patapsco River and sung by the audience in a theater.

The second War for Independence, like the first, was reported only by its officers and men, and the mysterious but conscientious eyewitnesses, whose letters were printed and reprinted until they had been completely circulated by the newspapers of the country. Conditions of transportation and communication were not much improved over those of the Revolution; there were more roads, better roads, and more postriders to race from relay to relay, but the news still reached the people weeks, even months after signal victories or defeats on land or sea. And news of home, news of other fighting fronts, and news of government reached American soldiers and sailors only after long, lonely intervals, demoralizingly empty of news that is a stimulant to victory and the prelude to peace.

Nameplate. Providence, January 1, 1820. The first use of a newspaper to promote editorially the idea of protection for American industry. Courtesy of John Carter Library, Brown University.

9

PUBLISHERS' PROGRESS

NEWS WAS THE SPICE THAT GAVE A ZEST TO CHURCH-
going. Sermons were preached on economics, politics, social, and other
current news topics. Births, deaths, and marriages were local news
worthy of clerical recognition, and sin was condemned with fascinating
allusions to familiar black sheep. But the coffee houses, not the churches,
were the real regional news centers.

To the coffee houses went men with real estate, pigs, produce, or
warming pans to sell. To the coffee houses went men with a little money
and a zest for a bargain. To the coffee houses went men who must

travel for news of the stages, coastwise sloops, and deep-sea sail. To the coffee houses went ships' owners and officers; coffee houses were the early market places for ships' provisions, ships' chandlery, ships' cargoes, and maritime insurance.

It was not by accident that mastheads of the newer newspapers described their distances and directions from the coffee houses; the nearer the London, the Merchant's, or the Exchange, the more frequent the visits of the news collectors. Everybody knew that news was first heard in these resorts hazy with tobacco smoke and cheerful with shouts of companionable laughter. Newspapers were on hand for the entertainment of customers; hosts kept registers to be signed by travelers whose calls for their letters always created a pleasant flurry, and clerks recorded marine and other news of interest to a dependable patronage. News became a coffee-house commodity, and when their newsbooks and newspaper files were opened for subscribers only, they were the active competitors of the newspapers in purveying the news.

The country's first successful daily newspaper, the Philadelphia *Packet*, so effectively supplied news in its advertising columns that the London, conducted for twenty-six years by William Bradford of the *Journal*, and reopened by Colonel Eleazer Oswald of the *Independent Gazetteer*, was permanently closed. Twelve years after the *Packet* became a daily the Boston *Polar Star*, unable to compete with Boston's popular coffee houses, expired; the *Federal Gazette*, after another two years, was unable to survive as a daily and retreated to semiweekly publication in three months.

The horse-express of Samuel and Ebenezer Hall was forgotten; and newsmen of 1800 were blind to the importance of John Lang's news pioneering. Every day the publisher of the New York *Gazette* had his servants row him into the harbor to hail new arrivals of sail; he asked where they were from, when they cleared port, who were the owners, the master and the mate, what was the cargo, who were the shippers, and to whom was it consigned? Getting back to his office Lang sometimes got this vital news composed, printed, and delivered to subscribers before it was entered on the coffee-house news books. Other New York publishers regarded this significant step towards building a newspaper with nothing but the utmost benevolence: "Lang likes the water," they explained.

In 1800 Jonathan Grout erected ninety miles of his "patent telegraph," using semaphores and flags, to send "Questions and Answers" back and forth between Martha's Vineyard and Dorchester Heights for the benefit of Boston merchants without disturbing the complacent routine of Boston publishers.

Raids by sea, the great danger of the War of 1812, were averted from New York City by the state-legislature-financed "telegraph" of Christopher Coles. Before the War was over Coles had organized a company of ship-owners, merchants, and newspaper publishers to be served by his "new and improved system"; more poles were used between the Narrows and a point visible from the Battery flagstaff. Operators relayed complicated news of the harbor in code by climbing to adjust pivoted wooden arms "each adaptable to twelve positions," and "Head Watchmen," catching through their spyglasses the news from the last operator, dispatched it to the trade.

The "French telegraph" employed in other coastal cities was invaluable in defense, important to commerce, but of only mildest interest to publishers. This greatest of boons to the wives and sweethearts of sailormen was too expensive for peacetime use because of the cost of the many operators and watchmen required.

According to a Boston news item, the news books of the popular Exchange coffee house of Samuel Gilbert were put into the sole charge of Mr. Samuel Topliff, Jr., in 1811. The industrious young Topliff not only rowed himself out into the harbor in successful pursuit of news of ships and shipping and bundles of foreign newspapers, but he sold news to local newspapers and then extended this business by forwarding his merchandise "by earliest Post" to newspaper publishers of New York and Philadelphia.

Within three years the coffee-house records were retitled: "Mr. Topliff's private Marine Journals," and seven fat ledgers opened for subscribers at ten dollars a year, contained general news, records of local deeds and documents, news of ships entering and clearing Boston, together with names of owners and officers, descriptions and values of cargoes, and names of consigners and consignees, news from other American ports, and news from the ports of Europe, and last, but not least, "the names of all the Gentlemen introduced by Subscribers, the names of the Introducers, and the Places the Introduced came from." The successful Mr. Topliff was soon able to acquire the Merchants Reading-Room, and in this well-appointed news emporium, in addition to marine and general news books, subscribers could find newspapers from all larger American and European cities, an excellent assortment of maps, and "a Good Clock."

An elaborate system of news-gathering kept Mr. Topliff's stock up to date with fashionably odd date lines and these, when copied by the hands of Mr. Topliff's many clerks, appeared in newspapers under the heading: "From Mr. Topliff's Correspondent."

With his glass the keeper of the light on Long Island in Boston Harbor could see for miles down the "President's Road," as the main channel into Boston was known to navigators. From atop a ninety-two-foot mast balls were dropped, probably pulley-operated, and in combination with flags flashed the news of the Harbor to the watchman atop Mr. Topliff's Boston home, and in turn the watchman dispatched the always ready, always waiting "Mr. Topliff's Boarding Officers" for the news. "Mr. Topliff's Visual Telegraph" station was so attractive that the light-keeper was obliged to warn "frolickers" that picnics and beer-drinking were not tolerated on government property.

In the new Topliff-quickened pace of news collecting, Mr. Aaron Smith Willington of the Charleston *Courier* had his slaves row him out to meet incoming ships, and his news, that came to Havana by swift Cadiz packets, was earlier than the news of Boston, New York, or Philadelphia, which was dependent on slower and more irregular sailings from London and Liverpool. News of the Treaty of Ghent, on December 25, 1814, for Willington's presses, came from Spain to Havana by packet, by sloop to Fernandina, Florida, by horse to Savannah, and by sloop or horse to Charleston for printing before the British sloop-of-war, the *Favorite*, with the news on board, dropped anchor in New York Harbor.

This was the same Willington who hired James Gordon Bennett, a young Scots immigrant, to translate Spanish newspapers. Here Bennett experienced the dizzy exhilaration of beating rivals to the presses with the news. And in Boston the country's first professional reporter, Henry Ingram Blake, regularly covered the waterfront by rowboat; and his was a familiar figure, running at top speed through narrow streets to compose in types for the *Palladium* his unquestionably "freshest of advices." News and newsmen were, astonishingly, beginning to have values measurable in cash.

News, newly evaluated, enabled the Boston *Daily Advertiser* to hold its own against the coffee houses and reading-rooms almost thirty years after Philadelphia, Charleston, New York, and even Alexandria, Virginia, knew the advantages of a daily newspaper.

Started in 1815 by W. W. Clapp, with Horatio Biglow as editor, the *Daily Advertiser* within a year or two became the property of Nathan Hale, nephew of the patriot who was hanged as a spy during the Revolution. Politically independent, knowledgeable in current economics, and sensible of coming benefits in future progress in mechanics and machinery, the editor wrote in his thoughtful salutatory of April 7, 1817: "One of the peculiar traits (of the public) is the unsatiable appetite which exists in all classes of people in this Country for news. It is a thirst so universal that it has given rise to a general and habitual form of salutation on the meeting of friends and strangers of 'What's the news?' This is an inquiry of such universal interest that one who can answer it is always welcome, while he who brings a second report of an event, although it may be much more full and correct in its details, is listened to with indifference."

Many publishers pondered long and profitably over Hale's remarks; many others continued to wield long scissors in search of ancient foreign "intelligence," the harangues of the political hacks who demanded of readers their attention to the last dull word if they were to be understood, and as news offered the dreary remainders scraped from last week's containers, indifferent or unaware of the new news zest and sparkle. The America whose word was "We've won the war, what next?" wanted earlier news, more news, cheaper news, and better news coverage. Talent and ability plus an understanding of the need for opinions on news, past, present, and future, gave the Boston *Daily Advertiser* a firm standing in reader appreciation, and made editorials regular features of dignity and importance.

It was news, newly appraised, that was summoned in a courageous attempt to give security to an industrial population suffering from postwar problems—problems even then pointing to the War between the States and today still beyond solution by either logic or propaganda. The Rhode Island Society for the Encouragement of Domestic Industries, concerned with the poverty caused by idle spindles, instituted as its organ on January 3, 1820, the *Manufacturers and Farmers Journal and Providence and Pawtucket Advertiser*. Its mission was to secure tariff protection for all domestic industries. Its publishers were John Miller and John Hutchens; its unpaid editor was William Richmond, and its address The Old Coffee House. This newspaper so faithfully kept its promise to eschew politics that, beyond mention in Congressional reporting, it was unsullied by news of the Missouri Compromise Bill that was hailed by the rest of the country's newspapers as marking the end of growing friction between the North and the South. Known for honesty and accuracy and sometimes spectacular achievements in getting the news, it soon carved the niche (a daily since July 15, 1829) it now fills as the Providence *Journal.*

It was news, local news, honestly and fully reported, that built the Springfield *Republican.* Ill and discouraged by a publishing failure, Samuel Bowles packed his wife and his baby daughter, his household goods, and a hired hand-press onto a flatboat and poled his way up the Connecticut River from Hartford to Springfield. On September 28, 1824, he got out the first number of the newspaper for which he had secured two hundred and fifty subscribers, and of which he was compositor, pressman, reporter, editor, and advertising manager, as well as advance agent. It was news alone that held his newspaper firm in reader affections when the anticipated Boston and Albany Railway brought to Springfield an influx of population and industry which encouraged no less than five rival newsmen to challenge the columns which subscribers had always found rich with news from almost every hamlet of the Connecticut Valley.

Another Springfield *Republican,* a daily newspaper and the first in Massachusetts west of Boston, was started just twenty years after the first by young Sam Bowles. It was a newspaperman's newspaper; it was respected by the country's editors for its opinions on national affairs, and was as potent an agent in the country's thinking as the weekly *Republican* that followed pioneering New Englanders with news and views of home.

Impressive talents were being attracted to the new professions of publishing and journalism; native ingenuity, faith, and courage found new application to that usefulness which was the ambition of every printer and publisher. In seaboard towns news of ships and shipping had made newspapers necessary; inland, new publishers found the touchstone of utility by publishing current prices for commodities on American and English exchanges. And in the prosperity of swelling populations, new publishers plunged into new newspaper ventures, especially for the religious, for farmers, for sportsmen, for travelers, for women and children, and for fun lovers.

The vast numbers of newspapers for church-goers, some with subscribers of only a few hundred, others counting circulations by tens and even hundreds of thousands, began, in these United States, with the *Christian Magazine* of the Reverend Elias Smith. It started in 1803, ran only two years, but was replaced in 1806 by the *Herald of Gospel Liberty* "almost a new thing under the Sun, I know not but that this is the first ever to be published in the World," wrote the Reverend

Mr. Smith, who issued the weekly from Portsmouth, New Hampshire, for ten years. Nathaniel Willis, who left the politics of the Portland *Argus* for Boston where he started the *Recorder* in 1816, made notable his children's department. The *Youth's Companion*, remembered by many men and women with unalloyed joy, was an outgrowth of the *Recorder*, and Deacon Willis was for many years Senior Editor of the weekly that provided generous entertainment, education, inspiration— and premiums—to generations of boys and girls.

News of interest to farmers was news for the most unpretentious of newspapers. Publications in this fertile field were initiated by the *American Farmer* which was begun in Baltimore in 1819 by John S. Skinner, who was influenced by the first serious American writer on agriculture, John Taylor of Carolina (i.e. Caroline County, Virginia). A close second on this list was Solomon Southwick's Albany *Plough Boy* of which he was the famous Henry Homespun, Jr.

The sporting prints also made a dignified beginning—forerunners of such barbershop classics as the *National Police Gazette*. First was the *American Turf Register*, a monthly published by the same John S. Skinner who witnessed the birth of "The Star-Spangled Banner;" its serious intent was to improve and encourage the development of American racing stock. Three years later and on a lighter note, William T. Porter gave the waiting world of sports fans the *Spirit of the Times—The American Gentleman's Newspaper*. Public devotion to unregulated horse-racing, boxing, and wrestling was served by the newspapers of professional "oracles" capitalizing on their gifts and suggesting that "wagers be left with the editor." Newspapers, oracles, and editors all too often vanished with the cash. Editors of general newspapers were long insensible to news that was to be found in sports. Early sporting editors were inept in translating the language of the track, ring, and sawdust; too long they featured only commercialized contests, scornful of amateurs denied the glories of "diamond-studded belts of gold," "crowns," "stars," or even "well-filled purses."

Wily artists in printers' inks glimpsed bonanzas in entertainment, usefulness, news, and gossip for the delectation of the ladies. Outstanding was the very literary New York *Mirror and Ladies Literary Gazette*, established by George P. Morris in 1825. Morris was the author of the deathless "Woodman, Spare that Tree." The first editor of the newspaper that lived to become the *New Mirror* (1843) and the *Daily Mirror* (1845) was Samuel Woodward, who wrote the words of the "Old Oaken Bucket." Nathaniel Willis, one of the Deacons' brood of nine talented little Willises, was associated with this newspaper. The *Daily Mirror* featured stories (that deviously arrived at highly moral endings), fancy work, the theater, kitchen recipes, recipes for home dosing, and also many appetizing formulas for beauty lotions using eggs, cream, and salad greens. Many newspaper titles slanted to feminine interests came and after a few years disappeared.

Anne Newport Royall, credited with "interviewing" President John Quincy Adams in 1828, roamed the country to produce sharp "pen portraits" of towns and their celebrities and to cultivate the gimlet eyes and waspish temper with which she unnerved strong congressmen in *Paul Pry*, started in 1836 and continued in *The Huntress* until 1854. Frances Wright, the visiting Scotswoman, called "the pride of Dundee," or "that old bird of evil omen," according to the moral pigmentation and gallantry of her editorial critiques, got out the *New-Harmony Gazette* with Robert Dale. After a year or two, the title was expanded to the *New-Harmony and Nashoba Gazette, or the Free Enquirer*. Failure of the Illinois colony and a general decrepitude of the Nashoba experiment sent the editors to New York, where they continued the *Free Enquirer* to advocate the many social reforms of the two Utopias where frail humanity was found incapable of achieving social ideals.

George Henry Evans, a Welshman, in 1822 edited the Ithaca, New York, *Working Man*, and in New York in 1829 inaugurated a vigorous American labor press with his *Working Man's Advocate*. Evans proposed to give the West to those who would make good use of the land. He advocated the abolition of slavery, sweatshops, and child labor. He called for a ten-hour working day, demanded easier and equal rights for all men and women at the polls, and reported the meetings of the newly-forming labor unions. His was an American view of American labor, opposed to the imported cults of Fourier and Owen, and his newspaper was the first to recognize the future importance of organized workingmen.

An ambition more limited, although as complex as, world reform was responsible in 1828 for one of America's most remarkable newspapers, the *Cherokee Phoenix*, printed partly in English and partly in the Cherokee alphabet (devised by George Guess, part-Indian and part-Dutch, who was known as Sequoia). Elias Boudinot, also an Indian, the editor, and Isaac H. Harris, Printer to the Cherokee Nation, turned out the newspaper regularly for several years.

"Simon Simple" dispensed some news in the Boston *Idiot* between January 1818 and January 1819; but humor was already creeping into

the general newspapers. The Croker Papers, celebrating in verse celebrities whose names were coyly concealed by rows of asterisks and
dashes, were answered in kind in the New York *Evening-Post* in 1819,
by Crow and others who had, it was reported, the Town in Stitches.
Nearly ten years later from a Broadway lottery office, the bons mots of
George Arnold, "the original Joe. E. Strickland," were delivered to the
newspapers to set a pace still imitated. And Seba Smith of the Portland
Courier in 1829 created "Jack Downing of Downingsville," first of
the cracker-barrel philosophers. Without the poise of Will Rogers,
Major Jack offered his advice to President Jackson and others, and thus
contributed through many newspapers to the befuddlement of readers
honestly trying to understand the battles between the President and the
Bank of the United States.

Over part columns of familiar jokes appeared familiar captions such
as All Sorts, Odds and Ends, Flashes, Quips, and Bright Sayings in the
Boston *Courier*, established by Joseph T. Buckingham, an impresario
of no mean ability, and published between 1824 and 1848.

In Boston the *American Traveller*, a biweekly newspaper, published
by Willard Badger and Royal S. Porter, supplied letters and articles
descriptive of American scenery and travel; for the more prosaic a
monthly compendium, a former rival, the *Stage Coach Register*, supplied
the timetables.

Newspapers of serious import and intent were being started in kitchen
lean-tos; battered presses were supported by two dozen, more or less,
subscribers who had very little money but who, from their poverty, gave
first support to ideas that were to change the world.

Experiments in news were as variegated in established editorial offices
as in the pressrooms of new enthusiasts. New ideas were given space, to
be retained or discarded in accordance with their usefulness. Most publishers of American newspapers were printers, workingmen of the American people, of whom many were still unable to read and more unable
to afford the luxury of a newspaper subscription; and newspapers then
and there made clear their conspicuous loyalty to Americans of the
same plain people.

The whole beguiling business of newspaper publishing had been given
a fresh impetus by lowered newsprint costs as the continued stream of
production processes of Fourdrinier, Thomas Gilpin, and John Ames
mechanically transformed rags into paper, and by new presses promising
new printing speed.

In Philadelphia in 1817 George Clymer perfected his Columbian, a press also of cast iron and lever-operated, but an improvement on the Stanhope. Its weight and bulk were less; and with less effort in each pull of the perpendicular bar that was elbowed and connected with a diagonal rod to force the platen against the type-form, the pressman could produce up to three hundred perfect impressions an hour. But the Columbian, long a favorite in Europe, with the wands of Hermes cast in its uprights, serpents and an alligator on its crosspieces, and topped with an American eagle that acted as a counterweight to lift the platen after each pull—and as magnificent as a circus chariot—cost four hundred dollars. This was usually too large an outlay for the average American printer. The lighter and less expensive Washington press, also of cast iron and embodying the toggle-joint of John J. Wells, was perfected and patented by Samuel Rust in 1829. The pressure of the platen of the Washington was controlled by a screw, and on it types were for the first time inked by composition rollers.

Steam was first applied to a hand press by Friederich Koening, a journeyman from Saxony, in London in 1811. With the help and encouragement of John Walter, Koening and an assistant, Andrew Baur, built a steam press with a revolving cylinder, automatically drawing news sheets over automatically inked types in flat beds, and automatically throwing off the printed pages. Angry printers, fearful that this mechanical miracle would deprive them of prestige and earnings, demolished the first printing machine, but it was replaced in another building, and the world's first mechanically printed newspaper, the London *Times* issued from it on November 29, 1814. An entire edition of 1,100 copies was printed in three—instead of the usual ten—hours.

Napier, Applegarth, Cooper, and Cowper, great names in English press-building, improved and simplified the press of Koening and Baur, and still faster printing of much larger news sheets resulted from their use of paired cylinders of reciprocating motion, the types clamped to one with wedge-shaped rulers, and the rolling platen printing the news sheets, as they were fed by the press attendants, who also picked them up as they were ejected, printed.

The first American steam press was the 1822 invention of Daniel Treadway of Boston. Improved and equipped with gadgets still valuable by the brothers Adam, the Adam Automized bore up with "getting out the paper" in many shops for many years. Slow and dependable, and so well built that they were an almost permanent investment (fifty to seventy-five years of service were not unusual), there may be a few of these steam presses still in regular use.

Robert Hoe, first great press-builder of America, contributed many designs and refinements which improved the contraptions and contrivances of old-time carpenters, joiners, and iron-workers, and increased the speed, capacity, and efficiency of this country's presses.

But it was only the publishers of books who were then interested in volume printing, and an important member of many of these concerns was the horse that turned the cylinders of their presses from a basement treadmill. For the book publishers the pairs of cylinders multiplied to four, six, eight, and twelve, and for the book publishers David Bruce introduced into America in 1812 the practical art of stereotyping.

News for American publishers still moved by horse, stage, river steam, and ocean steam-and-sail. But speed was anticipated by the many dreamers, speculators, inventors, and businessmen whose ideas and projects for hastening communications and transportation were rapidly materializing.

STEAM-BOAT
Walk-in-the-Water.

THE Steam-Boat WALK-IN-THE-WATER, will leave Black Rock for the Island of Michillimackinac, on the 11th day of June next. The Walk-in-the-Water is near 400 tons burthen —has a powerful engine—is schooner rigged, and in every respect a safe and commodious vessel. She will perform the voyage to Mackinac, (a distance of near 800 miles) and back in 2 weeks; remain two days at Mackinac, and a proportionate time at Detroit and the other principal settlements on the American shore, at which she will touch both going and returning. Persons desirous of visiting this delightful part of our country, may secure a birth and excellent accommodations, by addressing a line to Capt. FISH, on board the boat, or to   J. B. STUART,
Buffalo.

May 24.   4

Advertisement of tours, in Niagara Journal, Buffalo, May 24, 1819. Courtesy of New York Public Library.

10

THE STEAMBOAT WHISTLES

THE DAYS OF THE DREAD TECUMSEH WERE ENDED AT
Tippecanoe. In Florida, just purchased from Spain, Andrew Jackson's
Kentucky and Tennessee sharpshooters were in hot pursuit of the in-
hospitable Creeks and Seminoles.

Peace was returning to burned and bloody American frontiers and
the letter-writers, needing company, contributed through the country's
newspapers priceless information on the locations, habits, and present
dispositions of the Indians who still met invaders of their forests and
prairies with arrows, tomahawks, and firebrands.

Once more the lords of creation were travel-minded, and their destination was West. Printers, knowing their importance and the value of their art, slung their possessions over strong shoulders to walk all the way from Baltimore and Philadelphia to Wheeling or Pittsburgh, where they joined chance-assembled pioneers boarding flatboats and arks to float down the Ohio to homes, futures, and fortunes indefinite but rosy. By stage, by wagon, and on horseback printers followed new roads of plank and corduroy to Lake Erie's ports to resume their occupations as chance might dictate. Fortunate masters of the craft, who owned both press and types, breezed along the pike in gaudy Conestogas to take passage on cabined keel boats, queens of western rivers. Stopping at sizable towns and settlements along the way, all printers appraised local opportunities, gossiped with printers already arrived, and learned the news of interest to prospective gentlemen of the press.

Clinton's Big Ditch was actually started. Canal fever was a raging epidemic, and visions of man-made waterways linking the Great Lakes and the rivers to the sea thrilled the footloose public. Microscopic settlements along the rivers daily awaited the steamboats of Fulton and Livingston that would bring the world's markets to their very doors.

In enthusiasm's contagion printers halted to set up their presses and "strike off" newspapers which remained to live and grow. Others saw their fondest hopes bloom and fade as pioneers, scarcely settled, again packed up and set out for the greener grasses of farther fields. Some printers were left in ghost towns where friendly crowds would no more gather when the steamboat's whistle was heard around the bend. There were many empty towns at whose rotting wharves tall stacks would never again be made fast for the night. The boats would no more stand by for cargoes or jangle their engine bells for wood for the firepit. But the saddest tokens of what might have been were the newspapers of the forgotten river towns.

From the press of the Rochester, New York, Gazette, started in 1816 by Augustin G. Dauby for the benefit of that city's three hundred inhabitants, went John P. Sheldon to start, with Ebenezer Reed, Michigan's second newspaper. The Detroit Gazette was first issued on July 25, 1817, and about a quarter of it was printed in French.

After almost three years the printers and publishers of the Gazette were entitled to make a few pointed remarks; out of one hundred and fifty-two subscriptions only ninety were paid, and of the advertisers in that number, not one had paid for space. The customers were prodded, however, and soon reformed; business began to improve, and it was not

long before printers and publishers could mention with approval the
subscribers and advertisers who brought them a pig, a cartload of
pumpkins, or other produce in payment of their debts.

Sheldon was arrested, fined one hundred dollars, and locked up for
"criticising the judiciary"; against his wishes his friends paid his fine out
of contributions of twelve and a half cents each and welcomed his release
with a dinner in the jail courtyard. But despite this testimony of Detroit's loyalty, the Gazette was permitted to expire. It went out on April
30, 1829, on a familiar note: "Some light-fingered gentleman entered our
office and took from thence a double-cased silver watch with a steel
chain and two gold seals and a key. The man who would steal from a
printer ought to be compelled to drive a nail through the Black Swamp
to Boston in dog-days, and to suck a dry sponge for nourishment."

William Edward Woodruff, born at Fireplace, Long Island, was
apprenticed at the age of fifteen to Alden Spooner at Sag Harbor. As
a mastercraftsman Woodruff went West by the waterways, stopping
here and there to earn a little money and pick up information of any
printing opportunity.

And in Nashville, Tennessee, when Woodruff learned of the opening
he sought, he had funds enough to buy the press and equipment he
needed. This he packed into two lashed-together peroques. Floating,
poling, and paddling down the Cumberland, the Ohio, the Tennessee,
and Mississippi Rivers, he crossed the mightiest of them all to enter
the mouth of the Arkansas, up whose hairpin turns he worked his way.
The traveler with the printing press arrived at last at the Poste aux
Arcansas, oldest white settlement of the Louisiana Purchase, and on
November 20, 1819, just three weeks later, and without a single advance
subscription, William Edward Woodruff issued the first number of the
Arkansas Gazette from the log cabin that was his home, his print-shop
and his office.

When the government was removed to Little Rock, Woodruff and
his press and newspaper went along. On his weekly heading he described himself as: "Printer to the Territory, and Publisher of the Laws
of the United States, by Authority." The well-written, orderly, and well-
printed Gazette was a calming influence in the colorful and sometimes
turbulent land of the Ozarks and the Quachitas where the revered
marksmanship of Davy Crockett was legendary as confirmed by Woodruff's careful reporting.

In the great southwest the printing press was more than a rumor at
a date when there were but a few hundred scattered Americans in all

Texas. *El Mejicano* was an irregular publication in Nacogioches in 1813; its press was probably brought from Mexico City. In the same town six years later Eli Harris, a publisher from Tennessee, and Horatio Biglow, once editor of Boston and New York, and both members of the Americanization Expedition of Doctor James Long, got out the *Texas Republican*. Within three months the Mexicans rode in, drove the Americans out, and demolished the press.

Before this Samuel Bangs, Boston printer, had set up his press and done some printing before his long incarceration in the Saltillo jail. He had been with the earlier expedition of Francisco Xavier de Mina. A later and more peaceful printing-penetration of Texas was that of Godwin Cotton Brown who started his *Texas Gazette* in San Felipe de Austin in 1829.

To Yankees in Connecticut's neat salt-box homes, the new hamlets of their Western Reserve were as remote and unknown as the log cabins of Arkansas or the 'dobe dwellings of Rio Grande. In 1803, immigration to the West was a mere trickle; then Seth Comestock and Zachariah Griswold started their *Connecticut Herald* (later merged with the old *Connecticut Journal and New Haven Post-Boy* of Thomas and Samuel Green and, again, with the *Morning Courier* to make today's *Journal and Courier*).

In 1812 when Joseph Barber brought out his *Columbian* (now the New Haven *Register*) the impulse to travel was retarded by war with England and "Indian trouble"; but in 1817, when the prospectively powerful Hartford *Weekly Times* first made its appearance, subscribers to the press by families, groups of families, and half or more of the small townships, packed their goods into broad-beamed wagons, drove to the old, white-spired Congregational churches for the blessing of their ministers. Then they climbed over the big high wheels, waved goodbye, and with a fine clanking and the crackling of long whips, disappeared into the clouds of dust that marked the start of the long road West.

These pioneers, travel-grimed, aching and weary, arriving weeks later at ports of Lake Erie, found in those towns and settlements of the New Connecticut newspapers that cherished contacts with the world they had left behind them. Here were the old familiar titles, headings, and format, and new names in advertising columns to greet the curious.

In Buffalo, frontier metropolis risen from its destruction by British and their Indian allies in the winter of 1815, the Salisbury brothers had resumed publication of their *Gazette*. This little paper was delivered by post-walker Paul Drinkwater over a long route. By the following

Fourth of July the town boasted a second newspaper, the Niagara Journal of David M. Day and Isaiah Stillman. The all-important marine news was of sufficient volume to command several inches of advertiser's "cards." The public was notified of arrivals and sailings. Boats came in laden with pork, potatoes, flour, corn, fish, and furs, and boats sailed away carrying passengers, whole families and their freight—pots, pans, blankets, furniture, axes, plows, and tools.

In the Buffalo Journal of May 26, 1818, and probably also in the contemporary Gazette, appeared the first advertisement for tourist trade in the American press. The steamboat Walk-in-the-Water, whose engine had been sent up the Hudson by sloop to be hauled west by wagon, was launched with the aid of ten pairs of oxen and strong tow-ropes, a brisk "horned breeze" plus a big head of steam. She "clawed her way" through Lake Erie, stopping only in Dunkirk, Erie, Cleveland, and Sandusky to take on firewood, and arrived at the new wharf in Detroit to the din of a great public welcome.

In a woodcut illustration of the amazing Walk-in-the-Water prospective passengers could see for themselves the smokestack rising from the advertised "full steamer rigging" just forward of the paddle wheels. Under this picture sightseers and thrill-seekers were offered "Excellent accommodations from Buffalo to the Island of Michillemackinac and back," a two-week trip with a two-day stop-over in Detroit.

From 1820 on, mail coaches from Albany rumbled into Buffalo twice a week to disgorge the post. But west of Buffalo the mails still traveled horseback; at one time a woman rode the Lakeshore route. Pioneers and travelers could choose between this road and the sails or sails-and-steam that plied between towns and cities along the lakes. And by land and by water printers advanced steadily with the human tide of settlement.

In January of 1817 James Percival established a newspaper at Canadaway, New York. The thrilled inhabitants of that settlement's fifty dwellings by vote changed the name of their community to Fredonia, a name much favored by intellectuals as an improvement on the more prosaic "United States." The new newspaper, renamed the Chautauqua Gazette, became very shortly the business of James Carpenter and James Hull, and then of Hull only. Farther west, in Erie, Pennsylvania, Ziba Wilkes started in 1819 a Gazette that had already been preceded by a little paper printed on foolscap, called Genius of the Lakes.

A flickering press united pioneers in the Western Reserve and the home towns. Settlers had little but determination to reproduce the conditions and customs of the home state they had so excitingly abandoned. Towns were towns when three houses were erected, and the "public land" was cleared by the "public" in anticipation of a church, a school, and an academy. The *Trump of Freedom*, started in Warren, Trumbull County (Ohio), in 1812 by T. D. Webb, a lawyer with one leg, was first of many little papers that began to multiply. Until then the news was carried from the New to the Old Connecticut by sturdy souls who preferred to foot it.

In the news from the Western Reserve reprinted in home newspapers was detected a new and poignant note. The pioneers were exhausted by the rigors of primitive travel, overworked by clearing land, building shelter for themselves and animals, planting, hunting, and trapping; they suffered from malnutrition and exposure and were easy prey to diphtheria, dysentery, smallpox, consumption, and ever-present ague. Cemeteries were started too early and filled too soon; news of death was usually soon followed by news of remarriages of widows and widowers. News of weddings that enlivened the presses of both Connecticuts was often in doggerel, sometimes shy, if not coy, ironic, comic, and even vulgar. Rare was the weekly newspaper whose columns did not break their monotony with such gems as:

> Danbury: We would acquaint our distant friends that our marriage was solemnized on the 11th of July. We would also solicit their best wishes on so important an occasion;
>> We both before have married been,
>> and many happy days have seen;
>> We have a family well begun
>> with three daughters and a son.

> Bloomfield: Mr. Wm. Montgomery, aged 74 and Mrs. Sarah Short, aged 68:
>> Have courage men, ye frozen souls,
>> The ice is melting at the poles.

So the news of marriages burst upon the readers of the public prints, and dull the residents of the New Connecticut must have found the bleak notices under HYMENEAL that were to follow.

Cleveland, the "metropolis of the Reserve" had its *Gazette and Commercial Register* from July 31, 1818; Andrew Logan who brought his press and types from Beaver, Pennsylvania, was its publisher.

Apprenticed to the Salisbury brothers in Buffalo ("terms": forty dollars for the first year, fifty the second, sixty the third, and eighty the last, plus bed, food, and washing), Eber D. Howe worked as master printer for seven months on the Fredonia Gazette before arriving in Cleveland as the "Company" of Ziba Wilkes, late from Erie. Wilkes and Howe boldly issued the first number of their Cleaveland Herald on October 19, 1819, without a single subscription, so confident they were that this great and growing city of six hundred would support their venture.

The newest newspaper of the Great Lakes area and whose printing office was "directly opposite the Commercial Coffee House, Superior Street," was a weekly; its price was two dollars a year, "in advance," but "Pork, lard, tallow, butter, cheese, wheat, corn, oats and many other articles of produce at market prices are acceptable in payment." Corn was to be delivered at the distillery; whisky brought the publishers the neat, round sum of twenty cents per gallon. It was not long before the partners had three hundred subscribers, and paper for the folio had to be carted in from Pittsburgh by wagon.

The day after the partners struck off the newspaper, Howe filled a valise with copies of the Herald, mounted a horse and made deliveries as far as Painesville, thirty miles from Cleveland, and from Painesville his route diverged to Kirtland Flats. The trip took two days and the publisher always had with him "a fish-horn to notify the yeomanry of the arrival of the news that was generally forty days from Europe and ten days from New York."

The Gazette and Commercial Register ceased in 1820; thus the Herald was Cleveland's only newspaper until 1832, when Madison Kelly started the Advertiser, which became a daily four years later, and eventually today's Plain Dealer.

Limitations in page sizes imposed by platens, standard type faces and an almost uniform format gave the waterways newspapers a depressing sameness. The front and back pages of the weekly folios were entirely devoted to the cards and squares of the advertisers, illustrated by the same old woodcuts of horses, houses, and sailing ships, although pictures showing the tall stacks of the Walk-in-the-Water and the General Zebulon D. Pike were new. New also were the iron stoves, the cooking "rangers," offered for sale to purse-proud farmers and class-conscious farm wives in return for wheat. Western speed demons were shown velocipedes minus pedals and minus selling allure other than the flying coattails and rakish beaver hats of the riders. Inner pages featured the ads of the patent-medicine vendors. In the space left for news the doings of Congress followed the familiar engraving of the star-clutching eagle; these were interspersed with excerpts from political speeches and foreign news from eastern newspapers. Growing news of local deaths and marriages, prices current, and shipping notices made these thin newspapers valuable to subscribers in towns now well-rooted in the fertile West that was already being left in the rear of advancing frontiers.

Steam was news of first importance and of personal interest to printers and pioneers from the banks of the Hudson to the bayous of the Mississippi. Printers settled to set up presses along the Ohio, Wabash, Illinois, Cumberland, Tennessee, and Mississippi Rivers—and even the Missouri and Arkansas—in the faith that newsprint, ink, and news would be regularly delivered by steamboat. But often they saw the rivers rise and spring floods wash away their shops. Steamboats bringing supplies for which the presses waited often had to pass printers' wharves because the channels had suddenly changed, or because water was so low that captains dared not risk getting stuck in the mud.

A steamboat frozen fast in the Detroit River had on board all the essentials for a new print-shop to be set up by Henry Barnes at Niles on the opposite side of the Michigan peninsula. By this boon of refrigerated fortune Sheldon McKnight, whose shop printing the Detroit *Democratic Free Press and Michigan Intelligencer* was completely destroyed by fire on January 4, 1837, was able to purchase the press, types, and tools needed to continue the newspaper he established with his uncle John P. Sheldon, in May of 1831. At the time of the fire the *Free Press* had been a daily newspaper, the first in the northwest, for almost a year and a half.

Lafayette was news; his travels, his entertainment, and his glittering departure from the country for which he had fought were all faithfully, if belatedly, reported by the waterways newspapers without headlines or even headings. Daring printers were beginning to experiment in tall types to catch readers' eyes. HORRIBLE ACCIDENT over the subheading, Or Dangers of Sailing in High Latitudes would be followed by a paragraph beginning "In 1776 . . ." On the same page news of completion of forty miles of railway track by the Baltimore and Ohio Railway would be given no heading and only a fraction of the space devoted to the Horrible Accident; but it was there.

Publishing was still a printers' business and generally writers were still considered as unnecessary to newspapers as editors, advertising managers, circulation managers, and auditors. With the increased population and prosperity preceding the expected opening of the Erie Canal, small newspapers merged with small newspapers, and were, like the more ambitious publishing projects, the properties of men with capital.

The easy intimacy of publishers and their one or two hundred subscribers began to disappear from lake, river, and canal settlements. No more did newspapers address their subscribers as in the *Illinois Emmigrant* of Shawneetown in 1818: "Due to the protracted illness of the editor and the indisposition of the principal workman, there will be no further issues until Spring, when returning health and spirits will enable them to remunerate their friends and patrons who are thanked for their indulgence."

A well-known lawyer, writer, publisher, and Whig, Charles Hammond, arrived in Cincinnati in 1822. His contributions to the *Gazette* (started in 1815 by Charles Palmer, who, in the same year added by purchase, the *Liberty Hall*) were followed by further editorial labors. After several years Hammond had no doubt astounded the owner by asking for an annual salary of a thousand dollars; his talent was later awarded a third of the newspaper's profits.

Charles Hammond made the *Gazette* the newsiest and most influential of the western newspapers of the day. It attacked Negro slavery, fought Andrew Jackson, supported Henry Clay, and spared neither effort nor expense in getting the news while it was still news. It became the *Commercial-Gazette*, a daily newspaper, in 1827 and in 1930 merged with another centenarian, the *Enquirer*, which had been started in 1828 as the *Phenix* by Moses Dawson. It was sold to John Brough in 1840; eventually the *Enquirer* went to Washington and J. R. McLean.

Demanding more news of politics, government, wars abroad, Indian trouble at home, markets, prices, and transportation by land and sea, newspaper readers also wanted informed opinions on the day's news on which to swing their own interpretations of men, events, and affairs.

Writers with lucidity and leadership came to the western newspapers from unforeseen sources to give shape and substance to the crystallizing concepts of American life as it was going to be lived in these United States. But only occasionally was payment made for writing ability. Publishing costs, as hitherto, were largely limited to newsprint, ink, and outfits of types, plus the costs of compositors and pressmen.

Only a few publishers of those newspapers clearly beginning to break away from the bondage of job-printing were able to pay the few hundreds a year asked by editors and writers. But even the newspapers still set up in log-cabin offices and sheds at the printers' back door saw their editors and publishers bestir themselves as they added, to local news and extracts, the editorial views which were beginning to give all American newspapers new weight, new responsibility, and new direction.

NEW-YORK

A FREE PRESS, THE

BY M. M. NOAH.   THURSDAY MORNIN

THE NEW-YORK ENQUIRER, is published at No. 10 William-street, in the south room of Brew-er's New-York Coffer-House.
TERMS ... ...

FOR SALE,
The steamboat CHAN-
CELLOR LIVINGSTON.—
This valuable boat was built
by H. Eckford Esq. and is constructed of Oak, Locust,
... dimensions are ... Regis-

SELF DEFENCE.—WM. FULL
begs leave to inform his friends and the ge
men in general of New-York, that he has just retu
from England and proposes remaining a short ti
the city, and has engaged the rge room a
SHAKSPEARE HOTEL, corner of Nassau

Nameplate. Motto: A free press, the ARK of public safety. "Noah's Ark"—in the heavier seas of spectacular editorial rivalry—"Noah's Frigate." Courtesy of New-York Historical Society.

11

LOW BRIDGE

THE GREAT WORK IS DONE.

To the military music from bands of the state's elite regiments, the salutes of the artillery, and a confusion of cheers and laughter, Governor DeWitt Clinton and his official suite stepped aboard the *Seneca Chief* at Buffalo on October 26, 1825. And as the era-opening aquatic parade from the Great Lakes to the Sea started down the Erie Canal, a cannon boomed; before its echoes died away another and another, spaced at intervals, roared, "The great work is done," all the way to Albany and on down to New York City in eighty-one minutes.

The cannons' booming set in motion the plans and programs of welcoming committees all along the Big Ditch. Progress was slow as the survivors of uncounted serenades, countless collations, and uncountable toasts were joined by barges and boats from the canal towns where business was suspended and dancing in the streets was the order of the day. At Albany the flotilla carrying most of the state's prominent citizenry was met by a fleet of six beflagged steamboats whose whistles and bells drew townsfolk to the Hudson's banks as the stately procession continued to the sea, where on November 4, the Governor emptied a keg of water from the Great Lakes into the Atlantic.

Then came the parade. Crowds that had been packed aboard every craft that could be kept afloat for a glimpse of the important witnesses to the Marriage of the Waters swarmed ashore to join the still greater crowds that already lined the streets, found vantage points in doorways and windows, or clung to roofs to watch the long ranks of New York's greatest file past in New York's biggest celebration.

The draped car of the Typographical Society passed, drawn by four resplendent horses. On its wide floating stage were two brightly gilded printing presses, one made by Rust and Tourney, the other from the shop of R. Hoe and Company, together with type-cases and printers, who kept the presses busy as they struck off copies of the ode beginning, " 'Tis done, 'tis done." In the great chair of old Doctor Franklin himself sat the town's oldest printer, Mr. James Oram. Assisted by four boys costumed as Heralds and Mercurys, he folded the impressions and tossed them into the walls of applauding men and women. Presiding over all was the Freedom of the Press personified and enacted by John Louden in "robe and cap and accoutred with parchment scroll and brazen trumpet." The car's great banner proclaimed that printing was the Art Preservative of All Arts.

Behind the car marched three hundred master printers four abreast, each wearing a broad blue ribbon. Behind the masters walked the apprentices, also four by four. Then came the bookbinders with a huge volume in red morocco, gilt-trimmed and gold-lettered entitled The Statistics of the Erie Canal. After the binders came the booksellers at a dignified pace, and after them came the stationers.

Showers of silver rain and golden stars of evening fireworks fell over City Hall before all went down tree-lined streets to brick and frame dwellings that were still lighted by dying flames of burning tar-barrels. It had been a great day for printers, and an important one for those who published the news.

On the following Fourth of July, the fiftieth anniversary of the Declaration of Independence, the Typographical Society met to listen to rolling waves of oratory and spume of fife and drum. Solemnly they toasted the Great Document, President John Quincy Adams, two living ex-Presidents, General Lafayette, Charles Carroll, and other Founding Fathers. The dramatic news of the deaths of John Adams and Thomas Jefferson they were not to hear for several days.

The city's oldest newspaper, the *Commercial Advertiser*, was being published by Francis Hall and Company; its esteemed editor was Colonel W. L. Stone. The *Daily Advertiser* still served its faithful subscribers. The *Evening-Post* was newly in command of the able William Cullen Bryant, but still unchanged in the outlook that for twenty-five years had daily discredited foes and friends, and still claiming the first Secretary of the Treasury to be the heart of the old party newspaper. The *American*, the *National Advocate*, and *Statesman* also asked the confidence and support of the same political and commercial factions.

Most of New York's newspapers were ten dollars a year, as much as could be earned by the average working man in a week. Advertising was also sold on the per annum basis and copy was rarely changed. These cards and squares covered all the front and back, as well as most of the inner space of pages, all about sixteen by eighteen inches. In uniformly tiny types these newspapers for the business community were printed to six narrow columns to each page, and other than woodcuts sparingly used in the advertisements and an occasional engraving to give point to a heading, there were no illustrations. Payment for both subscriptions and advertising was so slow that publishers were obliged to exchange information discouraging to chronic debtors.

When the flutter of excitement over the opening of the Erie Canal was past, newspaper publishers, as far as news evaluation was concerned, settled back into the old grooves they had found comfortable since the War of 1812. Today's readers can discover little evidence of any acceleration in the life of the city to which canal barges were bringing loads of produce for shipping on the Black Ball Line. Nor was it considered news that ships returning from Liverpool were loaded to the gunwales with immigrants.

The editors, now accepted as necessary evils to the business of newspaper publishing, were often poets, and were expected by both their employers and their public to display their classical educations in pompous sermons for which party politics too often supplied the themes. Editorial clichés of their invention were long the subject of flattering imitation. And subscribers, accustomed to their mazes of verbage, welcomed the editorial quarrels in which the classic and academic were forgotten in favor of the short, sharp, and sometimes ugly words with which squirming enemies were impaled or dragged through mires of invective.

Occasionally publishers in bursts of enterprise sent agents scouting for domestic news, whose resultant letters gave to the newspapers a fleeting lightness. The featured news on page two was always heavily political or overbalanced with news from abroad; The Latest From Baltimore, Philadelphia, Boston, or Charleston now followed with courtesy The Latest From Europe or Washington.

The backbone of news in New York newspapers was commercial. Financial news of sorts, prices current for commodities, arrivals and sailings from the harbor comprised important news to an estimated ten thousand subscribers in the city whose population was nearing two hundred thousand. Theatrical advertisements, sometimes under column-heading cuts of Tragedy or Comedy, were handled as news and given good positions adjoining items reporting the brawls and fights between fans of various players, which more than once called out the constabulary.

Confusion, irritating to newspaper subscribers, amused rather than disturbed the aloof profession when the city's next addition to their numbers made its bid for circulation. Mordecai Manuel Noah, onetime editor of the powerful Charleston *City Gazette* and the author of the Muley Malack letters supporting the Madison administration in the Second War for Independence, had followed Henry Wheaton as editor of the *National Advocate*, and after ten years had left that newspaper in a violent political disagreement to start an organ of his own—using the same title!

After almost eighteen months of name-calling, legal bickering, and petty sniping, during which time subscribers to both newspapers were warned against taking in "the wrong *National Advocate*," Noah made a fresh start on July 6, 1826. He claimed to be improving on "my former newspaper" and "my newspaper of a similar name" with Number One of Volume One of the New York *Enquirer*. At Noah's heading was a woodcut of the Ark of Public Safety—the free press—complete with American flag and dove.

Noah had a new press; it was slow and he had to apologize to subscribers for late deliveries. He also had a new outfit of types and the *Enquirer* was the most cleanly and legibly printed newspaper in town

Noah's news was a little livelier than that of his competitors, too. He had a certain modest grace in writing that should have been admired; he was a playwright and his interest in the theater made that department interesting.

On May 3, 1827, publishing lethargy was really blasted by the New York *Morning Courier*, described as a "commercial paper for the mercantile community." Its strong plea for a place in the well-worked fields was: "We have engaged an active and experienced news-collector with swift and able oarsmen; this is a very heavy part of our expense but insures to merchants and underwriters later news than they might otherwise receive. We have also made arrangements in the various cities of the Union, as well as foreign, which, in a short time will assure us a correspondence of much utility to our readers."

The apprehension felt by the established newspapers was promptly expressed in the columns of the *Commercial Advertiser:* "The *Morning Courier* published by Skillman, Brooks and Lawson made its appearance this morning. It is handsomely executed. We hope they will flourish and get rich, but we fear we are 'getting too much of a good thing.' At the rate we are now going on, everybody will soon set to publishing his own newspaper, which, strange as it may seem, has its advantages."

In the same number a scanty news summary was followed, a little painfully, with the explanation that "Our news-boat was late last night." A few weeks later the desirable News From the Springs had to be lifted from a local rival's columns, and the peevish editor whose scissors discovered the list of famous, fashionable, and the titled personages then "taking to waters" at Saratoga, plaintively and querulously added to his purloined news: "Why does our correspondent remain silent? The important information in the above paragraph ought to have been sent to us by express. In a very few years we expect to see every paper in our plain Republic with a table (as in the English journals) of Fashionable Arrivals and Fashionable Departures. It is very important for the world to know where their fellow citizens sojourn."

Perhaps to save wear and tear on the belaying pins of crews of rival news boats soon scurrying down the harbor in pursuit of news, the publishers of New York organized the Morning Newspaper Association and in peace shared the annual expense of collecting the news. Two thousand five hundred dollars was paid for the small craft and their crews which were held in readiness to meet any ships sighted and reported by the watchers.

In the following October another publishing flurry disrupted offices just returned to normal calm. Arthur Tappan, a wealthy silk merchant, established the New York *Journal of Commerce* on a scale that meant war. William Maxwell, lawyer and educator from Virginia, was installed as editor, and David Hale was made business manager. It was the policy of the owner to refuse "theater, lottery, and other immoral advertising," thus adding a strong voice to the current campaign for strict observance of the Sabbath Day and thus giving support to the temperance and anti-tobacco factions. Both owner and editor were ardent and active members of the American Colonization Society and gave time and money towards the transportation of free Negroes to Africa, where it was proposed to reestablish the victims of the world's greatest social evil. Arthur Tappan was an honest and an upright man "conscious of his obligations as a steward of the Lord"; he was also stern and humorless and incapable of compromise with his fellow men of less rigorous principles than those which he had seen fit to adopt.

Almost at once the *Journal of Commerce* was admitted to membership in the Morning Newspaper Association. Publishing settled back to its pleasant hibernation—until that December when James Watson Webb secured control of the *Morning Courier*.

As a boy Webb had run away from home to join the Army. He saw service in the Second War for Independence, and had since acquired a reputation for Indian fighting. He was known for a hair-trigger temper and a readiness to challenge any opposition to a duel when he arrived in New York as a Democrat, a dyed-in-the-wool anti-abolitionist, and a militant supporter of Andrew Jackson. He backed the President in his fight against the Bank of the United States. His political views, like his opinions of some politicians, shifted until they were completely reversed, but whatever they might be at any time, James Watson Webb could never endure either criticism or competition.

In 1829 he purchased sufficient interest in Noah's newspaper to merge its title with his own to make the stronger New York *Morning Courier and Enquirer*. On the *Journal of Commerce* William Maxwell had been succeeded by Gerard Hallock, an editor who gave his readers not what they thought they wanted, but what he knew they needed. He was a newsman who led New York newspapers in news-collecting associations. David Hale, a former publishing partner of Hallock, was a writer and reporter whose devotion to duty was so strong that he slept in a room adjoining his office, and so never missed a fire. He was a genius in organizing the collection of news. To Hallock and Hale, Arthur Tappan and his brother, Lewis Tappan, turned over their newspaper to be conducted in accordance with the principles of the originator who made possible their full ownership within two years.

Webb, tall, with military bearing and flashing dark eyes set deeply in an unusually large head, was the natural enemy of the frail and incorruptible Arthur Tappan, whose stubborn strength was the prop and stay of so much gospel diametrically opposed to Webb convictions. He sharpened the rivalry between the city's newspapers by withdrawing from the Morning Newspaper Association. The Association, wrote the publisher of the *Courier and Enquirer*, was "altogether too fond of its dollars to suit our view of procuring the latest intelligence." He then put the fast schooner, the *Eclipse*, into service of collecting harbor news for his exclusive printing. He later built the Baltimore clipper, the *Courier and Enquirer*, also for this newsworthy enterprise.

In retaliation and also overcoming scruples against printing news collected on the Lord's Day, Hallock and Hale put two schooners, one called *Journal of Commerce* and the other *Evening Edition*, into the harbor and were promptly expelled from the Association which was then faced with the expense of replacing its light craft with the sails of the *Thomas E. Smith*. (The *Journal of Commerce* permitted no work to be done from midnight Saturday until midnight Sunday and in consequence always came out an hour or so later than other city newspapers on Monday morning.)

Within three years New York newspapers were maintaining a fleet of half a dozen news boats at a cost estimated at twenty-five thousand dollars a year. These swift schooners and clippers sailed from fifty to a hundred miles beyond Sandy Hook; skilled pilots maneuvered for position alongside incoming vessels, snatched the bags and packets of newspapers and news from pursers, and raced back to waiting presses. And New York suspended all business as soon as the signals were reported to gather in the streets outside the printing offices, place their wagers, and watch for the horsemen who took the news on shore near Fort Lafayette, dashed for the Fulton Street ferry, and drew up their lathered steeds amid cheers, applause, boos, and groans.

The Semaphoric Telegraph, financed by newspapers led by Hallock and Hale, merchants, and the Black Ball Line, was once more "perfected"; it was extended to the Nevasink Highlands rising four hundred feet above sea level on the Jersey coast beyond Staten Island. On a clear day the watcher stationed in the dome of the old Merchant's Exchange at the corner of Wall and Hanover Streets had an unobstructed view through his telescope thirty miles to seaward. And from the frequency with which David Hale was reported to have mounted a chair on the floor of the Exchange to read the latest from Europe to the merchants, it would seem that the sails of the *Journal of Commerce* were either the speediest or the best managed. Hallock and Hale also brought the horse expresses to new efficiency; their riders brought in the Washington news hours before it reached other publishers by the Government Express Mail—at triple postage.

News in New York newspapers, beyond the dubious values of the expensive "foreign intelligence," news in subscribers' letters, a spattering of local news, and the long-winded "advices" of politicians, was a commodity in which the pungent-penned James Gordon Bennett was soon undisputed master.

In town from Charleston and suffering from a financially disastrous experience on the *Sunday Courier*, the Scotsman had happily fallen heir to the job as editorial assistant to Noah on the *Enquirer*, the former incumbent, W. W. Graham, having been the unfortunate party to a duel. From Washington Bennett sent to the *Enquirer* a series of gossipy letters about the capital's bigwigs and their ladies. It was from Salem, disputing the testy Perez Morton, Attorney-General of Massachusetts, on his right to report—without special permission of the Court—the Knapp brothers, accused of complicity with Richard Crowinshield in the murder of Captain Joseph White (the State was represented by Daniel Webster), that Bennett gave America that exquisitely balanced truth: "The newspapers are the living jury of the Nation."

It was Bennett who suggested to Colonel Webb that he buy the *Enquirer*, urging that the combined newspapers could be made a great force for liberalism. To the *Morning Courier and Enquirer* Bennett brought a well-tutored mind and an innate news-sense plus courage, capability, and ingenuity. Acting on his principles, Bennett so ably supported President Jackson in the scandalous fight with the Bank of the United States, that Noah, in behalf of that institution, bought a share in the newspaper and easily forced the silence of the writer. Bennett at once resigned.

And when the alliance between the *Morning Courier and Enquirer* and the Democratic party came to an abrupt and noisome end and James Watson Webb became a Whig, his newspaper knew no restraints in reviling President Jackson and "Noah and his mob." Bennett was replaced on the newspaper by Matthew Davis, who wrote as the "Spy in Washington" and the "Old Boy in Specs," and also as the "Genevese Traveller" for the *London Times*. He was considered one of the best of the less than a dozen capital correspondents. A one-time henchman of Aaron Burr, Davis had witnessed the shooting of Alexander Hamilton at Weehawken and had kept his memories green by charges, countercharges, and challenges resulting in many affairs of honor among newspaper men. And he died naturally, an old man who had acquired a dashing reputation without exposure of his own person to the awkward inconveniences of sudden death.

Washington correspondents cost money and so did the clippers, schooners, their captains and crews, the operators and watchmen of the French telegraph, and the mounts and the horsemen of the land expresses. And in the excitement of the New York newspaper publishers' new competition for personal and political prestige, mere subscribers were the almost-forgotten men. To newspapers whose subscription rates were so high that news was a luxury to men of moderate means, publishers added a new and appalling stipulation: "Subscriptions will be continued until ordered stopped and all arrearages paid." And to revenues made doubly uncertain could be added the modest, unappreciated, and perhaps uncounted sixpences of the poor or eccentric, who left their coins on print-shop counters. As far as the publishers were concerned, the economical were welcome to subscribe to the numerous reading-rooms where they could sit all day on stools at high desks to read newspapers and periodicals from many cities.

As costs soared above revenues haughty impresarios of the printing presses blindly turned to advertisers to bail them out of the difficulties which threatened to sink them one by one. The cards and squares were still sold by the year; thirty to forty dollars paid for an indefinite number of lines inserted as often as the insistence of the customer required, and for good measure the advertisers received free subscriptions. To accommodate all the needed business, newspaper pages were increased in size and, making a virtue of what they considered a life-saving necessity, publishers belabored their fellow publishers, advertisers, and the public to impress them with the quantity of newsprint they could manage to cover with ink rather than with the quality or quantity of news, information, or entertainment.

News boats were laid up, dismantled, and sold and incoming sails were again hailed from harbor rowboats. Express riders and their horses returned to their plowing. Publishing rivals concentrated grimly on size. Inch by inch New York newspapers, especially the *Morning Courier and Enquirer* and the *Journal of Commerce*, extended beyond the reasonable dimensions of a readable newspaper. Each additional inch was celebrated as a great achievement and their vast folios, the talk of the country, were imitated as far west as St. Louis. The World's Largest Newspaper, no matter what its momentary title, could have been nothing much more than a source of exasperation to all serious and sensible subscribers. At length they found themselves confronted with news-sheets that the publishers advised ironing, so creased were they from folding for delivery. They reached from the eye level of a tall standing adult to the floor, and were so wide that outstretched arms could scarcely hold the pages open. A common quip was that it was too wet—or too cold—to read the newspapers!—the implication being that they were too big to be opened indoors. The *Morning Courier and Enquirer* boasted proudly of its "specimen copy" of eight pages of eleven columns each, and sent it for exhibition to the London Crystal Palace Fair in 1851; and by 1853 the *Journal of Commerce* was turning out a sheet of three by five feet.

Publishers clinging to the idea of bigness in newspapers were either unaware of growing public indifference, or refused to admit defeat or acknowledge their shrinking importance. Soon their worn-out insanity was gently capped by a bit of ribbing. In 1859 George Roberts got out the *Illustrated Quadruple Constellation: the Mastodon of Newspapers—Eight Mammoth Pages, Thirteen Columns to each Page and Each Column Forty-Eight Inches Long.* Twenty-eight thousand of these enormous newspapers, well illustrated and without too much advertising, were printed and sold by the country's printing offices as a novelty at fifty cents each. The editor and publisher promised to get out the *Constellation* once every hundred years; he was confident that he would hold the record for size until his next because, wisely noting the weakness of the whole towering structure, "Anybody can catch an elephant, the problem is what to do with the elephant when you have got him."

From the first pale rays of dawn until twilight's deepening dusk the jingle and rub of harnesses and the songs of the Canawlers were heard on the banks of the Erie where patient horses and mules plodded the towpaths. East went produce of farms, mines, and trap-lines, and west went barges bearing the immigrants bound for the free lands of the West.

At Albany, where canal and river traffic crossed, the old *Argus*, a daily newspaper since 1824, continued to weather newspapers of opposing politics as well as the even more hostile press of its own party factions. The *Argus* was the authentic voice of the "Albany Regency," and Edwin Croswell was the greatest of the three great political propagandists of the day. Thomas Ritchie of the Richmond *Enquirer* and Francis Blair of the Washington *Globe* completed a trio which could make other party editors jump through hoops when they snapped their imperious fingers.

An interesting supplement of eight pages, about seven by ten inches each, was issued by the *Argus* on September 30, 1828. It contained quotations from the country's newspaper editors on the "suitability" of Andrew Jackson for the presidency. There was no resemblance to modern summaries of editorial opinion other than format; no contrary voice was admitted to curdle the lyrical praise for the Saviour of his Country, and abuse, not only of the Whigs but of disgruntled party "slivers" was liberally included and Old Hickory lost this election to John Quincy Adams.

Barges and packets brought printers and their presses to every booming canal town between Albany and Buffalo. New newspapers were frequent events and stirred the interest and curiosity of settlers just arriving, who welcomed any news but hoped for news from home. In cheerful disregard for the unadvertised values of good will, new publishers changed the titles of new newspapers and then changed them again as improvement caught their fancies. New publishers started new newspapers that promised to prosper, then succumbed to the lure of travel and sold out to rivals or newly arriving printers—at so much per head per subscriber.

Looking always to the west for more desirable locations for their presses, printers from Albany, Amsterdam, Canandaigua, Utica, Herkimer, and other up-State towns joined wandering fellow-craftsmen, passed Buffalo, a thriving city, as a mere way station en route to rumored settlements of fifty or a hundred buildings—little settlements constantly threatened by Indians where they could expect few comforts and none of the amenities. Miraculously York-State printers produced, from the Great Lakes to the Coast, first numbers of long-living newspapers known, or remembered, for their rugged pioneer virtues.

To Chicago, then numbering not more than two hundred men, women, and children who, on nights when the wind blew in from the prairies, could hear the howling of the wolf-packs, went John C. Calhoun, printer from Watertown, New York. From the little building he helped erect Calhoun issued on November 26, 1833, the first weekly *Democrat*. Three years later he sold out to John Wentworth, his editorial assistant who in 1840 made the newspaper a daily. The famous title was absorbed in 1861 by the *Tribune*, first published in 1847 by

Forrest, Kelly, and Wheeler who changed their "literary" weekly, Gem of the Prairie, into the Sunday Tribune in 1852, only a few years before the Chicago Tribune carried the famous name of Joseph Medill at its masthead.

The church sent to the new world its first printing presses; in Mexico City, Mexico, in Lima, Peru, and in Cambridge, Massachusetts, printing was permitted only because of its necessity to Faith. The printed word that upheld the authority of the church on religion's new frontiers also upheld that Authority uneasily representing uneasy crowned heads. The printed word was the unfailing implement of the skilful proselytism, and with printed words the apostles of the cloth spread the propaganda of their churches among the natives of North and South America —after they had mastered the native languages, created the alphabets, and taught their savage charges to read.

Filled with the valiant aspirations of the Reverend John Eliot of Roxbury in New England and the Reverend Señor Don Fray Juan Zumárraga, first bishop of Mexico, teaching and preaching and printing humble men continued westward by way of the Erie Canal. They passed through Albany where Thurlow Weed was beginning a frustrated political career with the Evening Journal he had started in 1830, and Rochester where he'd edited the Telegraph, and where a Daily Advertiser had been started by Luther Tucker and Company in 1826. In Buffalo, where printing missionaries barely paused to change to road or lake, Guy H. Salisbury, son of Smith H. Salisbury, one of the founders of the old Gazette, was editing, in 1835, a Daily Commercial Advertiser.

Only a few of these printers had presses, but most carried small assortments of well-worn types. They built presses and obtained impressions with hand rollers, made or begged the paper, and made their ink to print in the languages of many Indian nations messages supplemented by more worldly almanacs and monthly or semimonthly "newspapers."

Following Lake Michigan's shore to the west, another York-State printer, Albert Ellis, from the Herkimer American, chose to remain in Green Bay as an Episcopal missionary. With John V. Suydam, a teacher in the Navarino mission, he issued for this hub of the fur trade the Green Bay Intelligencer on December 11, 1933. Irregularly published for only three years, this weekly was made interesting for future readers by "ungarnished" descriptions of the "traits and characters of the Indian Nations." And in Green Bay in 1835 was born and lived for the promotion of Morgan L. Martin, a congressional candidate, the *Wisconsin Free Press*.

In 1836 in Juneautown, that ancient rendezvous of swarthy pigtailed traders and trappers, Daniel H. Richards from Burlington started Milwaukee's first newspaper, the *Advertiser*. On June 27 of the following year John O'Rourke from Watertown established its second paper, the *Sentinel*, which became a daily late in 1844. And other printers bringing their presses from the East through the Erie Canal joined printers and presses already arrived to the quiet of primeval forests where they had hoped to convert the Indians to Baptist, Catholic, and Episcopalian faiths. They remained to become publishers of the newspapers that were the only contacts with "home" and without which the world and all its people would have faded to dimly remembered dreams to men and women lonely in the lovely land which is now Wisconsin.

T H E

"IT SHINES FOR ALL"

NUMBER 414.]   NEW YORK, THURSDAY MORNING, JANUAR

PUBLISHED DAIL
By BENJ. H. DAY and GEORC W. WISNER. | [For the Sun.] | [From the O
[OFFICE 222 WILLIAM STEET.] | THE WAY THE WORLD WAS MADE. | TIGER HUNTIN
  | The manner in which our little world was made, | We proceeded towards th

Nameplate. New York, January 1, 1835. The second nameplate in two years; first use of the motto: "It shines for all."
Courtesy of New-York Historical Society.

SUN.

[Price One Cent.

r 1835.] 1 ... were beating a jungle upon an elephant, when a
, large tiger suddenly sprang upon the animal's flank,
reached the seat on which the officers were sitting.

12

THE PENNY DREADFULS

CHANGE WAS IN THE AIR AND CHANGE WAS ALL
around. "Don't blow out the gas" was the password to plenty.

New York's population was sweeping up the narrow island: modest
surburban homes had already gone, mid-Manhattan's farmers were going, and the country squires of the exclusive solitudes of Spuyten Duyvel
were worried. Sober citizens wrote to their newspapers with warnings
that the town was fast becoming an enormous way station, an immoral,
irresponsible, and unruly junction for the temporary accommodation
of travelers by land and sea.

And in the composing rooms of the city's newspapers trained hands somehow lost their cunning and dipped into the wrong cases to confound proofreaders with strangely misplaced roman and italic and, worse, even dropped the contents of composing-sticks as they transferred set lines to waiting galleys.

The *Penny Magazine* of the Society for the Diffusion of Useful Knowledge, without a single subscriber in America, or in England, was coming into the United States in quantities sensational to printers, the public, and prospective publishers.

The respectable cheap press of England had died by slow government strangulation. Taxes demanded by Queen Anne in 1713 to suppress "seditious papers and factious rumors, by which designing men have been able to sink credit and the innocent have suffered" had steadily spiraled from a halfpenny to fourpence on every pound of newsprint. The newspapers to which Defoe, Swift, Addison, and Steele had contributed—the *Review*, the *Tattler*, the *Examiner*, and the *Spectator*— had vanished before the long shadows of the excisemen. The tax was threepence when in 1832 Charles Knight, son of a Windsor bookdealer, a prolific writer, a publisher of experience, and an editor of vision, was given the management of the Magazine of the Society, of which he is credited with having originated.

The *Penny Magazine* was amply financed and had the moral support of an eminent committee headed by Lord Brougham, Chancellor of the Exchequer. Each of its eight pages of about seven by eleven inches was printed to two columns, and every page was crammed with a wonderful miscellany of "useful and interesting knowledge"; people, places, arts, architecture, animals, birds, construction, and machinery of the ancient and modern worlds were presented with illustrations made from especially drawn and prepared woodcuts. The *Penny Magazine* carried neither advertising nor news, thus avoiding taxation, and soon achieved a circulation of nearly one hundred and sixty thousand weekly copies.

The printing of the *Penny Magazine* was done in the shops of William Clowes, where the stereotype plate of the unfortunately advanced William Ged, further developed by the Earl of Stanhope, Tillock, and Fouldis, Wilson, and Cooper, was used with far-reaching effects.

In the Clowes shop composed pages, types, and woodcuts were assembled in molding frames into which plaster of Paris was poured; when this became dry and firm beautifully sharp reproductions were removed to be baked until hard. This process could be repeated as many times as required. These molds were then sent to the foundry to be clamped into shallow iron boxes with small corner openings. They were plunged by cranes into molten type-metal, lifted, swung, and dropped into cold water with a terrific sizzling and steaming, and cooled. Next the boxes were pried apart and the metal type-plates removed and readied for the Clowes' many presses. This reproduction of composed pages so reduced the expense and risks of volume printing that cheap literature was, from this time, an accomplished fact. No longer could the printing crafts deny themselves or the public the benefits of mass production of the printed word.

From its beginning the *Penny Magazine* was sold at a discount to the wholesalers of the book trade who, in turn, supplied "book-sellers, shop-keepers, vendors and hawkers," and the pennies of its fascinated readers were, amazingly, able to maintain a network of distribution so extensive that anyone, almost anywhere within the kingdom, could easily purchase it, at an accumulated return to the Society which publishers agreed was "handsome."

The London Plan of wholesaling and retailing the magazine for cash was brushed aside by New York's established newspaper publishers, who could foresee no security without subscriptions and whose sales at six-pence a copy were too small to encourage experiment. Missing from the American scene was the first and most important individual in this new method of merchandising the news: the newsboy or newswoman, fa-miliar figures in London since the days of Sir Roger L'Estrange, who, however, would not permit his *Observator* to be sold by hawking. Amer-ican publishers, sensitive to the superior estate they condescended to share with their subscribers, had occasionally been moved to run off a hundred or so copies of their newspapers to be sold by their carriers, but it was understood in New York of the 1830's that extra newspapers were a favor to the boys on the part of the publishers who considered hawking beneath their dignity. The hawking of the many scurrilous broadsides of the time probably gave publishers an uneasy feeling of being on the same level with the name-callers; writers of broadsides screamed that their enemies were "crazy"; starchy editors of New York's most respectable newspapers thought nothing of flatly stating that theirs were "mentally deranged, and should be shut up in Bedlam."

The *Penny Magazine* raced along to an imagination-staggering two hundred thousand. At the turn of its first year Mr. Knight announced that Jackson, of New York, would supply the American trade; and the name Thomas H. Jackson and Company began to appear in city direc-tories. Before the news that the English plates would be sent to New

York for American printing was made known, another Jackson—Solomon M., Printer, 163 Chatham Street—started a New York *Penny Post*, quite freely lifting material—minus pictures—from the London original. The first newspapers sold in America "as in London" advertised: "Wanted. Boys as Carriers for the Penny Post. Carriers supplied at wholesale prices. Customers to pay on delivery," and listed several city bookdealers as agents in quite the Knight manner, for several months of early 1833.

Newspapers smaller in size and smaller in price (all about four dollars a year) had already been successfully started. First was the *Daily Courier* established by Seba Smith, in Portland in 1829. In Boston the 1830 *Transcript* of Lynde M. Walker had been followed by the 1831 *Morning Post*, Charles Greene's gift to down-east Democrats; and in 1833 the *Mercantile Journal* was made famous by Hawser Martingale (Captain John S. Sleeper) and Stephen N. Stockwell.

In New York on October 29, 1832, James Gordon Bennett got out the first number of the *Globe*, "neat and manageable" and containing only the "cream of intelligance" for only two cents a copy, but before another month rolled around the daily *Globe* had expired.

The *Globe* was scarcely forgotten when Horace Greeley and Francis V. Storey took from their press the first copy of the New York *Morning-Post*, which Doctor Horatio D. Sheppard, the publisher, had intended to have sold on the streets for a penny. The dubious printers, however, insisted on a price of two cents. The first issue came out in the season's worst snowstorm, January 1, 1833, and too late the price was made the magic One Cent. After twenty-one days the little newspaper vanished along with the young doctor's entire capital of fifty dollars in cash and two hundred in credit.

But in the brilliant light of success, parts of the London Plan were being measured and fitted for a color-splashed picture sometime to be recognized as the modern American newspaper. It was no wonder that young printers sat for hours in ale houses discussing the prospects for the future.

Benjamin Henry Day from the Springfield *Republican* found work on the *Evening-Post*, the *Commercial Advertiser*, and the *Journal of Commerce* before setting himself up in business as a job-printer. Business in New York was becalmed, but not the responsibilities of this twenty-three-year-old husband and father of an infant son. Day's thoughts turned again and again on possibilities for success with a small penny newspaper to be sold "as in London"; this he often discussed with Dave Ramsey, a fellow compositor on the *Journal of Commerce*. The *Sun* was the stunning name (its origin credited to Ramsey) that dominated the printer's imagination, and the *Sun* was the *Sun* from the moment Day readied his old press and types and with the help of his scissors compiled copy, including advertisements from any local newspapers, for his epoch-opening first number.

With the help of a journeyman, Parmlee, and a boy, Day worked through the night to run off a thousand copies at about two hundred and fifty an hour, printing first one and then the other side of the sheet. The *Sun*, a morning newspaper, rose on September 3, 1833, under a spread-eagle, the folio with pages, each printed to three columns, about the size of a letter-sheet of stationery. The dawn of the penny press was viewed with contemptuous silence by the established newspapers blissfully unaware of its coming heat.

The *Sun's* salutation was simple, modest, and forthright: "the object of this newspaper is to lay before the public, at a price within the means of everyone, all the news of the day, and at the same time afford an advantageous medium for advertising. The sheet will be enlarged as soon as increased advertisements require it—the price remaining the same. Yearly advertising (without the paper) Thirty Dollars per annum—Casual advertising at the usual rates charged by City papers. Subscriptions will be received, if paid in advance, at the rate of Three Dollars per annum." And as he wrote the last line no doubt Mr. Day's firm young chin thrust itself forward belligerently;—he had no intention of shouldering the dead weight of a deadbeat subscription list; he wanted only cash customers at six cents a week.

In the *Sun's* first number appeared a notice: "To the Unemployed: A number of steady men can find employment by vending this paper. A liberal discount is allowed to those who buy to sell again." The first unemployed, steady man to apply was Bernard Flaherty, aged ten, who grew up to become Barney Williams, the popular Irish comedian of New York's music halls. One hundred copies of the *Sun* were sold outright to carriers for sixty-seven cents, or for seventy-five cents on credit. The *Sun* was "hollered in the streets" on its third day.

Religiously the *Sun* abstained from dipping a finger in politics. The doings of the president, the governor, and of Congress were but grudgingly allowed space. Its news of the Police Offices was a novelty in American newspapers; and this news was the business of Mr. George W. Wisner, who was employed by the publisher at four dollars a week. So successful in finding circulation was Mr. Wisner (who rose from his bed each day to attend court sessions starting at three or four o'clock in the morning) with his humorous stories of drunks, derelicts, and other unfortunates swept in by a zealous constabulary, that he was rewarded with a half interest in the newspaper. This interest was to be paid out of profits. But Mr. Wisner, whose ideas of what made a newspaper were quite different from those of Mr. Day, relinquished this interest for fifty-two hundred dollars, cash. From its first number the *Sun* carried news and anecdotes with a new human-interest angle, and within a week initiated the animal stories that still delight newspaper readers on dull Mondays. The *Sun* was a success; circulation zoomed; and to the astonishment of Benjamin Henry Day, before the end of the year the *Sun* was counting its thousands, to the anguish of Colonel James Watson Webb.

The following spring competition reared a singularly unlovely head as the *Evening-Transcript* arrived in New York to rival its model in all its worst features. The *Transcript*, also One Cent on the London Plan, was published by Hayward, Lynde, and Stanley, of 34 Ann Street, Front Room, Second Story. Its police reporter was William Atree, a genuine English import with Bow Street training. The *Transcript* frankly catered to the flashier gentry of the racetracks and prize rings; it was not only vulgar, but it was salacious in reporting crime and moral degradation, and its columns of advertisements of patent medicines and quack doctors were revolting to many people. But the *Transcript* was also a success; its circulation expanded to almost that of the *Sun* in New York and probably exceeded that newspaper's out-of-town distribution.

A third penny newspaper intimated, and not shyly, its coming blessings to New York. On May 3, 1833, James Gordon Bennett sent out the Introductory Number of his planned *Morning Herald*. This experienced journalist, who had a realistic appreciation of the cash value of news while it was still news, brought new vigor and enterprise to New York newspapers which were groping to find a middle ground between the old titles slowly stifling in their newsprint swathings and the unformed offerings of the first cheap-for-cash brigade.

In his Grace before Meat said Bennett: "We shall support no faction or coterie, and care nothing for any election, or any candidate from President down to Constable. We shall endeavor to record facts, on every proper and public subject, stripped of verbiage and coloring, with comments when suitable; just, independent and good tempered."

On May 11 came Bennett's further promises in his first *Morning Herald* of regular issue. "The broad relief which the lively HERALD will afford to the dull business air of the large morning papers, will naturally induce every patron of the former to take in a copy of the later . . . amusement and agreeableness are not our sole aim. We shall give a correct picture of the world—in Wall Street—in the Exchange—in the Police Office—in the Opera—in short, wherever human nature or real life best displays its freaks and vagaries." Then, having made arrangements for printing and having completed his carrier organization, the publisher, whose war cry was "We're here to stay, and so up and away," settled down in his Wall Street cellar office. It was elegantly furnished with two planks resting on barrels, a kitchen chair for the editor, publisher, advertising manager, circulation manager, business manager, proofreader, folder, counter, distributor, salesman, cashier, bookkeeper, and clerk and another kitchen chair for any visitor on business. He had to succeed before his five hundred dollars were gone.

The instant success of the *Morning Herald* rewarded Bennett and justified his appraisal of his target. He provided indispensable news with a lighter touch for intellects weary of wading through the ponderous sheets, and also the sensationalism which was the steady diet of devotees of the *Transcript* and the *Sun*. By thus securing customers from both he made himself the common enemy of all New York newsmen.

Bennett was well grounded in economics because of his Aberdeen Catholic Seminary training. In the first regular number of the *Morning Herald* appeared an article on "the money market": a feature that opened the doors of the most conservative bankers, merchants, and businessmen to his newspaper. Within three months the publisher could boast an income big enough to meet expenses; then came the fire that destroyed the print-shop, and publication had to be suspended for nineteen days while new quarters and a new press were found.

It was while Bennett's newspaper was crippled that Day published in a series of seven articles, the story of the "Great Astronomical Discoveries, lately made by Sir John Herschall at the Cape of Good Hope, as reported by him in the Edinburgh Journal of Science." The construction of the great telescope through which the flora and fauna of the moon were clearly seen was no less convincingly described than the bat-men and bat-women lazily floating over the eerie landscape. Awed comments were drawn from most of the country's editors; sermons were preached on the meaning of life in empyrean spaces, and the *Sun's* presses groaned and complained ten hours a day to turn off the nineteen thousand copies demanded by a palpitating public.

Quite innocently Richard Adams Locke, an English writer employed by Mr. Day at the famous White Plains trial of "Matthius the Prophet," (and colorfully described by his friends as "cross-eyed and pock-marked but handsome, with a lofty brow and a noble presence"), remarked that he had written the story as a satire. The hoax was exposed by infuriated rivals, but the *Sun* smugly "awaited confirmation from Edinburgh" and did not lose a reader. The public, amused but unresentful, was never again quite so susceptible to clever deceit.

Returning to the fray "larger, livelier, prettier, saucier and more independent than ever" on August 31, 1835, the *Herald* made no admission of being outsmarted by the *Sun*; but the editor, whose impact on American newspapers was as great as that of any individual during their long history, fought for circulation supremacy with every weapon the day's news might provide. Led by the *Herald*, both the *Sun* and the *Transcript* whipped up the emotions of the unthinking public with growing expertness. It was Bennett who first sensationalized murder, outmoding old-fashioned editors and their hair-raising descriptions of "the remains." Bennett's reporting of the Robinson tragedy, for which he interviewed Rosina Townsend who discovered the body of Helen Jewett, led to permanent improvement in reporting of all "spot" news. He also started throngs of the morbidly curious on their way to court-rooms, funeral parlors, and cemeteries.

Bennett restored advertising to the news by insisting that copy constantly be changed until finally he could write: "Advertisements renewed every day." Bennett first reported New York's Anniversary Meetings of church organizations; he also made sermons and church news a regular weekly feature. He first found news in the society he provided with a capital S. The religious were, at first, furious and the elect scared. And the blanket sheets, stung into the defense of people suffering these invasions of privacy, burst their self-imposed bonds of silence and no longer ignored the little upstarts. Only the *Journal of Commerce* could find a kind word for the pennies: "they are superior to their six-penny contemporaries . . . let all classes of the community read, and they will think . . . and become less the dupes of designing individuals."

Imitations of New York's penny dreadfuls appeared in Boston, Philadelphia, and Baltimore; the *Times*, the *Public Ledger*, and the *Sun* were, for a time, all faithful copies. The cheap-for-cash newspapers multiplied in amazing numbers, and none was long without competition to nudge them into further coarseness, or in extreme instances, into respectability.

Steamboats, railroads, and locomotives were all top news for the spreading penny congregation. The Best Friend, a locomotive built in New York and shipped south by schooner, hauled newspapers and express shipments over the one hundred and thirty-six miles of railway track, the longest in the world, from Charleston to Hamburg, opposite Augusta, on the Savannah River, South Carolina. The directors of the railroad boasted that this transfer consumed only twelve hours. Express companies delivering newspapers to out-of-town dealers by rail and horse, and the wholesale news, periodical, and book companies now combined in a vast network of news-distribution. All had their roots in the London Plan, and owed much to the circulation promotors who went out to drum up business and keep it moving in the raids, forays, and battles they plotted, planned, and fought with the owners and editors of local newspapers.

Sinclair Tousey, once a carrier boy for the New York *Herald*, a New Haven, Connecticut, agent for the New York *Transcript*, and Philadelphia circulation promotor for the New York *Sun*, after he unsuccessfully tried his hand as a publisher of a penny newspaper in Louisville, Kentucky, turned his talents to the wholesale distribution of newspapers and books. Of the great news networks that also owe much to the London Plan of news merchandising, Tousey's genius built the American News Company.

Not all the penny papers were dreadful, however. There was *The Man* of George H. Evans, who expounded many of the theories of Henry George, another printer, forty years before Henry George. These radical ideas demanded votes for women, a ten-hour working day, and labor unions. Naturally there was a penny paper for the ladies too—called the *Woman*; its mysterious editor was one Ann Oldbody.

And in the *Ladies Morning Star* of 1836, William Newell shed crocodile tears for the "operative class of females," the "ten thousand orphans and widows who once walked the velvet of refinement and ease; dignity and gracefulness played like rainbow reflections along their pathway as they walked. Due to death and creditors it is their melancholy fate to ply the needle and fold the printed sheet for bare subsistence." The ten thousand orphans and widows scorned his dreary loaf, however, and missed the lovely advertisements of the "Bowery Steam Confectionery Company, always ready to supply the SWEETS OF LIFE, including Jelly and Cordial Drops, Pyramids and Crystal ornaments for cakes." Or perhaps they ate the jelly and cordial drops as they enjoyed the *Splifincator*, which was "Devoted to Mirth and Sarcasm with Comic

Engravings," but which did not neglect the news, and was also, Price, One Cent.

The best of New York's pennies was the *Tattler*, wisely and wittily edited by Park Benjamin; for businessmen it was published at NOON —right on the Meridian. In October of 1839 the soul of the *Tattler* was transfused into the *Evening Signal*, also published at NOON. And from its reinforced soul the *Signal* immediately fired the first gun of the Great Moral War to Exterminate Bennett.

James Gordon Bennett was charged with libel, indecency, and blackmail; the showmanship that pleased many was considered vulgar by others. His worst crime, apart from his success as a publisher, was the only crime not mentioned—a flippancy in handling the news not appreciated by Americans who were still accustomed to regarding the printed word seriously. Committees called on advertisers to demand they withdraw their patronage from Bennett's columns, and ministers preached that "Christians compromised their characters before the world by buying or reading that infamous sheet." The climax, sobering to many, was a long and well-written letter, skilfully skirting libel, but implying that Bennett had daily insulted the civilized community and had perverted the country from nearly every national virtue. This remarkable epistle of July 21, 1840, was signed in simple good intention—A Brother.

A similar comment, appearing in the *Evening Signal* of July 1, 1840, colorfully expressed the widely-felt sentiment:

The *Herald* says of late great numbers of citizens have ordered their *Herald* to be regularly served at their houses instead of buying it in the street. As to "great numbers," we believe that part of the assertation to be a ——, Bennett, but we can readily believe that any decent citizen must by this time have found out that it is infamy to be seen buying it in the street.

James Watson Webb and Mordecai Manuel Noah were the self-appointed generalissimos of the brawl which finally involved most of the country's newspapers. It was later charged that the owner and editor of the *Morning Courier and Enquirer* had with Noah's help coolly used the *Signal* as a catspaw to regain his lost circulation. In the *Signal* a year or so later the editor wrote: "Mr. James Watson Webb, who is eternally lugging his personal opinions into his columns says that Bennett is a disgrace and that the Herald is beneath his notice. Bennett makes up a better newspaper; the Herald is now decent. The Courier is fifty years behind the times; people stop it by the tens and fifties every day." To tell the truth the older newspapers, now "big enough for a bed-blanket and an extra pair of pillowcases with enough left over to paper the pantry shelves," were slowly and surely being starved out of existence by the livelier penny dreadfuls.

The London Plan revolutionized the business of publishing newspapers by putting it on a cash basis. Publishers could now pay their own way, independent of politicians' purses and government plums. And when publishers gave their readers more than a penny's worth of newsprint, news, and entertainment, a myriad of advertisers supplied the funds for publication. New problems were submitted to the long tests of trial and error. Time alone could disclose the answers.

Nameplate. Courtesy of Library of Congress.

Oberon—"Be thou here again,
　　　　'Ere the Leviathan can swim a league."

Puck— "I'll put a girdle round about the earth
　　　　In FORTY MINUTES.—Shakes.

BOSTON, JANUARY 5. 1833.

GAZETTE.

:IENCES, LITERATURE, RELIGION, COMMERCE. &C.

PRICE THREE DOLLARS
Per Annum, in advance....Two Dollars for Six months.

THE SEA DIVER.
BY H. W. LONGFELLOW.

13

"WHAT HATH GOD WROUGHT?"

UNDER THE RIPPLE AND MOTION OF NEWS RAN STRONG
tides of responsibility, their origin, strength, and direction more mysterious than those of the sea.

Editors leapt upon editors, brandished canes under editorial noses,
ripped off each other's buttons and tore out overcoat sleeves, and rushed
to get the news to their presses, some to boast of victory and others to
claim the title of "the most-abused." But newspapers of New York, port
of entry for the prized foreign news, honored the newsman's profession
by assuming the labor and expense of furnishing that news to the rest

of the country's newspapers. Western farmers were notified of suspension of England's corn laws when markets for their grain were open. Southern planters learned of fluctuations in cotton prices on the Liverpool Exchange, and Yankee traders looked to New York for news when mapping markets for ice, cheap clocks, tinware, and sperm oil.

There was urgency in the drumming of the hoofs of the news-express horses as they sped across the wooden bridges of all roads leading from Washington, bearing the messages of Andrew Jackson, reports of debates in House and Senate, and the gossip of the Kitchen Cabinet. Post-riders carried news-slips to other newspapers; special couriers coordinated their services with those of steamboats, railroads, and stagecoaches to hurry news of nullification, the Compromise Bill, the Withdrawal Act, the Specie Circular, and other administrative sensations to a people who sensed a threat of change to the American political concept—a change they did not understand and to which they would not blindly subscribe.

Pride forced Amos Kendall, Postmaster General, to prod his riders into delivering the new court journal, the Washington *Globe*, in which he, together with Editor Francis Blair and Printer John Rives, retailed the views of the President, excommunicated refractory leaders and editors, and held together the splitting Democratic party with such skill that even enemy editors were forced to read and admire.

The expresses of the *Journal of Commerce* recaptured the honors for speed in news by land. Their twenty-four horses and riders in eight relays often covered the almost two hundred and thirty miles from Washington to New York in twenty, and sometimes fifteen hours. And theirs were the envied beats in political news, which they published a full day ahead of all other New York morning newspapers.

Competition flared to fire the imaginations of the public as the *Herald* and the *Sun* challenged each other and dared the blanket sheets to outdo them. A news-express organizer who combined all methods of transportation to beat his rivals was Moses Y. Beach, brother-in-law of Benjamin H. Day, and in 1836 the owner of the *Sun*. James and Erastus Brooks, Portland brothers who established the New York *Express*, a commercial newspaper, in 1836, also won laurels in the races to the pressrooms. And Frederick Hudson, right-hand man for James Gordon Bennett, was one of the most resourceful of all American news collectors. The Boston *Atlas* of Richard Houghton (who had been an employee of the speed-conscious *Journal of Commerce*, importantly collecting and collating election returns) and the Providence *Journal* got the news to New England—fast. And in the West subscribers as far as Cincinnati marveled at news hurried by day and by night, by road and by river, from Washington.

The public, growing sophisticated, inflated the value of early news. Men with reports less than world-shaking set out for presses in gigs and arrived mounted on spent steeds, their wrecked vehicles left on the road-sides. Compositors on steamboats worked through the night to get the latest items ready for waiting press beds. From Utica reports of a murder trial were taken to Schenectady by special trains; a coach with Otis Dimmick at the reins made the Albany boat, "sixteen miles in forty-nine minutes," crowed the *Sun*. And the *Sun*'s Exclusive Express that left Albany by stage mounted on runners in January of 1841 with a copy of Governor William H. Seward's annual message and sped through wind, rain, and hail, with fresh horses every six miles in record time was met at Goshen by a locomotive. The news, whizzed over the rails of the Erie to Piermont and a waiting steamboat, was set on board by twelve compositors, and the forms were locked into the *Sun*'s presses just twelve and a half hours after the great man's words left the capital, to be forgotten the next day.

Light sails and oars continued to skim out into New York's waters and as leisurely return until the aggressive Bennett put the *Fanny Elsser* into service. The *Fanny*, said the *Herald*, "danced lightly past and left far astern the *Dot-and-Go-One*, the old tub of the Wall Street press." The blanket sheets met this challenge with bigger and faster news boats and once more the harbor was the scene of lively battles to get the news and get it first.

It was not long before fair warnings of news arriving by sea were flashed to the newspapers of New York, Boston, Portland, Charleston, and Savannah by the Semaphoric Telegraphic Companies using the marine signal flags approved by Mr. A. A. Leggett, Conductor of the Telegraph of the New York Merchants' Exchange. Wigwagging the news was such a success that had the country been spared the depression that followed the administration of Martin Van Buren, it would have been extended inland. One M. Gannon, formerly of France, but more recently from Russia, and his associate, M. Servell, were reported in Baltimore in 1837 making arrangements for a line of telegraphs from New York to New Orleans; with the system of their invention "that casts in the shade all others" they expected to send one hundred words including punctuation marks and capital letters over the entire distance in thirty minutes.

Prospects of earlier news from Europe exhilarated all American publishers when the arrivals of the *Sirus* and the *Great Northern* crowned the editorially advertised Age of Steam that was celebrated by big wood-cuts of the ships in most newspapers. The ever forward-looking James Gordon Bennett returned to England with the *Sirus* to arrange for reports from Special Correspondents.

An odd commentary on this celebrated era was the pigeon-service proposed by Daniel H. Craig, printer from New Hampshire and news-collector extraordinary. Arunah S. Abell who, with William M. Swain and Azariah H. Simmons had established in 1836 the Baltimore *Sun* and Philadelphia *Ledger*, penny newspapers, found the experiments so successful that the *Sun's* big flock of carriers made wings as necessary to newspapers as hoofs.

A pigeon loft with rows of nests in neat tiers, feed boxes, water troughs, and a little wire-covered door that rang a bell to summon a handler as it was pushed open by a returning messenger was an up-to-date feature of the building erected to house the New York *Sun* in 1842. Part of the New York *Sun's* flock was imported from London where the pigeons had regularly delivered news from Dublin and Paris for the *Morning Chronicle*. A famous member of the *Sun's* flying staff was Pigeon Sam Patch, who brought news-slips from the Boston steamboat no matter how late the ship or how heavy the weather. His reward was a place in contemporary slang: people who fell neatly and without injury were reported to have "executed a Sam Patch."

Pigeons carried news from Washington to New York in the course of a morning, from Albany in two and a half hours, and went to the Narrows in twenty minutes. Many of the country's newspapers noted with sadness the fate of the feathered martyr trained by Aza D. Banker to bring news from the mainland for the Nantucket *Inquirer*; he was shot and eaten by a miserable wretch who claimed he had mistaken the messenger for a crow. As an independent news collector Craig packed his birds into big baskets and carried them out to ships he hailed and boarded far beyond Boston Harbor, and his tissue-thin news-summaries "tucked under pigeon's wings" reached his clients, including the penny dreadful Boston *Times*, so early, they were printed and sold long before the ships were sighted and reported by the usual signals. Some publishers were furiously resentful of Craig's enterprise but many others saw no reason to get excited about news that someone would bring them when it was convenient.

Bennett raised the price of the *Herald* to two cents in 1836, and three years later the *Transcript* suddenly expired, thus leaving the *Sun* in the enviable position of being the only New York general penny newspaper. This ideal state of affairs lasted until April 10, 1841, when the New York *Tribune*, also Price One Cent, was first "hollered in the streets."

Born in Amherst, New Hampshire in 1811, Horace Greeley was nourished on the Bible, Shakespeare, and Burns and his imagination was stimulated by the Amherst weekly *Farmer's Cabinet*. At an early age he was learning to print on the East Poultney, Vermont, *Northern Spectator*. Ten years after he arrived in the city where he knew frustration and failure, he was able to establish his famous "New Morning Journal of Politics, Literature and General Intelligence." To American newspapers Greeley brought a new earnestness, a strange assortment of personal enthusiasms and antipathies—the "isms" on which he frittered away time and talent—and the aspirations which helped to make his weekly the country's most important and himself the most influential editor any American newspaper had.

The *Signal*, for which Greeley collated the returns in the election in which he had supported Harrison ("Tippecanoe and Tyler, too," with words and music of campaign songs in his *Log Cabin*, a campaign newspaper), reported that the *Tribune* after only a month had a circulation of nine thousand copies daily. The same newspaper for July 31, 1841, said: "The publisher of the *Sun* has, during the past few days got up a conspiracy to crush the New-York *Tribune*. The *Tribune* was from its inception very successful, and, in many instances, persons in the habit of taking the *Sun* stopped that paper, wisely preferring a sheet which gives twice the amount of reading matter and always contains the latest intelligence. This fact afforded sufficient evidence to Beach, as it did to all others who were cognizant of the circumstances, that the *Tribune* would, before the lapse of many weeks, supplant the *Sun*. To prevent this, and if possible, to destroy the circulation of the *Tribune*, an attempt was made to bribe the carriers to give up their routes; fortunately this succeeded in the cases of only two men, who were, likewise carriers of the *Sun*. In the next case all the newsmen were threatened with being deprived of the *Sun* if in any instance they were found selling the *Tribune*. But these efforts were not enough to satisfy Beach. He instigated boys in his office, or others, to whip the boys selling the *Tribune*. No sooner was this fact ascertained at the office of the *Tribune* than young men were sent out to defend the sales of that paper. They had not been on their stations long before a boy from the *Sun* office approached and began to flog the lad from the *Tribune*; retributary measures were instantly resorted to; but, before a just chastisement was inflicted, Beach himself and a man in his employ came out to sustain their youthful emissary. The whole matter will, we understand, be submitted to the proper magistrates."

This earliest of circulation battles won public sympathy, advertised the superior qualities of the new newspaper, and increased the newsboys' sales of the *Tribune*. It was first of the wars disgracing publishers who later failed to hear of bloodshed and the destruction of property, including the burning and inking of whole editions of newspapers resented for telling the truth.

Speed-achieving publishers and speed-conscious readers were alike curiously immune to the promises of the Electro-Magnetic Telegraph, for which the inventor had secured a grant of thirty thousand dollars from a Congress reluctant to squander the taxpayers' money for its demonstration. It took dramatic news from a crowded and smoke-filled convention hall where the tensions of whipsawing backers of favorite sons and deserving Democrats were at last eased by the emergence of an acceptable dark horse as candidate for the Presidency to convince the country, including the newspapers, that the electrical transmission of news-making words was a fact to reduce their triumphs in newsspeed to absurdity.

Along the wire stretched from Washington to Baltimore by Ezra Cornell traveled, on May 1, 1844, news of the nomination of Henry Clay by the Whigs; and that news "arrived one hour ahead of the train." On May 24 when Samuel F. B. Morse, formally opening the wire in Washington, clicked off "What Hath God Wrought?" to Alfred Vail at the receiving instrument in Baltimore, neither the newspapers nor their readers realized the significance of the event. But on May 29 when news of the nomination of James K. Polk, breaking the convention deadlock, came through, both editors and public regarded the invention rather with surprised respect than enthusiasm. The awed James Gordon Bennett was the exception; he wrote: "It must be borne in mind that the distance between Baltimore and Washington is thirty-six miles." Then came news of the nomination of Silas Wright of New York for Vice President. Back over the wire went: "Mr. Wright is here and says, say to the New York delegation that he cannot accept the nomination as Vice President." Later went the message: "Mr. Wright is here, and will cheerfully support Mr. Polk, but cannot accept the nomination as Vice President." Unbelieving politicians and newspapermen settled down to await confirmation by horse-express of this astounding news and not until then did they know of the selection of George M. Dallas of Texas.

Now wrote James Gordon Bennett in the *Herald*: "The Magnetic Telegraph at Washington has totally annihilated space—what there was left of it by steam locomotives and steamships." And almost a year later he predicted, truly: "Mere newspapers—the circulators of intelligence merely—must submit to destiny or go out of existence. That journalism, however, which possesses intellect, mind, and originality, will not suffer. Its sphere of action will be widened. It will, in fact, be more influential than ever. The public mind will be stimulated to greater activity by the rapid circulation of news. The swift communication of tidings of great events will awake in the masses of the community a keener interest in public affairs. Thus the intellectual, philosophic, and original journalist will have a greater, a more excited, and more thoughtful audience than ever."

Enemies consolidated with enemies to wage war against the common arch-enemy. There was high mystery in the advertisement in—of all newspapers—the *Herald* of February 26, 1846: "A vessel of extraordinary speed and with choice sailing-master and picked crew, will leave New York for Liverpool on the 9th inst. at 12 o'clock, and returning will leave Liverpool on or about the 26th or 27th inst. Letter-bags will remain open until Monday at 10 o'clock." Newspapers and their readers spluttered with curiosity; the sudden sailing, the emphasis on speed, and the quick return indicated that there was something in the wind. Was it a great international coup or something on the Oregon Question? Rumors spread like wildfire: would disagreement mean another war with England? The crowd that gathered at the Battery cheered when the pilot boat *William J. Romer* sailed as advertised. They noticed that there were only two passengers on board—"two men with shiny black caps" —so they lingered as she disappeared in the distance far ahead of the packet *Patrick Henry* which sailed at the same time.

On scenting mischief in the smug aura of satisfaction about the offices of the *Sun*, the *Tribune*, and the *Journal of Commerce*, and with newspapers combining with others in Boston, Philadelphia, and Baltimore to beat him in getting news of the Oregon Treaty—by sending Captain Brogan, ships' news collector, for the *Sun* and Mr. Gale, assistant foreman of the *Tribune*, as their secretly speeding emissaries—Bennett made arrangements to have the Cunarder *Cambria* met at Halifax. Captain Judkins was persuaded to hurry with the coaling and to push his engines hard all the way to Boston. In Boston a locomotive was waiting to speed to Allyn's Point where the smoke-grimed messenger climbed from the cab to hurry aboard Commodore Vanderbilt's yacht *Traveller* at

Norwich. Crossing Long Island Sound the *Traveller* deposited its passenger at Greenpoint for the railroad to the New York ferry. So, while the express horse of the others was racing down Nassau Street to the office of the *Journal of Commerce*, the newsboys of the *Herald* were swarming after him with EXTRAS of the news: the Holy Alliance was beaten again and by five hours!

Excitement over the Oregon Question gave way to the equally agitating Texas Question, and when the Texas Question was submerged in the hue and cry of War with Mexico, speed in the collection and communication of news began to find its perspective in the daily news picture.

New Orleans, port of departure for the troops and supplies of Winfield Scott and Zachary Taylor, and also the port of entry for news from the theaters of action, saw its newspapers brace themselves for the responsibilities and expense of keeping the country informed. Public interest and public demand for adequate news combined to create and shower with stars the world's first war correspondents, those romantic newsmen who so nonchalantly risk all to send to newspapers their observations made in the perils and discomforts of fire and sword.

George Wilkens Kendall, first of these, was born less than two years before Horace Greeley, at Mount Vernon, a New Hampshire hamlet, near the birth-place of the famous editor. Also a printer, Kendall worked in Washington, New York, and Mobile, where he acquired a reputation as a raconteur with a weakness for epigrams. He went west to New Orleans and in association with Francis A. Lumsden established in 1837 the *Picayune*, the town's first cheap-for-cash newspaper, which soon won an enviable place in the country's affections for its light-hearted gaiety. Comic editorial paragraphs were admired as "bantering" and news items, with sheer genius, managed to avoid all the basic rules of journalism: "We understand that a couple of gentlemen were engaged in a fight in one of the short streets near the River one night last week."

The publisher, who had an unquenchable thirst for adventure, had been a part of the ill-fated Santa Fe expedition of Mirabeau Lamar in 1841. He was captured and marched to Mexico City and jailed with lepers. Kendall long believed war with Mexico was inevitable, and when, on May 11, 1845, Congress declared that "a state of War existed," he was ready to leave for the Rio Grande to serve under Ben McCullock in the Texas Rangers before joining the staff of General Scott.

To get his reports to his newspaper Kendall had to organize an express. Daring horsemen, mostly mere boys, rode in relays over more than a thousand miles of open desert and brush, with little protection from Indians and guerrillas; and such was the dependability of Major Kendall's express that it was the preferred method of transportation for all but official papers.

Arriving in New Orleans by boat, Major Kendall's news soon came from the *Picayune's* presses in EXTRAS, and as these were hollered in the streets, great bales were hurried to the wharves along the Mississippi for delivery by tall-stacked, paddle-wheeled steamboats to Natchez, St. Louis, Cincinnati, and even Pittsburgh. First copies from the presses were rushed from New Orleans to Milneburg on "old" Lake Ponchartrain and the steamer for Mobile. And over the two hundred miles of stagecoach road from Mobile to Montgomery raced the horses of the expresses of the eastern newspapers, sharing the expenses of getting the news early after only a few brushes with C. A. Wicliffe, Postmaster General, who wanted a law to make beating the United States mails a punishable crime. Over this road once rode Fred Taylor, a lad of fifteen, in thirteen hours, stopping in the night only to saddle fresh horses; his modest reward was a purse of seventy dollars. From Montgomery the goal was the terminus of the telegraph wires, at first Washington, then Richmond, and before the war was won and over, Petersburgh, Virginia.

All the country had the news in a week or ten days. The stories of Major Kendall, and James M. Freamer who signed himself Mustang for the New Orleans *Delta*, and almost a dozen other correspondents from other cities, all somewhat florid and rather strong in clichés, were considered and accepted as accurate and honest portrayals of the fighting.

Freamer was made official army messenger, and was entrusted with news of the peace of Guadaloupe Hidalgo for delivery to a government agent at Mobile. Under the angry glares of Kendall's couriers, Freamer steamed out of Vera Cruz on the *Iris* while they were detained on the *New Orleans* for two days by army order. Records were broken and the great news over the usual route reached Baltimore for printing in the *Sun* seven days after it left New Orleans and two days before "official" army messengers ambled into Washington.

Kendall is credited with preserving—if not inventing—"Give 'em a little more grape, Captain Bragg." He stirred American affection with his presentation of General Taylor as an honest, homely old soldier whose attachment to his horse, Old Whitey, was so great that he could not bear to be deprived of the animal though it made him a conspicuous target in the battle.

The American Army newspaper, like the American war correspondent, first appeared during the War with Mexico. Three gadding printers, R. G. W. Jewell, John Peoples, and J. P. Darnard, set up a press and opened shop in Vera Cruz, and got out the *American Eagle* in April 1847. Four small pages carried late army orders, lists of the dead and wounded, a grouch against the Post Office Department—"no one cares about us"—a story of General Scott, who with his party went to church on Easter Sunday to the astonishment of the natives, and the really exciting news that Hart and Wells, with "their full and efficient theatrical company" had arrived on the S.S. *New Orleans* "just as we were beginning to wonder how to kill time." The weather? "Hot as Thunder." Still other presses followed the troopers of the U.S.A. to Jalapa, La Pueblo, Metamoras, Chichuahua, Saltilla, and Tampico with the *American Star*, the *American Pioneer*, the *Anglo-Saxon*, the *Picket Guard*, the *Sentinel*, the *American Flag*, the *Republic of the Rio Grande*, and other newspapers, which seemed priceless to soldiers far from home. Besides home news they contained also not too restrained commentaries on life as lived in the Army.

Peace came early in an election year. Betting ran high on the four prospective candidates for the nomination of the Whigs meeting in Philadelphia convention. The brokers' system for getting early and dependable news in New York was decided upon. Every weekday morning at eleven o'clock a flagman stepped to the roof of the Merchants' Exchange to wigwag the news of the prices of stocks and bonds to a watcher in Jersey City, and that news was passed along by flag all the way to the Quaker City. Signals for this occasion were a white flag for General Taylor, a red flag for Henry Clay, two white flags for General Scott, and two red flags for Judge McLean. The watcher for the *Courier and Enquirer* caught the white flag of the brokers' tower and in elation released the news that lighted bonfires and boomed cannon all the way to Portland, and Zachary Taylor was nominated next day.

An undocumented, unrecorded, and incredible event occurred sometime within a few weeks after the close of the Mexican War. Gerard Hallock called on James Gordon Bennett "to talk about the news," and it was not long before Hallock and Hale of the *Journal of Commerce*, James Watson Webb of the *Morning Courier and Enquirer*, the Beaches of the *Sun*, the brothers Brooks of the *Express*, Horace Greeley and Thomas McElrath of the *Tribune*, and Bennett and Frederick Hudson of the *Herald* (the country's most temperamental of news talents) were meeting regularly with an amity engendered of mutual acknowledgement of the coming dominance of telegraphic news. Problems arising from the physical limitations of each paper and the expense of the new method could be solved only by cooperation.

Gerard Hallock was first president of the budding New York Associated Press; its first General Agent was Doctor Alexander Jones, who employed the Association's first correspondents and received their telegraphed reports in an office up a flight of wooden stairs at the corner of Broadway and Liberty Street. The historian of the early telegraph forwarded news to the members of the Association, often by his own hand, by day and by night, in fair weather or storm, and never entirely neglected his medical practice. Frederick Hudson and Henry Jarvis Raymond, who represented the newest cheap-for-cash newspaper, the New York *Times*, newly a member, comprised the Association's first Executive Committee.

In the first number of the *Times* on September 18, 1851, Raymond charted the course that he, together with George Jones and Edward B. Wesly, intended to pursue, i.e., they would "present all the news of the day, from all parts of the world" through a newspaper pledged "always upon the side of Morality, of Industry, of Education and Religion." Further, he wrote:

We do not mean to write as if we were in a passion unless this shall really be the case; and we shall make it a point to get in a passion as rarely as possible. There are very few things in this world which it is worth while to get angry about; and they are just the things that anger will not improve. In controversies with other journals, with individuals, or with parties we shall engage only when, in our opinion, some important public interest can be promoted thereby; and even then, we shall endeavor to rely more upon fair arguments than upon misrepresentations or abusive language.

This new note of moderation was welcomed by New Yorkers, who were beginning to weary of the intensely personal journalism of the day. The novelty of a cheap easily purchased newspaper had lost its original allure and was no longer capable of sustaining readers of its own creation. The public had grown sceptical of editorial St. Georges, who lashed at mice and ignored the dragons of political friends and foes. They were tired of a press whose news all too frequently consisted of no more than bold and biased accusations. "Mealy-mouthed" was Greeley's retort to the *Times* after Raymond had reproved him for beginning a news article with "Governor Seymour is a LIAR." It was current editorial belief that strong feelings could be expressed only with strong words. James Gordon

Bennett had already put in his two-cents' worth with "Galvanize a large New England squash and it would make as capable an editor as Horace Greeley."

And there were many men and women in the lingering exaltation of the Great Revival who wanted a religious penny newspaper of such high moral tone that it would not only bar advertisements of lotteries and theaters, but all other "objectionable and improper matter." No longer would all news columns carry stories of crime and sex, scandal and slander, or even reports from police and divorce courts. To this lofty aim the New York *World*, a daily with weekly and semiweekly editions, was dedicated on June 12, 1860.

Promising to "refuse to pander to corrupt tastes" and to "rigorously exclude everything unfit to be read in pure households," the *World*, under the expert guidance of Colonel Alexander Cummings from the Philadelphia *Bulletin* presented, in a style suggesting the modern news magazine, much information of interest under such captions as, "The Scientific World," "The World of Art," and "The Literary World." Its news of the day was flat:

FROM HAVANA.

> Charleston, June 13th.
> The S. S. *Isabel* arrived last evening, from Havana, June 10th.
> Sugars are advancing.
> Molasses is quiet.
> Claussen and Carbondell, merchants in Havana, have failed for a large sum.
> It was officially declared that the International Bank has collapsed.
> A noted highwayman named Sallez was arrested on board the schooner, the *Merritt*, from New York.
> Twelve of the crew of the slaver, *Don Juan*, were arrested in Havana.

The *World's* advertising, strong in books for the religious, also advertised the poisons of the vermin-destroyers and the soothing syrup of the well-known Mrs. Winslow.

Underestimating the frailty of human nature and the ease with which curiosity can toss the noblest of aspirations out the window, the new *World* was not a success because "it hadn't any news."

Early in its career the *World* absorbed the *Morning Courier and Enquirer* of the once fire-eating James Watson Webb, but this had little effect upon its anemic circulation. And while it continued to languish in the hands of its more or less earnest editors and owners, the "Devil continued to whisper into the ear of James Gordon Bennett every night and tell him just what the good people of New York wanted to read next morning."

Nameplate. San Francisco, September 21, 1860. Steamer Edition: Letters in newsprint for the people back home. Courtesy of New York Public Library.

14

THE WESTERNS

COCKILY INDEPENDENT AND CRACKLING WITH PIO-
neer verve was the first western newspaper of the twenty-six United
States which were still shouting themselves hoarse with "Fifty-four forty
or fight."

Flumgudgeon's Gazette and the Bumble Bee Budget, "A newspaper . . . Edited by the Curl Tail Coon" and "Devoted to Scratching
and Stinging the Follies of the Times" was in manuscript. Its publisher
was Charles Pickett, one of the Virginia Fighting Picketts, who were
then disputing the claims of the Methodists to most of the Williamette

Valley. Pickett got out his little *Budget* free to all during the Territorial Council in Oregon City in the summer of 1844 under: "Don't stroke us backwards! There is enough villainy going on to raise our bristles without that!"

To Spanish California in 1838 came a printing press from Boston 'round the Horn in the *Lagoda*. Press and types had been ordered long previously by Don Augustin Vincente Zamorano, Secretary to Governor Don Jose Figuerno, and who had been printing from seals. Zamorano promptly opened shop to "serve the public with the greatest exactness and care," and although his interesting price list offered "more equitable prices to gentlemen who may wish to establish any periodicals," there is no record of any such enterprise. Within two or three years the press became the property of the government, and was for a time operated by one Santiago Aguiler, who expressed his opinions of his social betters by always printing the word *aristocrata* neatly, but upside down. Last of the Spanish printers to use the Boston press was the versatile José de la Rosa.

Barely three weeks had the Stars and Stripes floated over Monterey when the frigate *Congress* in command of Commodore Stockton sailed into port to aid and uphold Fremont and Sloat. Aboard the *Congress* was Walter Colton, the chaplain who was a printer from Vermont and a journalist from the Philadelphia *North American* as well as a Congregational minister.

Looking about the town, Colton "in a collection of junk" came across a printing press, probably the one first used by Zamorano. Colton thought it was "old enough to be preserved as a curiosity; there were no rules, no leads and the types were rusty and all in pi." In excitement and with the help of two printers, Joseph Dockrill and Robert Semple, Colton cleaned and restored the outfit. "It was only by scouring that the letters could be made to show their faces. A sheet or two of tin was procured and these, with a jack knife, were cut into rules and leads." Colton and Semple were seized with a desire to get out a newspaper. Colton described his partner as "an immigrant from Kentucky, who stands six feet eight in his stockings. He is in buckskin dress, a fox-skin cap; is true with his rifle, ready with his pen and quick at the type-case." "Luckily," he wrote, "we found the greater part of a keg of ink; and now came the main scratch for paper. None could be found, except what is used to envelope the tobacco of the cigars smoked here by the natives in sheets a little larger than common foolscap; a coaster had a small supply of this on board and this we procured, and this is the size of our first paper which we have christened the *Californian*."

The first number of the first newspaper printed on the Pacific Coast was dated August 15, 1846, only five weeks after California was declared American territory. "A crowd was waiting when the first sheet was thrown from the press. It produced quite a little sensation. Never was a bank run upon harder; not, however, by people to get specie, but exactly the reverse." The little folio's pages were oddly freckled by the solid inner spaces of the *a*'s and *e*'s, and the lower case *w*'s were contrived of two *v*'s. Half the two-columned pages were printed in Enlgish and the rest in Spanish. The *Californian* was "as full of news as a walnut of meat"; much of its news was local and more had been secured from travelers and from officers and others stationed at the regional military posts.

When Walter Colton, who had been elected *alcalde* of Monterey, was appointed Judge of the Court of Admiralty for the Territory, he resigned his publishing interest. The *Californian* appeared on April 24, 1847, over the name of Robert Semple only; and after only two more numbers the Kentuckian moved the old press to San Francisco to continue as of May 22, 1847.

Number Two of this breezy young western newspaper had noted the arrival of the *Brooklyn* at Yerba Buenna. This was the ship chartered by Elder Samuel Brannan to bring two hundred and thirty-eight Mormons from New York; the voyage took nearly seven months and great was the surprise of the passengers, the Captain, and the crew to see the Stars and Stripes billowing over a country that had been Spanish when they set sail. Aboard the *Brooklyn* was the second printing press destined for California; it had already been used by the Mormons for printing the *Prophet*.

It took time to hang quilts and blankets from the ceilings of the old Spanish barracks to make living quarters, and it took time to get the immigrants' belongings, their supplies, their cattle, pigs, and chickens ashore, all sheltered and settled; so it was September before Brannan opened a printing office and not until the end of the year did he get around to getting out a newspaper. Nearly six months later Niles' *Register* of Baltimore, acknowledging a copy of the first number of the *California Star*, dated January 9, 1847, described it as "small and neat." Sam, remarked the *Register*, had been brought up by Joe Smith and was well qualified to unfold and impress the tenets of the sect. But the *Star* was a general newspaper, non-sectarian, and special news and communications for the Mormons were published in supplements and as extras.

The first editor of the *California Star* was E. P. Jones; its second was Edward C. Kemble, a youthful printer from Troy, New York, who was also a passenger on the *Brooklyn*. And in November of 1848 the *Californian* and the *California Star* combined under the name *Alta California*, a newspaper which became famous during the great days of the gold rush. Its new owners were Kemble & Co.; the Co. comprised two other York State printers, E. Gilbert and G. C. Hubbard.

To Sacramento, rip-roaring camp of six thousand adventurers, prospectors, and pioneers, went on the *Dica Me Nana* (Says My Mama) the following spring California's first journalist and the historian of her early newspapers. Edward C. Kemble set up his Washington press in a little building he helped erect of 'dobe, wood, and cotton cloth, cut a nameplate with his jackknife, and went to press on an odd assortment of paper with the first number of the *Placer Times* dated April 28, 1849.

Kemble & Co.'s first Sacramento newspaper was printed three columns to each of its four pages and carried three advertisements. J. T. Sutter offered a handsome reward for the return of two stolen horses and also gave notice of the forthcoming sale, at auction, of Sutter's Grist Mill that had been deserted by workmen and customers since the day Sam Brannan ran through the town holding two bags of gold aloft and screaming: "Gold! Gold! Gold from the American River." The last was the professional "card" of the same Sam Brannan: "Brannan and Company, Wholesale and Retail Forwarding, Storage and Commission Merchants." Freight was being hauled at two thousand dollars a ton.

In early January of the flaming '49, William Faulkner, publisher of the Norwich, Connecticut, *News*, and his two sons set sail for "Caly-forni-a," and in their luggage was the lumber for a house and a printing press. On this press in late August of 1849 the *Pacific News* was started, just one of seven daily newspapers launched in San Francisco. Of this Jonas Winchester, a one-time partner of Greeley, was later a part owner, and it was the first west-coast newspaper produced on a power press.

In February of '49 the *Henry Lee*, chartered by one hundred and twenty-five from Hartford, Connecticut, insurance offices, left for the diggings. No doubt with beaver hats newly ironed they entered the ark with solemn tread, two by two, a little self-important because safe on board they had a printing press and two able-bodied printers to get out a newspaper when wind and weather permitted.

The *Old Harry's* news included reports of storms, tempests, a bolt of lightning that struck a spar, and a Sunday afternoon bullfight in Rio de Janeiro. The *Henry Lee* was used as a store ship until all the five-thousand-dollars' worth of goods and commodities in her hold were sold. Then she was abandoned as gold-seeking storekeepers joined gold-seeking passengers and crew. Left to rot the *Henry Lee* finally sank in the mud of San Francisco Bay. The press was probably sold to some printer whose pockets bulged with nuggets of gold and who craved nothing in this world but the acrid odor of printers' ink. On it may have been started more than one of the many early newspapers demanded by the news-hungry, news-conscious West.

Three California Numbers were published by the New York *Herald* in December, 1848 and January, 1849. Maps, directions, and advice to a world intent on getting to the gold-fields made this an appreciated public service. With the rush, by regular steamers around Cape Horn, went Special California Editions of newspapers of New York, Boston, Philadelphia, and New Orleans, and eager men tossed dollars into the baskets of the vendors for news from home. Single copies of newspapers of later dates, carried overland, commanded fabulous prices and were passed from hand to hand and from camp to camp until the rag-stock was worn bare of ink. Eastern newspapers took on glamour from the descriptive articles of famous writers who were sent to report at first hand the gold-rush spectacle that stirred the imaginations of more sedentary men and women. And in the traditional exchange of news between frontiers and home, Steamer Editions of California newspapers, made up for home-bound ships whose names and pictures topped their nameplates, and sold at fifty cents a copy, supplied news of utmost value to eastern newspapers. These were the "letters home" from boosters, luring to the West the women who later made the homes which converted many of the forty-niners to true Californians.

Less than twenty years after the first broad wheels of the Great Migration turned to follow their pilots over the unmapped Oregon Trail, and only two years after the brief summer of *Flumgudgeon's Budget*, Oregon City had its first printed newspaper on February 5, 1846.

The *Oregon Spectator* of the Oregon Printing Association, of which empire-building Jessy Quinn Thornton was president, was edited by W. G. T' Vault, Postmaster General of the Territory. Under a wood engraving of an American eagle and the motto: "Westward the Star of Empire Takes Its Way," he promised in a long political dissertation that politics would be shunned in the newspaper, and proposed to bring subscribers twice a month such foreign and domestic news as could be secured. Frankly he admitted that without the benefit of the exchanges he could not hope to compete with the newspapers of New York and London. The objective of the Association's publication was immediately plain in the light of its editorial boasting of climate and waterpower "unsurpassed on the Globe." Scant news was supplemented by a short poem on Love, and in one of the few advertisements in this first number, the proprietor of the City Hotel offered Horse-ferriage free to those who would favor him with a call from the west side of the river.

Came the Fourth of July and the *Spectator* was doing very well with news, both foreign and domestic, extracted from newspapers brought into the Columbia River by ships from the Sandwich Islands. Editorial gratitude was slightly soured, however, by the impolite *Polynesian's* chortles over the idea of Love in the pine forests: it expected to hear any day that bustles and ice-cream were also common in the deep woods. The *Spectator* also found good, serviceable news in the *Seamen's Friend*. Honolulu not only got the news by clipper ship and by whaler but published it in its own newspapers. A Ramage press was sent to the Islands in 1820 by the American Board of Foreign Missions, and printers and printers' wives who were also printers were among the first American missionaries to the South Seas.

The *Oregon Spectator* within two years had a rival in Oregon City: the *Free Press*, published by George L. Curry, the fourth editor of the *Spectator* who had established a record by holding his editorial chair for a year and a half. Explained Mr. Curry: "Some months ago when we were unceremoniously deprived of editing the Governor's paper, and no longer permitted to bask in the sunshine of official favor, we were, of course, dreadfully cast down . . ."; but this had not been for long. With the help of Victor M. Wallace a wooden press that "Mr. Wallace thinks will tell the truth quite as well as an iron one" was constructed. Types were bought from a French Catholic missionary to the Indians, and the future governor of Oregon Territory proceeded to give his former employers a little competition before all hands, including his subscribers, decamped for California's glittering river beds.

The old Ramage, which was brought around the Horn by the Mormons and on which the first issues of both the *California Star* and *Alta California* were printed in San Francisco, was taken to Portland by T. J. Dryer and A. M. Berry. On it they printed the *Weekly Oregonian* on December 4, 1850. Henry L. Pittock from Pittsburgh was a compositor on this newspaper in 1853 and its proprietor from 1860. A daily from 1861, the *Oregonian*, famous for its industry in collecting news by horse, stage, steamer, and telegraph, supported with its considerable influence the development of the modern Northwest. The same old press two years later turned off the *Columbian* for Olympia until publishers Wiley and McElroy celebrated territorial elevation with a new nameplate: the *Washington Pioneer*. The press did further service, printing the news in Alaska; the Sitka *Times* of T. G. Murphy managed to survive from April of 1869 to September of 1870. Moved to Seattle the same press in the hands of the same publisher produced the *Alaska Times and Seattle Dispatch* for a few months before coming into the possession of C. H. Larrabee and Beriah Brown. Brown was a legendary journeyman from Canandaigua, New York, who had a hand in starting western newspapers beyond counting. On this same press they began in late 1871 the *Puget Sound Dispatch*. This old Ramage press, so intimately associated with news for the West in its pioneering days, is now in the Museum of the University of Washington.

A Ramage, types, paper, and ink were taken to the Land of the Honey Bee with the first wagons of the Mormons. After three years, on June 15, 1850, the first issue of the *Deseret News* appeared in Great Salt Lake City. Its publisher was Brigham Young, its editor Doctor Willard Richards, and its printer W. K. Whitney.

Weekly the little newspaper begged for RAGS! RAGS! RAGS! but there were not enough old wagon covers, tents, quilts, shirts, etc. to provide pulp for paper-making. Publication was made semimonthly and suspended from August to November of 1851 when, continued and enlarged, the *Deseret News* reappeared. In an early number there was an interesting bid for the cash of transient trade: "Names and places of travellers and immigrants, together with the dates of arrival and leaving will be inserted for twenty-five cents an issue, and in companies of twenty and up, twenty cents an issue." Sent east by a rare post or carried by accommodating travelers who had "paid to see the elephant," copies of this newspaper were scanned by home-town editors and publishers eager to print news of fortune-seeking friends and neighbors.

To Genoa, neat little Mormon settlement and haven for weary men and beasts on the Carson River just east of the high Sierras, in the fabulous Washoe country, William L. Jernegan and Alfred James brought an old Washington press from California. In late 1858 with worn types and tools they started the *Territorial Enterprise*, and news from the outside world was packed in on snowshoes. Within a year the publishers moved to Carson City and sold out to Jonathan Williams and Isaac B. Wollard, who moved both press and newspaper to Virginia City, where they were printing daily before they sold to Joseph T. Goodman and Dennis McCarthy. Tall stories well told and giddy battles with rival newspapers, publishers, editors, and reporters of this booming Nevada mining camp earned an early reputation as a wit for the best-known employee of the *Enterprise*, that "beef-eating, blear-eyed, hollow-headed, slab-sided ignoramus, that pilfering reporter Mark Twain."

Los Angeles, goal for some and way station for others of the westward swarming hordes, had a newspaper from May 17, 1851, when John A. Lewis and John McElroy issued *La Estrella* on the press of Theodore Foster. The print-shop was in a dwelling newly erected by Foster on a town lot given him by the city council, which was anxious to secure the public benefit of a printing press. *La Estrella*, a quarto with five columns to a page, was printed in both English and Spanish, and was split to make the Spanish half the *El Clamor Público*. According to rumor the little *Star* was so mettlesome that it once published an account of one of the town's many hangings, complete with gallows-side confession, before the noose was sprung in order to make the San Francisco steamer with the news.

A printing press was set up in Santa Fe in 1834, from which came *El Crepúsculo de la Libertad* of Lic Antonia in 1835, but this Dawn of Liberty was short-lived. Ten years later from the same press came *La Verdad*, of Donaciano Vigil, and this was followed by *El Payo de Nuevo Méjico* of *Jesús Maria Baca*. Yankee hustle following trade over the famous trail got out the Santa Fe *Republican* in September, 1847, a good six months before the close of the war with Mexico; Hovey and Davis were its publishers. The *New Mexican* was established two years later by Davis and Jones, and this newspaper, started before American government was organized, was a daily for forty-four years before the Territory was admitted to the Union.

To all the vigorous southwest went printing presses. Newspapers, with the color of local news threading its sturdy way through very ancient intelligence and editorial horseplay, gave mining camps and cattle towns a sobering sense of permanence and responsibility.

From the Central Foundry Company of Cincinnati the Wrightson brothers bought a Washington hand press; its serial number, 25, indicating the path already being beaten to the Queen City to make it the country's new center for publishing supplies and equipment. Shipped down the Ohio and Mississippi Rivers, through the Gulf of Mexico, around Cape Horn, and up the west coast of South America, it was landed at Guaymas, Mexico, and transported by ox cart to Tubec, Arizona. On it was printed in February, 1859, the *Arizonian*, by William Wrightson; its publishers were the Salero Mining Company. It moved to Tucson, from where publication was intermittent until 1871, when it was revived as the *Citizen* by W. S. Oury, and is still so published. The press, on which was also started the Tucson *Star* and the Tombstone *Nugget*, is now in the possession of the Arizona Pioneers Historical Society.

Over two rough roads leading up and up through thin, clear, Colorado mountain air panted the men and mules of two printing outfits both heading for the mining camps (in country soon to be named Jefferson territory) now becoming known as Denver City. John L. Merrick reached the destination first and was readying his press for job-printing and the publishing of a weekly newspaper when William B. Byers arrived with the same plans.

Warily the disconcerted rivals who had neglected to bring with them the "cards" necessary to an affair of honor, looked each other over, inspected each other's presses, and weighed the strength of local sympathies before reaching an agreement satisfactory to both; the one who got out his newspaper first would stay, the loser would clear out of camp and leave the winner in undisputed possession of all Denver City's printing prospects, whatever they might be. So they set to work with approximately equal experience, talent, and zest and the entire population of the camps, electing themselves the referees in this strange contest, declared a holiday and seesawed back and forth from one press to the other for three days. Byers beat Merrick by twenty minutes. It was April 23rd of 1859 and Saturday night and the event was fittingly celebrated. Then the proprietor of the *Cherry Creek Pioneer* of Denver City, Arapahoe County, Kansas, sold out for a grubstake to the winning publisher of the *Rocky Mountain News* of Auraria, Kansas Territory, and left to prospect for gold.

Early issues of Denver's first newspaper extracted its news from well polished bones; its entertainment consisted of ancient anecdotes and relied heavily on conundrums. But the publisher soon had correspondents in neighboring camps to supplement local news, which became increasingly generous in quantity and honest and accurate in quality, for subscribers at twenty-four dollars a year, delivery by broncho. News also improved when Byers secured a post office, and the mail for Denver City, formerly delivered to Laramie, began to arrive more or less regularly once a month. The true flavor of the pioneer West permeated the newspaper which carried advertisements of such simple honesty as: "A. F. Peck, M.D. Physician and Surgeon. Cache-a-La-Pondre, Nebraska. Where he may at all times be found when not professionally engaged or digging gold." In Byer's prospectus he wrote: "The character of this important region will depend much upon the influence brought to bear upon its early settlement, and no influence is so powerful to dissuade from disorder, or assist to organize dignity and order as a Free Press." This the editor and publisher believed so firmly that he was obliged to write with his rifle at hand, and he was once abducted by desperados who objected to editorial denunciation. Byers was so harassed by newsprint shortages that he sometimes went to press on brown wrapping-paper borrowed from Denver merchants, and his was the experience of seeing his shop, which diplomatically straddled Cherry Creek, swept away by a mountain freshet one clear, moonlit, spring evening. "Where a few months ago wild beasts and wilder Indians held undisputed possession, now surges the advancing waves of Anglo-Saxon enterprise and invigoration." News was brought in by horse riders until the telegraph and locomotive gave Byers' press the stability to make it a western institution.

All the big brave West ached for news from home. Somehow presses came even to forts and stockades housing Army barracks, general stores, and trading posts. Space for printing newspapers was found in back rooms of dance halls, "shaving salons," and news depots offering books and newspapers of latest dates. New newspapers were greeted with the roar of shooting irons and the heavy stamping of silver-spurred feet. And to all news was added the editorial "humor" spawning tent-town comic opera. Advertisements called for skilled workmen in staggering numbers, offered the comforts of hotels (which outnumbered all other buildings!), and provided a directory of smiths, wheelwrights, barbers, dealers in arms, ammunition, salt and dried meats, blankets, buffalo robes, picks, pans, and spades. Publication was occasionally "unavoidably delayed" while the publishers or editors were in jail, and the business of getting out almost any western newspaper was apt to be considerably impeded after western sheriffs learned the ease of confining their prisoners by merely handcuffing them to the presses.

The first horse of the Pony Express, the promise of speed in the news of the nation, was given royal welcome in the San Francisco *Bulletin* as a "veritable Hippogriff who shoved a Continent behind his hoofs so easily; who snuffed up sandy plains and sent lakes, mountains, prairies and forests whizzing behind him like one great river forever rushing forward."

By clipper ship, by steamer, by prairie schooner, by stagecoach, ox cart and hand cart, all America was going West where the rich black earth was yet unturned by the plow, and where the crash of the ax and the crack of the rifle were still unheard. And with each onsweep went the printers and publishers who wove their talents, their minds, and their hearts into the basic warp and woof of the life-fabric known as American.

Nameplate. Boston, April 23, 1831. Vol. I, No. 17. Courtesy
of New York Public Library.

15

TRAMP, TRAMP, TRAMP

OVER RIVERS AND ROADS SEPARATING FREE STATE
from slave there drifted to desks of editors and publishers of newspapers,
from 1814 on, tinted broadsides foretelling the spilling of blood.

They came in long envelopes accompanied by small sums of money
to pay for the publication of "the enclosed" in the esteemed publisher's
esteemed newspaper and all read very much alike: "One Hundred Dollars Reward For Information Leading to the Return of the (described)
SLAVE RUNAWAY." At first details of these transactions were CON-
FIDENTIAL, but, growing bolder, slave-owners directed that their

property be returned forthwith, shipping expenses and reward to be paid on delivery. To many publishers of the border states these advertisements represented rare and welcome cash; editors and subscribers alike regarded slavery as commonplace, until the catching and returning of men and women became an organized business conducted with cold-blooded cruelty, exposing at last the mockery of humanity concealed under the sanctimonious wrappings of "benevolent paternalism."

Across the river from Wheeling, Virginia, in the tiny Ohio town of Mt. Pleasant, Charles Osborn, a Quaker, in August of 1817 started a little newspaper, the *Philanthropist*, that was partly devoted to the plight of the slave. This was the first printed advocate of immediate emancipation and the first voice, small though it was, lifted against the socially powerful American Society for the Colonization of Free People of Color in the United States.

In Wheeling another Quaker, Benjamin Lundy, a harnessmaker from New Jersey, watched the fugitives as they were driven from the ferry and back to punishment, and in 1815 brought about the organization of the St. Clairsville, Ohio, Union Humane Society. A year later he sent out a circular letter urging more of these anti-slavery societies. Lundy who had already contributed to the *Philanthropist* one of the most powerful of pleas for abolition, was invited by Osborn to join him, but before the association was completed the publisher sold his newspaper. With no capital and only six pledged subscribers Lundy, in January of 1821 in Mt. Pleasant, began his *Genius of Universal Emancipation*, which he soon removed to Greenville, Tennessee. Writing for his newspaper, walking miles to get it printed and delivered to his few subscribers, Lundy met with encouragement—if not financial success—leading to his removal to Baltimore. Here he was joined by an expert printer and fiery editorialist whose energies had already been cast in a single-minded mold by Lundy's influence—William Lloyd Garrison.

It was Lundy and his little newspaper which kindled the fires of the many effective Anti-Slavery Societies of the North. Garrison's more vituperative pen involved the publisher and his *Genius* in lawsuits and violence before he retreated to Washington. Garrison, rescued from jail by Arthur Tappan, retreated to Boston where on January 1, 1831, he started the *Liberator*, through which he continued to "speak harshly" for thirty-four years until his work was done.

Multiplying Anti-Slavery Societies found church doors closed and business communities hostile. The immediate emancipation demanded by the radicals seemed to most people an alarming proposal to cure the disease by suicide. General newspapers for a long time were silent, and when they spoke they were as divided, as confused, and as violent as their readers. Missing was that spark of newspaper leadership that might have given soul and substance to the great reform. Editorial acrobats attacked the problem obliquely, charging that the Colonizing Society in sixteen years had sent twenty-five hundred free Negroes to the African Colony, but that in that time had uttered no word of protest against the illegal importation of half a million human beings for impressment into Southern bondage. The whole thing, asserted northern editors, was "trumped up" and managed by Southern slave-owners whose inter-est it was to protect their "property" from possible contamination by free men of their own race. And, they raged, the "Hypocritical old Humbugs" spent the money they collected from churches, individuals, businesses, and even state legislatures to purchase the fourteen hundred barrels of rum they shipped to Liberia: Liberia, "their modern Golgotha to which they shall not send us" vowed editor Samuel S. Cornish in the November 17, 1838, *Colored America.*

The drums of the Southern newspapers took up their monotone; their stories emphasized the necessity of slaves to the South. Led by the Charleston *Mercury* they declared the rights of Southern states to declare null and void any laws of the United States unacceptable to the fire-eating few who ruled the vast Cotton Kingdom. Southern editors kept their duelling pistols oiled and ready for that inevitable day des-tined to end in a blaze of glory for one and a green mound under a weeping willow tree for another.

Resigning from the Colonizing Society, Arthur Tappan sent out a call for the organization of a New York Anti-Slavery Society, proposing to return free Negroes to their homeland. An ugly mob prevented the meeting set for October 2, 1833, but fifty men, including two Tappans and three ministers, slipped away to form the Society of which Arthur Tappan was made president. Indignantly the *Morning Courier and En-quirer* screamed for the "immediate crushing of this many-headed hydra as the only course to meet opposition to the Constitution." And the cry was echoed through the very press it branded. The same newspaper labeled the Abolitionists "tools of Tappanism"; this profundity evoked flattering offers for the bodies of the merchants "dead or alive."

The following summer some Negroes belatedly celebrating the Fourth of July and a Sacred Music Society bent upon a rehearsal fought for the use of the Chatham Street Chapel; and James Watson Webb demanded "meetings of protest." In response there was a riot that lasted three days. The homes of the Tappans were looted and burned, the churches of the Reverends Cox and Ludlow demolished, and the Negroes were beaten and run out of town as other hoodlums burned their homes. At last "two troops of Horse" led by Mayor Cornelius W. Lawrence, who was early felled by a well-aimed brickbat, sallied forth to restore law and order. Only the *Evening-Post* condemned the outrage without quibbling; the *Courier and Enquirer* smoothly charged that newspaper with inciting the "sooty usurpation" and causing shame to a supposedly civilized city. And only the *Evening-Post* and the *Journal of Commerce* published the facts supporting the claims of the Negroes given the use of the Chapel.

Burned out but unintimidated, Arthur Tappan continued his contributions to the financing of the *Liberator*, the *Emancipator*, the *New Era*, which serialized Harriet Beecher Stowe's *Uncle Tom's Cabin*, or, *Life Among the Lowly*, and other publications of abolitionist valor.

Tossing a little tinder into smoldering fires, Amos Kendall, Postmaster General and politician extraordinary, promised in 1835 that by "No Act or Order" would the government aid in circulating Abolitionist newspapers, and postmasters freely censored the United States mails to burn those they considered "incendiary or insurrectionary." Wrote William Leggett, editor of the New York *Evening-Post* in the absence of William Cullen Bryant: "If the Government once begins to discriminate as to what is orthodox and what heterodox in opinion, what is safe and what is unsafe in tendency, farewell, a long farewell to freedom." And for this potent and much-quoted paragraph Leggett's political head was neatly removed by administration ax-man Francis P. Blair.

The Enemies of the Constitution, the Abolitionists, met in Utica, New York, in 1835, and were dispersed by men who then wrecked the shop printing the anti-slavery Oneida *Standard and Democrat*. The *Philanthropist* owned by James G. Birney was attacked in the following summer. Windows of the print-shop at New Richmond, near Cincinnati, were stoned, books, papers, and types were thrown out, and the press was dragged to the river, broken up, and thrown into deep water. Elijah Lovejoy, Maine-born "preacher of Abolitionism" was driven from St. Louis to Alton, Illinois, and on the night of November 7, 1837, his crusading spirit was forever stilled, and the press which he lost his life in defending followed two others (previously seized from him) to the bottom of the Mississippi. News of this last brutality spread quickly through the Northern newspapers, which were now outspoken in their condemnation of a "murder that would disgrace the Algerian Coast."

John Greenleaf Whittier was editing the *Pennsylvania Freeman* when its Philadelphia office in Pennsylvania Hall was attacked; the building was burned to the ground with little hindrance from law or firemen. The modest *Free South* of William Bailey whose daughters set types in their Newport, Kentucky, home was visited by thirty men as a "warning." And when Cassius Marcellus Clay, ambitious to rid only Kentucky of slavery, started his *True American* in 1845, a self-appointed committee concerned with the commercial purity of their 'Fair City' called in his absence to crate his two four-pound cannon, his rifles and Mexican lances, gunpowder, and other editorial equipment for shipping to Cincinnati; but Cash Clay continued his newspaper as the *Examiner*. It was printed in Cincinnati but edited from Lexington with the limited protection of a bowie knife and two pistols worn on his person.

Steadily, month after month, year after year, were heard the mosquito-thin protests of Abolition newspapers, the relentless rattling of Southern swords in newspapers ever demanding more of the new acres of the country for working by slaves, and the rumble of angry debates growing angrier in legislative halls. Of peculiar distaste to northern log-rolling politicians and for professional apologists for the slave kingdom alike was the woodcut of the Washington slave block with the dome of the national Capitol in the background that had topped the nameplate of the *Liberator* from its seventeenth number. Its justification ended with Henry Clay's Omnibus Bill of 1850, but in tensions that had continued to tighten, the news that click-clicked from the telegraph wires for publication on January 6, 1855, brought consternation to editors and their readers who were still hoping that slavery could be eradicated without violence. Wrote Horace Greeley in the *Tribune* next day:

Senator Douglas today reported a new bill providing for the establishment of two Territories . . . the bill, in so many words, declares the Compromise Act of 1850 renders inoperative the Missouri Act of 1820. . . .

And Henry Jarvis Raymond wrote in the *Times*, with clairoyance:

Its very success will sow the seeds of a future contest that will admit of no compromise, its passage will root out from the Northern mind the last vestige of confidence in the good faith of the advocates of slavery and create . . . a hatred of the institution that will crush its political power at all hazards and at any cost.

The Kansas-Nebraska Bill became the law, and the peace promised by its proponents was promptly proved illusory. Conflict moved into the new Territories and disturbed settlement. The *Kansas Weekly Herald* was set up by W. J. Osborn, W. H. Adams, and S. M. Myers on September 15, 1854, when Leavenworth was a town of four tents and their office "a big shingle."

Over the border from Missouri rode proslavery men bringing Robert S. Kelly and John H. Stringfellow, who in Liberty had published the *Democratic Platform*. In Atchison they started the *Squatter Sovereign* on February 3, 1855, and the firm editorial policy of this organ of the Border Ruffians was to "Lynch, hang, tar, feather, and draw every white-livered Abolitionist who dares pollute the soil of Kansas."

Free Soilers sent by the New England Emmigrant Aid Society, of which Eli Thayer, Lord of the machicolated castle on Goat Hill, Worcester, Massachusetts, was the mainspring, were late in reaching the battleground. Their newspaper, published by George W. Brown, was first printed in Conneautville, Pennsylvania, and its date line was Wakarusa, Kansas Territory; when Brown and the *Herald of Freedom* at last arrived the name had been changed to Lawrence. The second number of this well-planned organ was printed on a press used twenty years previously by Jotham Meeker, printer and missionary, to turn out the *Shawanoe Sun*, a bimonthly newspaper in an Indian language. Types were set in an office newly erected of green cottonwood before the roof was on; at hand were "four tons of paper, plenty of ink and a supply of plain and fancy job-types," and a new steam press awaited transporation.

The newspaper, "Devoted to Humanity and the Interests of Kansas," had news, some local, and much edifying entertainment such as the Interesting Discourse of Mr. Beecher. It was strong on information for prospective immigrants, a feature guaranteeing it nationwide circulation.

On the night of May 21, 1856 a posse of Border Ruffians left the *Herald of Freedom* a smoking ruin. Three nights later mad John Brown of Ossawattomie dragged five proslavery men from their beds and in cold blood shot them down; civil war flared and crackled in the warm spring winds of the prairie. "Who is responsible?" inquired the *New York Journal of Commerce*. "Those who first set afoot and afterwards maintained and encouraged the Border Ruffians' proslavery war against the Free Labor settlers of Kansas," answered the *Tribune*. The *Herald of Freedom* was revived and published until 1860 when its supply of job-types was melted down to be shot from Union cannons.

Into the open wounds was rubbed the salt of utterly un-American propaganda seeking welcome in the fertile midwest for Southern gentlemen, slaveholders, who would "save that country from greasy mechanics, filthy operatives, and factory workers." And shallow-souled intellectuals hastened to fatten on the carrion of the Republic, which they pronounced a "proven failure." Dazed northern newspapers produced erudite lectures recommending for the United States a government by Patronal Economy. In this happy state the land would be forever held by the aristocratic few and all the rest, black and white, would be forever tenants, fed and clothed in accordance with their patrons' notions of their merits.

The politically unpredictable New York *Herald* gave its support to Fremont, candidate of the new party. Two days after the inauguration of James Buchanan, the Supreme Court delivered its Dred Scott decision and the Black Republicans were a party resuscitated. Wrote Greeley in the *Tribune:* "The decision . . . is entitled to just as much moral weight as would be the majority of those congregated in any Washington bar-room."

Greeley was at the zenith of his power and fame; his tersely vigorous editorials gave clarity to issues nearing the great decision now becoming unescapable by either North or South; and the scissors that hung over his desk from a pulley were used with such acute discrimination on incoming newspapers that readers of the *Tribune* knew the sentiments of the rest of the country. There was more than a touch of the showman in the little editor whose pink baby face was fringed with pale whiskers, and whose sharp blue eyes peered from behind thick lenses of steel-rimmed spectacles at a world he longed to save. He was always dressed in a long white woolen coat cut wide and full; always one trouser leg was tucked into a high boot while the other rode an ankle and always his neckerchief was askew.

And Greeley, whose importance in the thinking of plain people at a critical time has never been exceeded by any American editor and who loathed slavery, still could not bring himself to unconditional support of the Abolitionists. Greeley was devoted to the Union, and considered the threat of rebellion that of a "violent, unscrupulous, desperate minority who have conspired to clutch power"; but he was willing to temporize, saying: "If the majority want freedom from the Federal Government, let the erring sisters go." And he who had assembled the ablest talent yet engaged by any one newspaper, whose *Tribune* was daily evidence of an unerring appraisal of public intellect, sadly miscalculated the quality of leadership demanded by that same public which had become so astute in its own interpretation of the news.

When John Brown's raid on Harper's Ferry threw into sharp focus the fuse leading to gunpowder, Greeley praised the man who marched to mad silent music although he did condemn the attack. And Bennett, always more interested in news than in its connotations, made journalistic history by sending a reporter to Peterboro, New York, for an interview with Garritt Smith, wealthy Free Soiler suspected of financing the disaster.

Verbatim accounts, made by reporters of the Lincoln-Douglas debates, brought Lincoln's homely phrases to a people now grown suspicious of political horse-trading. Encouraged by the enthusiasm of Long John Wentworth of the Chicago *Democrat*, leading newspaper of the West, and of Joseph Medill whose Chicago *Tribune* was beginning to oust Greeley's weekly from midwestern homes, a host of able editors rallied to support the Rail-Splitter whose reputation seemed to thrive on the ridicule heaped on his humble origin, his ungainliness, his " 'hain'ts" and " 'tain'ts," his big feet, and his funny clothes. With a mighty heave they led former Whigs, discontented Democrats, political independents, and chronic malcontents meeting at the Chicago convention into the nomination of Abraham Lincoln and Hannibal Hamlin.

Daily the Charleston *Mercury* preached the terrors to come if the Black Republicans gained control of the federal government. "It means the loss of everything—liberty, home, country—everything that makes life worth living." "The contest for slavery will no longer be between North and South, but between men of the South"; "Property will depreciate, the value of slaves will be reduced by one hundred dollars each; men will leave the South and confusion, distrust and pressure will reign." Boldly the *Mercury* led its editorial satellites in calling for prompt secession should Lincoln and Hamlin be elected.

Northern editors cheered, sneered, praised, and scoffed; Wide Awakes marched with bands and torches, and oratory spouted from every political stump. And between the puffs for Ayer's Liver Pills, Concentrated Dew for the Perfect Complexion, and notices of superior tombstones made by local artisans, the "fists" of Northern country weeklies steadily pointed to such paragraph captions as: "How Lincoln Learned to Cipher," and ancient jokes such as: "Lincoln is a dead letter in the County. *Eastern Argus*"; "Like all dead letters Lincoln will go to Washington. *Washington-Groton Mercury*." And in November these same country weeklies celebrated with tallest types at tops of their editorial columns (usually fifth on the second pages of big folios): "Glory! Glory! Glory! There is Joy in the Land! Lincoln and Hamlin the Choice of the People!" And in the Charleston *Mercury* for November 7, 1860, wrote Robert Barnwell Rhett:

The Agent for the Associated Press telegraphed that Lincoln's election was certain, and trifling details were unnecessary. Upon the announcement of the news at the MERCURY office, which appeared to be the headquarters for information, the crowd gave expression to their feelings by loud and continuous cheering for a Southern Confederacy. The greatest excitement prevailed, and the news spread with lightning rapidity.

News of secession followed news of Lincoln's inauguration; then news from the South reached the *Times*, the *Herald*, and *Tribune* in code through banks and businessmen from reporters who, when recognized, were treated as spies and threatened with lynchings. Northern news in Southern newspapers was captioned News From the United States or merely Foreign. News of the Confederacy and its seizure of arms and arsenals brought shadows into every home, and churches opened for prayer were disturbed by the heavy tramp of marching feet as General Beauregard attacked Major Anderson in Fort Sumter. To the New York *World* B. S. Osbon sent his story of the surrender, and in the *Tribune* for April 12, 1861, Greeley wrote: "Fort Sumter is temporarily lost, but the Country is saved. Long live the Republic."

Then came the President's Proclamation of War and his call for troops. Newspaper offices hummed with the excitement of organizing, equipping, and dispatching their Special Correspondents charged with keeping the home towns informed of the successes of home regiments. Six weeks later the *Tribune* first lifted its voice in the daily battle cry: "Forward to Richmond! Forward to Richmond! The Rebel Congress must not be allowed to meet there on the 20th of July. BY THAT DATE THE PLACE MUST BE HELD BY THE UNION ARMY!"

It was a bitter pill for newspapers loyal to the administration as well as a shattering blow to their confidence in the War Department when they had to follow columns captioned: "EXCITING NEWS! Bull's Run Taken!" Henry Villard, who had covered the Lincoln-Douglas debates for the New York *Staats-Zeitung*, got in his report of the debacle to the New York *Herald* (he was later chief war correspondent for the *Tribune*). The reports of Edmund Stredman of the *World* and John Russell Young of the Philadelphia *Press*, also witnesses of the rout, were also much reprinted and there was an ominous lack of editorial comment on the official news release. Greeley denied responsi-

bility for failure traced to his newspaper; his distress was so deep that
he suffered brain fever.

Vividly, clearly, and often brilliantly writers for the country's newspapers described the engagements of the War Between the States. They
rode away to the wars on horses—supplied by the home offices—clad in
army blue greatcoats with capes, their kepis at jaunty angles, revolvers
in holsters and field-glasses on straps. Some were followed by their servants driving wagons to carry their impedimenta including big tents with
the names of the newspapers in big black letters. "Cheeky rascals,"
grumbled an envious opposition.

Franc B. Wilkie, who went to war with the First Iowa Regiment of
Volunteers, wrote for the Dubuque Visitor until he joined the staff of
the New York Times to send from the theaters of the West and southwest his reports signed Galway. Grant's early victories were also reported for the Boston Journal by Charles C. Coffin (Charlton) who
was also with the iron-clads off Norfolk. He was one of the few correspondents to report the entire four years of the war; another was Doctor
George W. Hosmer of the Herald who, at Cemetery Ridge, saw the ap-
proach of the Rebels in time to warn the Federalists. Murat Halstead,
who saw the hanging of John Brown, wrote for the Cincinnati Commercial, and Whitelaw Reid wrote of the war's awful carnage under the
pseudonym of Agate for the Gazette of the same city.

There was no censorship and the War Department moved with
cloudy objective to promote ill-feeling between the army and the newspapers. Correspondents were accused of puffing some generals and abus-
ing others. General Sherman, who hated all reporters and called them
liars and spies, had Thomas H. Knox of the Herald court-martialed.
With its small army of writers the Herald gave the country its most
accurate and complete war news and the Tribune was its close second.
Almost all northern newspapers had one or more reporters at the front,
and editors and publishers made frequent trips for first-hand news of
the fighting. Circulations—and expenses—soared and Sunday editions
of daily newspapers were, for the first time, generally issued.

From the war's beginning Horace Greeley and Robert Barnwell Rhett
were determined to hold steady the spinning cycle of relations between
newspapers, their readers, and their government. The Tribune and the
Mercury had been the most important vehicles articulating the creeds
for which men were dying, and neither editor would relinquish his
position on the driver's seat for mere presidents or generals. Daily and
in almost identical phrases, Lincoln and Davis were lashed with crit-

icism, flayed with contempt, and showered with advice. The generals of both the Union and the Confederacy knew the scorn of these experts who devised or exploded military strategy as easily as they concocted diplomatic coups sure to snare the elusive Dove.

The petulant Greeley and the carping Bennett were loyal to the Union; William Cullen Bryant, from whose pen came *The Union, Now and Forever,* joined these critics of the administration and the army. The *Commercial Advertiser* was utterly loyal; the *Journal of Commerce* was so against "this unholy war" that it was barred from the mails, at which time Gerard Hallock retired. The *Express,* loyal only to business, brushed extinction. The *World* edited by Manton M. Marble was loyal to its owner, August Belmont, supposedly the agent of the European Rothschilds, and was, like the *Daily News* of Benjamin Wood, close to treason. The *Sun* was in the hands of Archibald M. Morrison who was trying to make a "religious" newspaper of Benjamin H. Day's child. Morrison spent much energy in trying to persuade the generals to stop their fighting on Sundays.

The Southern newspapers that lacked paper, ink, and labor shrank as the blockade tightened. They found it hard to replace the news from the Confederacy's own London *Index* and the English Tory press with an apt belittling of Lincoln (the Baboon, they called him) and his soldiers and sailors. Because of the break-down of telegraph and railroads the official organs gradually grew smaller, and war news was reduced to what could be gleaned from letters, as during the Revolution; and this dribbling intelligence was often printed on wall paper and sometimes with shoeblacking.

On wall paper went to press the *Southern Sentinel* of Alexandria, Louisiana, to advertise for job-printing on the same stock "pressed smooth." And when this newspaper went to fifty cents a copy, publisher T. G. Compton of the Ice-House Hotel, who would accept only Confederate, Louisiana, or Rapides Money, reminded customers that a "glass of vile rum or corn whiskey, or an ounce or two of inferior tobacco now costs a dollar," and ended with "You no like him, you no take him."

Editors who begged in every number for the privilege of reading any newspapers that might reach their readers, printed as important news wonderful recipes such as the following from the Memphis *Daily Avalanche:* "COFFEE: Brown and grind equal amounts of corn and rice and boil as coffee. This is an excellent substitute and now that coffee is selling upwards a dollar a pound, it is well worth your trying."

Southern newspapers fled, press and all, before Union occupation. The Memphis *Appeal* wandered over four states on a flat car, moving under fire and printing where it could. The Chattanooga *Rebel* followed the flag of Tennessee until it was ostracized for criticism of General Bragg. Not all Southern newspapers supported the Confederacy; Parson Brownlow, owner of the loudest voice in Tennessee and editor of the Knoxville *Whig*, was evicted by hands that also destroyed his press. And William Holden of the Raleigh *Standard* stridently demanded that North Carolina secede from the Confederacy and make a separate peace with the United States. "This," thundered Holden to his Heroes, "is a rich man's war and a poor man's fight."

Farragut was planning to cut the chains across the Mississippi; with him was B. S. Osbon, reporting the Navy for the New York *Herald* as signal officer. And Albert D. Richardson and Junius Henri Browne of the New York *Tribune* with Richard T. Colburn of the *World* proposed to run the batteries of Vicksburg in a tugboat. A cannon ball killed the captain at his wheel, pierced the boiler, and crashed into the firebox. The correspondents leaped into the Mississippi and were rescued by the Confederates who immobilized them in the Salisbury Stockade for eighteen months before they escaped to walk three hundred miles through enemy country, by night when possible, to the Union lines at Nashville.

The Vicksburg *Daily Citizen*, printed on wall paper, as the long siege drew to an end recommended mule steaks and fricasseed tomcat to subscribers living in trenches and cringing under the earsplitting whine of Whistling Dick. It reported to them that the Glorious Union was now very weak in the knees, and that soldiers were rapidly deserting; but on the Fourth of July, 1863, General Grant "Caught his rabbit" and had enough men to get out an edition of the newspaper.

North of the lines of Blue, Freedom of the Press was stretched to cover a multitude of crimes against men in that uniform. The Copperhead newspapers, relying on the American instinct to preserve freedom of speech, curbed disloyalty only in fear of those who might resort to tar and feathers and riding offensive editors and publishers out of town on rails. Capitalizing on war-weariness, the crusaders for Peace (the Holy Grail that was promised to dues-payers who remembered the passwords composed by using old and new newspapers to conjure fear, need, grief, and anxiety into new political parties) wrapped their perfidy in piety and clothed treason in Bible quotations for large followings.

The victories at Gettysburg and Vicksburg were hollow victories to an America saddened by its losses, and the rioting of the able-bodied objecting to the first American draft seemed like a mockery to grief. Within ten days after these bloody milestones of the War Between the States the wheel was turned in the Draft Office at the corner of Third Avenue and Forty-Sixth Street, New York, and the four-story building, wrecked by flying bricks and stones, was left in flames by men who marched to loot, shoot, fire, and murder at will for three days.

Singing "We'll hang H. G. from a sour apple tree," the mob swarmed into Printing House Square. A few police aided by rain saved the offices of the *Times* and the *Tribune* until guns, swivel cannon, sandbags, and hoses attached to boilers could be installed for the protection of these presses.

Recalled state troopers on the third day shot a Howitzer loaded with canister down Third Avenue, fired, "and not with blanks," into skulking groups, and poked marchers with their bayonets to make them "skedaddle on the double-quick."

By Thursday the town could gather up its dead and on Friday men gathered before the Very Reverend John Hughes were warned to avoid disorder and the disorderly, given his blessing, and sent to their homes.

Soberly northern newspapers discussed the Draft Riots. They published the address of the Archbishop in full, and for many newspapers this ended the long American editorial enmity against the Pope. They published in full the headliner of the previous Sunday's *Herald*: "What is the real reason for the draft? Does it mean war with England?" For this Bennett was charged by some with inciting the riots with his hint that the Confederacy might have succeeded at last in obtaining the help of British ships, men, and money. And a gossiping press capped a busy week with the story that Horace Greeley had hidden under a table at a nearby restaurant during the riots in Printing House Square. This the great man dignified by an indignant denial.

Even the President, who had added to his cares the visiting of camps and hospitals—accompanied, usually, by Noah Brooks, "Castine," the Washington reporter for the Sacramento *Daily Union*—read the comics for a chuckle. There was that old showman Artemus Ward (Charles Brown) in whose "wondrous collecshun of wild beasts" were many familiar animals. Much of Artemus Ward was reprinted from *Vanity Fair* ("just like *Punch*, only not so dull"). Petroleum Vesuvius Nasby (David R. Locke) with humor, a dash of malice, and much bad spelling lambasted the Copperheads. Orphus C. Kerr (Robert H. Newell) reported human nature in sharp mock-serious caricatures, and Josh Billings (Henry Shaw, ex-auctioneer from Poughkeepsie) supplied many an apt phrase, politically useful, in his essays.

The Confederacy had its own Bill Arp (Charles F. Smith) who addressed Mr. Abe Linkhorn from the *Southern Confederacy* of Rome, Georgia, for Southern circulation.

Beyond the reach of newspapers still dependent for illustrations on wood engravings were the photographs of Matthew B. Brady. Brady drove his "what-is-it wagon" where he would, without concern for shot, shells, generals, or drummer-boys, to make the world's first photographic record of a war; and the products of his traveling darkroom, laboriously copied for reproduction in the many new pictorial news weeklies, stripped military life of its glamour.

Atlanta was burned, Nashville lost and retaken; Sherman was marching towards the sea, and there had been butchery in the wilderness and at Spottsylvania. Around two in the morning of May 24, 1864, to the night editors of New York newspapers came, on paper of the Associated Press and written in a familiar hand, copies of a Presidential message calling for a draft of four hundred thousand men.

The *Times* learned that the message was forged. The *Tribune* did not receive its copy because the messenger had gone to the wrong door; the *News* and the *Express* were warned; the *Herald* had printed 20,000 copies, fortunately, not distributed; but the *World* and the *Journal of Commerce* printed it and put it on the streets. Before the day was over General John A. Dix, provost marshal, stopped the presses and closed the doors of the two newspapers printing the Bogus Draft Call.

Angrily the country's Copperhead newspapers denounced "this further exhibition of the contempt of this despotic Administration for America's traditional freedom of the press," but the small-town weeklies, with their impersonal view of the problems of big-city publishers "thought it strange that the Proclamation should be published only in these two newspapers, and also that it was strange that these two should become the organs of the Administration. . . . The *World* and the *Journal of Commerce*, both shameless proslavery newspapers, were so anxious to get the bad news on the streets that they could not wait to verify its truth."

Joseph Howard, Jr. and Frank Mallinson of the Brooklyn *Eagle*, the confessed authors of the false Call, had planned to buy gold cheap on the release of the news and sell it high next day. They were arrested by General Dix and confined in Fort Lafayette. Howard was freed without trial after a plea to the President by Henry Ward Beecher; his accomplice was held for a year.

Politics, pitting Lincoln for a second term against his former Commander of the Army of the Potomac, found loyalty to the President strong in the Chicago *Tribune*, the New York *Times*, the Springfield *Republican*, the Philadelphia *Inquirer*, and the Washington *Chronicle*. When George B. McClellan—Gunboat McClellan, the little Napoleon —advanced his muddled platform including more of the same war from which he had been retired, Josh Billings said: "Nobudy but a phool gits bit by the same dorg twict." And the country newspapers whittled to splinters the platforms of the Peace Democrats and summoned Lincoln votes with "Rally 'Round the Flag, Boys" to reelect their candidate.

Newspaper headlines, column-wide in two-line banks, editorialized with: "Grand and Glorious News!!! 'Atlanta Ours, Fairly Won' Says General Sherman." Then George Washington Smalley made history by riding through the night to telegraph his newspaper of the defeat of Lee at Antietam. The operator insisted on sending the news to Washington, and the exhausted reporter set out for New York writing for the *Tribune* his story so soon followed by the dramatic THE END LEE SURRENDERS.

Before the rejoicing ceased the New York Associated Press received from its Washington agent, Lawrence A. Gobright, the news that Lincoln had been shot. THE PRESIDENT MURDERED ran the headlines that shocked the nation.

Famous war correspondents including George A. Townsend, who was Garth of the New York *World*, furnished the country with the details of the tragedy. They supplied news of Johnson taking the presidential oath, of the deep grief of the people, of the long journey of the black-draped funeral train, and of the little groups of men and women standing with bowed heads as it slowly steamed past, and of the simple ceremony in Springfield, Illinois.

Then came the crashing anticlimax: MOBILE OURS.

It was news—day-to-day news—that from the first printed word in behalf of freedom for all Americans led and held the will and faith of the people as stubbornly as fighting men led their armies to free the world to new decency and dignity. And before the War Between the States passed into its niche in world history, American newspapers and newspaper readers had found a new intimacy with new responsibilities to be shared—someday, fully—by both parties to the country's oldest partnership.

MAP SHOWING THE POSITION O

The Cable Celebration Number of Frank Leslie's Illustrated
Newspaper, New York, August 21, 1858. Courtesy of Library
of Congress.

16

PEANUTS, PIE, AND GUTTA-PERCHA

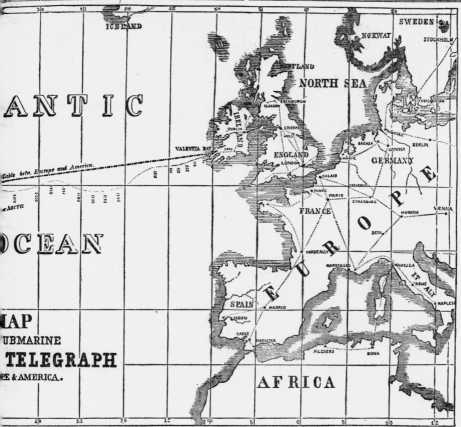

STEAM LURED, EVADED, AND FINALLY CAPITULATED TO Yankee imagination. Paddle wheels churned the waters of spring-flooded rivers many miles from the water highways they raced to join. American-built locomotives, spouting smoke and cinders, chug-chugged noisily over American-mined and -milled rails to disgorge passengers and freight at terminals of short tracks—to be pulled by still useful horse to the next "depo" one or several miles away. Up-to-date editors and publishers matched their eye-filling HYMENAL and OBITUARY columns with the newer CATASTROPHES, under which was printed news of steam-

205

boat collisions, conflagrations, and boiler explosions, collapsed viaducts, disregarded highballs, track-jumping locomotives, and the resulting drowned, burned, mangled, and crushed, and sometimes lists of the survivors.

The telegraph had steadily advanced in mechanics and mileage since that first news of the Mexican War was sent from Washington to New York to Baltimore by wire, to Wilmington by horse, and again by wire to Jersey City, whence by ferry to the main office of the Morse wires in a basement room of Number 10 Wall Street. Telegraph companies, like the railroads, operated from city to city independent of each other, each with its own notions as to rates, as well as to what messages and whose messages they would give precedence in their services. Delicate questions, worthy of the attention of the world's most skilled diplomats, concerned newspaper reporters: should the use of wires be allocated to newsmen as they came? Or, should news for important newspapers be given preference to those of smaller circulations? Or, should all reporters alike be given five minutes each in rotation? The growing New York Press Association and the forming regional news associations reduced telegraphic traffic, added to telegraph companies' earnings, and multiplied worries of agents, operators, and linemen.

There was a Morse wire from New York to Boston in 1846, which was soon paralleled by the wires of the patents of Royal S. House and Alexander Bain. Then the first was extended to Portland to the slight disadvantage of its rivals. In the same year Theodore S. Faxon, Utica newsman, was responsibile for a Morse wire from Albany to Buffalo, and when poles were erected for sixty miles up the east bank of the Hudson to a narrowing where the river was crossed, New York had its first direct-wire connection with the mainland of the United States. Telegraph wires that started to the West and the southwest under the spur of war hummed atop the on-marching poles of Henry O'Reilley. But floods washed out the masts, and storms splintered the stoutest of poles and disorganized communication for weeks.

As early as 1845 Ezra Cornell wrapped twelve miles of copper wires in cotton cloth, encased them in lead pipes, and laid them under water from New York to Fort Lee, New Jersey. But ice broke the pipe! Henry Armstrong of Brooklyn in 1852 coated wires with gutta-percha, which had already been used in Europe. These wires, unreeled from the stern of a small boat, were drawn across the Hudson. Secured only twenty feet below the river's surface they were frequently pulled up and broken by the dragging anchors of ships passing above, but the "submarine telegraph" was so satisfactory that men, and especially newsmen, began to think and talk seriously of an under-ocean wire.

Twice a day Doctor Alexander Jones received news telegraphed in code, at weekly rates, from the correspondents of the New York Associated Press. The Association's foreign news was the business of pilot boats plying the swells just outside the harbor. The out-of-town customers of the Association reduced if they did not absorb the costs of producing the commodity at last discovered to be valuable as well as perishable. Daniel H. Craig was made the Association's first foreign agent. He was stationed at Halifax, Nova Scotia, to intercept incoming ships from a little steamer which had been added to the Association's fleet for this purpose. He summarized the news and forwarded it by horseman to Digby, where a yawl, warned by cannon, was waiting with steam up, ready to cast off for the Portland, Maine, terminal of the telegraph wire.

Craig had an iron determination and was considered by his enemies too shrewd and too ruthless; and he was detested by the telegraph men who objected to his use of pigeons as unfair in the race for the news. The Morse wire from Boston to Portland was practically the private property of Francis Ormond Jonathan Smith, a telegraph man known to newsmen as Fog—cold, penetrating, and impenetrable. As a member of Congress and Chairman of the House Committee on Commerce, he recommended government financing of Morse's Electro-Magnetic Telegraph, of which he thought so highly that he lost no time in insinuating himself into patent control. Fog was as determined and as ruthless as Craig and much more autocratic; his unsmiling face was framed with a ruffle of iron-gray whiskers and every whisker was briskly belligerent. Craig and Smith quarreled constantly, and as Mr. Smith's gorge rose, so rose Mr. Smith's charges, and the already overburdened general agent had to devise new ciphers to keep the tolls down.

The feud reached its climax over control of a new wire from Portland to Halifax. To a new ruling that three code letters equalled one English word, Smith added another to the effect that unless the Association fired Craig forthwith, his wire would be closed to their news. A locomotive was hired to shuttle back and forth between Boston and Portland with the latest advices, until Mr. Smith was by-passed by the wires of the Bain patents that opened a through wire from New York to Halifax. And when Doctor Jones resigned from the Association to join the staff of James Gordon Bennett, Daniel H. Craig was made its second general agent.

Demands for more news and less inspiration from the Seat of Government were few, and these few made little progress until the telegraph shattered the Washington news vacuum which had been so long and carefully cultivated that administrative control of its news had become accepted as a condition of political fortunes pleasing to the ins and opposed only by the outs. The victory of Philip Freneau, opening the sessions of the United States Senate to newspaper reporters had, by political conniving, been converted over the years into the privilege of excluding representatives of all but "useful" publishers. All publishers were more than welcome to lift extractions from Court Journals, and advance copies could be had upon request from administration-favored printers.

The absorbing question of "who will play the stops on the party organ?" after the inauguration of William Henry Harrison was boldly answered with: "We have made arrangements to station two or more correspondents in Washington for the purpose of giving the Public, through the columns of the HERALD, the first and most authentic information on the movements and policy of the new Administration . . . of which the HERALD can be considered the leading Independent Organ." Great and loud was the wrath of James Gordon Bennett when Samuel Southard, Whig from New Jersey and president pro tempore of the Senate, flatly refused seats to the reporters from the New York *Herald*. The administration was almost ceaselessly blasted by its frustrated organ that took satisfaction in the acute discomfort it caused "those lazy favorites," the *National Intelligencer*, that had been restored to prestige by Harrison, and the newer *Madisonian* of Tyler. Both newspapers were publicly branded as a "mendicant press, living on the Government and dependent on the Government for its very bread." The collapse of the administration was further hastened as Bennett disclosed the fantastic sums paid to these political agencies for the public printing.

Four years later when James Knox Polk succeeded John Tyler, he ousted the Whig organs to restore Andrew Jackson's *Globe* (renamed the *Union*) with Thomas Ritchie as editor. The interest of the country's newspapers could almost be summarized by the Charleston *Courier's* bored: "The GLOBE, installed as the Court Journal, lauds the speech from the Throne. They who are paid for praise—shall they not lay it on thick?"

Undermined by Bennett who fought and fought hard instead of tamely submitting to precedent, and weakened by the competitive bidding for public printing forced on the government by opinion aroused by the same editor, the Court Journals received their *coup de grace* from the telegraph that got government news to the country's newspapers before prettified versions could be concocted, printed, and delivered to the Washington post office. It was not until one day in June, 1860, that Congress authorized a Public Printer and the establishment of the Government Printing Office. And at about this time the seating of reporters for House and Senate began to be managed with the justice which is still generally satisfactory to newspapers, their readers, and the government.

So far beneath the notice of the Court Journals was local news that Washingtonians had been obliged to buy a Baltimore newspaper to find out what was going on. To the *Evening Star* went Crosby S. Noyes in 1855 to make it Washington's "Star-paper." In 1861 John W. Forney, who succeeded where James Gordon Bennett failed with the Philadelphia *Pennsylvanian*, left that city's *Press*, which he founded in 1851, to begin the Washington *Sunday Chronicle*, which soon became the *Daily Morning Chronicle*, active in the support of Lincoln, although never an organ of administration. Last of the newspapers more adept in concealing than in revealing true news was the *National Republican*. This paper gave gallant backing to President Johnson in his hour of need before it lost its identity in the *Evening-Post* of Stillman Hutchins. It is now by editorial alchemy the Washington *Post*.

Far from sources of important news, publishers and prospective publishers watched short-line railroads joined together to make longer lines. Horace Greeley, on a western trip, reported to the *Tribune* one of the many peanut wars against progress. Rails were torn up, road-beds plowed, bridges destroyed, and station-agents pelted with over-ripe eggs by townsfolk protesting against loss of revenues earned by hauling freight, baggage, and passengers from one depot to another; even profits on "apple pie and milk," "oysters and coffee," and "bags o'peanuts" would vanish when hungry passengers no longer transferred from one railroad to another.

TELEGRAPH NEWS ! ! ! lost its fringe of exclamation points and a little of its glamour when steam roads opened this country to domestic news; but steam on the high seas lifted THE LATEST FROM EUROPE from the anecdotal and, underscoring speed, restored foreign news-intelligence to favor with newspaper readers.

An English engineer, F. H. Gisborne, in 1851 secured concessions for a telegraph wire between St. Johns and Cape Race, Newfoundland,

and proposed forwarding news from incoming ships to Cape Breton, Nova Scotia, by pigeon, and thence by wire to the United States and Canada. Overhead and underwater rights-of-way plus an exclusive franchise for landing a cable from Europe gave the New York, Newfoundland and London Telegraph Company an importance not depreciated by pictures of its St. Johns Station, which showed an old-fashioned sending-instrument standing on a crude table, open and unprotected in deep forest, its two wires carried from view by stubby, closely-set and crazily-leaning poles.

Coming into the possession of Cyrus Field, the Gisborne concessions became the Atlantic Cable Company financed in England, and public interest in the many miles of gutta-percha wires now expected to unite two continents was aroused to high pitch. Small town weeklies matched big city dailies with tall type captions. Under CABLE NEWS, NEWS FROM THE TELEGRAPH FLEET, or NEWS FROM THE WIRE SQUADRON they printed reports from letter-bags picked up in the mid-Atlantic. Everyone who read the newspapers knew the ocean-news; on board the U.S. frigate *Niagara* was a Mr. Mullaly of the New York *Herald*, and H.M.S. *Agamemnon* berthed writers for the London *Times* and the *Daily News*.

There was unashamed exaltation in the news welcoming of the landing of the cable August 5th, 1858, at the head of Trinity Bay, Newfoundland, which was to be connected with the land-lines some two miles away. A salute of one hundred guns awakened New York on August 18th. Flags of the United States and England whipped over public buildings, the church bells rang all day, and by night the city was illuminated. The cupola of City Hall caught fire and was consumed. Headlines and Cable Numbers swept through the newspapers. For weeks readers were regaled with such unusual out-of-town items as: "Syracuse, New York: Twenty locomotives at the Station screamed out their notes of Joy with all the power of their whistles—what a noise." "New York: Tiffany and Company, the well-known Broadway jewellers, have purchased eighty miles of left-over cable that is still on board the *Niagara*; it will be cut into small parcels for distribution."

And all America gasped with awe as it read such delightful trivia as what the dear Queen ate for breakfast, no less than at news of war and rumors of peace—and all within twenty-four hours of the Royal morning tea. And newsmen noticed the few words necessary—at such high prices—for the conveyance of the news.

The cable fluttered, grew weak, died, and was all but forgotten in a country engaged in Civil War, as ingenuity succeeded where science and financiers failed. Newspapers and news-summaries were sealed in gallon-sized tin canisters and each canister outfitted with an American flag on a short flagpole. Handed to the pursers of ships of the Cunard and Collins lines just before sailing from Liverpool or Galway, they were thrown overboard when the ship approached the continent by the Great Circle and Cape Race was sighted. Warning was by rockets or the booming of a cannon and depended on time and weather. The first cannonade of a nervous sea-captain sent coastwise inhabitants out to see what was going on. Men in small boats collected the floating canisters that were marked by their flags, and the news, telegraphed, reached this country's newspapers three to five days before Boston or New York landings, and only ten to fourteen days from foreign ports.

New financing, new knowledge, and new energies (under Field, who had a printing press on board the *Great Eastern*, on which members of the crew got out a small illustrated newspaper in the summer of 1865) saw the cable relaid and in working order in 1866. For the public whose appetite had grown insatiable for news unprecedented in quantity and quality, newspapers established listening posts in Europe. When George Washington Smalley cabled the first under-water "beat": "Peace certain. Prussia carries all her points. Liberals support Bismarck's foreign policy," he was doubted, in print, by his competition.

Eager for more foreign news for swelling circulations, the regional press associations, all subservient to the New York association, were beginning to protest control of the small end of the news-funnel by the monopoly to which they were so firmly yoked.

Publishers were having trouble with Indians who scalped telegraph operators to silence the humming of the wires, with cowboys who took pot shots at transmission boxes just for fun, with teamsters who cut off as much wire as they needed to mend their wagon wheels, and with buffalo that used the telegraph poles for scratching-posts, pushing them out of the ground in a few hours; therefore they were not, it was loudly complained, getting enough foreign news. Most fretful and most critical of the parent news-collecting agency was the Western Associated Press, and to calm all these early isolationists the New York Press Association opened a London office under the experienced Alexander Wilson.

"Patent insides" and syndicated features provided readers with stories and articles by well-known writers. A dash of interest and style was added to their appearance by the "boiler-plate," the syndicated text and pictures on stereotype plates mounted on wood for flat-bed presses.

These brought on publishers the charge of using saws instead of scissors to make up their newspapers. An outgrowth of the war, the Readyprints were made by the millions on city presses and went to small-town editors and publishers with space reserved for local news, editorials, and advertisements.

In 1865 when newsprint soared to twenty-seven cents a pound, "Daniel H. Craig, General Agent of the New York Associated Press acting for the editors of the Country who have control of a new patent process for making paper from cornhusks" sent out a call, printed in many country newspapers, for "prices on the same in bales and on contracts of one, two and three years." Experiments in blending rag pulp with wood pulp, ground tree-bark, fine-cut straws, and *esparto* (Spanish grass) were made with usable results. Twelve years later the Pagenstetcher brothers brought from Germany two of the machines devised by Friedrich Gottlob Keller to make paper of wood fibers; and wood gradually replaced rags and all other materials for newsprint.

News of the War Between the States was printed by presses of almost every European and American version of the original old Gutenberg press. Strong arms of city crank-men had been replaced by the steam that turned multiple printing cylinders. Papier-maché molds, perfected in this country by Charles Craske, were used in casting curved type-plates unbroken by the old column rules; and city streets missed the boys who had dashed back and forth between foundries and pressrooms with type-trays balanced aloft, as the work was done in print-shops. And William Bullock, mechanical genius in the American tradition, in 1865 built for the Philadelphia *Inquirer* his rotary "perfecting" press that printed on both sides of the paper at once from a web, or continuous roll of newsprint.

Of the post-war changes in editorial offices and in pressrooms, the strangest was the new edition of Horace Greeley. In the Norwalk, Connecticut, *Gazette* there was advertised on November 16, 1865, the coming lecture of the Distinguished Philosopher, Mr. Horace Greeley. The subject of his discourse was: The Self-Made Man. Editorially "it was assumed" that "the lecture is in no way political and members of all parties may attend"; and editorially the lecturer was recommended with: "The Old Philosopher is certainly a self-made man, and he is also an honest man."

"Dry and solid and quite interesting," was the report of this lecture; what really captivated the critic was: "The old philosopher was neatly dressed and respectable in a good black dress coat, a black velvet vest, dark pants and a clean white shirt. The knot of his black silk necker-chief, however, from force of custom, strayed off to one side and under an ear!"

And Greeley "put on his old white coat and hurried to catch his train," and that was all; not a word about the lecturer's somewhat special editorial eminence nor a mention of his famous newspaper. The world of steam, telegraph, and cable was hurrying on, too busy to mark the end of a great era of newspaper progress, to which the Old Philosopher had contributed as much as, if not more than, any man.

Trans-Continental

"LET EVERY STEP BE AN ADVANCE."

Vol. 1.   Omaha, Neb., May 26, 1870.   No. 2.

Nameplate. Omaha, May 26, 1870. Published daily on the Pullman Hotel Express between Boston and San Francisco. Courtesy of Mr. E. J. Brehaut, Boston.

17

NEW NEWS FRONTIERS

THE BUFFALO GRASS WAS GREEN ALONG THE PLATTE; convoys of mule and ox-drawn prairie schooners plodded towards Kearney, Nebraska Territory, the hub from which radiated the five main trails to the Far West. Here trains were reassembled and here in the shadow of the Fort, travelers could relax. Here were supplies of arms and ammunition; jerked beef, bacon, beans, cornmeal, coffee, and tobacco could be purchased; here were the needed blacksmiths, and wheelwrights, and the busy manufacturers of ox-yokes and whiffletrees, and here was a triweekly newspaper with the latest telegraphic news of the world.

An old printing press, abandoned by General Joseph E. Johnston when he left Council Bluffs in a hurry, was treasure-trove for Frederick K. Freeman from Culpeper County, Virginia, who had come West with his brother Legh to recoup their war-ruined family fortunes. They took their find to Fort Kearney and soldiers who were printers helped to recondition it. And on it they produced sometime in May of 1869 the first number of the *Frontier Index*. Telegraph poles had been erected and wires were strung all the way from Omaha to Great Salt Lake City by Edward Creighton and Brigham Young who generously "gave the boys the privilege of taking the news off the wire." This novel diversion was sometimes interrupted by calls to the aid of soldiers lassoed by fast-riding Indians who dragged their victims over the top of the stockade, or by the chore of going outside to shoot a cannon into wildly stampeding herds of buffalo.

But the publishing brothers deserted the effete security of the Fort and the boon of free telegraph news for livelier and more remunerative business. Loading the press and their other possessions into a wagon drawn by three yokes of oxen, they moved into North Platte to serve, at outrageous prices, the motley population of the Union Pacific Construction Company's camp. Their job-printing was strong in broadsides advertising tickets for lotteries and admissions to dance halls and for lost dogs and other property. And they continued to print the paper as they moved West with roadbed construction. The next stop was Julesberg, Colorado, home of Jules Beni whose ears an enemy had claimed to wear as watch-charms, and of the teamster, Blacksnake Lachut, of the murderous whip that so easily flicked the ash from the cigar of a passerby or removed his hat—or broke his neck.

Cheyenne, laid out by the Union Pacific in July of 1869, had a newspaper three months later when J. M. Gates and N. A. Baker, printer from New York state by way of Denver, got out the weekly *Leader*, at twelve dollars a year. Two months later Hell on Wheels arrived and with it the Freeman brothers who set up shop under a tarpaulin. Pushing steadily westward with the railhead six mules replaced the oxen, and at Laramie the publishers enjoyed the luxury of printing under a roof, and renewed with zest their bickering with Mr. Baker, who had come from Cheyenne to begin the *Sentinel*. Promoted to the dignity of an office in a boxcar, the *Frontier Index* went all the way over the Rocky Mountains with the first steam train over the Great Divide, and after publishing at other construction stops came to a violent end, with maledictions on the Crédit Mobilier at Bear River City in northern Utah.

The last spike was driven into the rails and the railroad at last crossed the continent. Gold, silver, and lead strikes brought the fortune-seekers who were, no matter how high or how remote, always supplied with news from presses packed into camps by burros, mules, or oxen. If presses did not come quickly enough, committees were sent for them, and, on at least one occasion, when impatient residents of shanties high above the timber line wanted the news and wanted it now, men went on a long journey and returned with a printer, drunk and kidnapped, along with his press and his types. And the new publisher quite contentedly got to work on a new newspaper as soon as he learned the name of the camp which was to be his professional new home.

Slowly that immense and beautiful country where the Missouri wanders in crazy convolution between the Mississippi and the Rockies saw settlers break its rich, black earth. Single isolated chimneys and sparse communities, connected only by a few rough roads and the rivers, were held in their emerging pattern by the developing pioneer press that defeated loneliness even as it drew in the telegraph, the railroad, and more and more pioneers with their seed-bags, plows, skill, and capacity for hard work.

Dubuque, ancient town of lead mines on the Iowa bank of the Mississippi, had a newspaper from 1836 when John King, boomer-minded citizen, went back to Ohio for printer William Carey Jones and his press. His *Visitor* was the first of several newspapers started before Iowa became a state. Missionaries to the Lapwais brought Idaho its first press, and gold brought its first newspapers. The *Golden Age* of A. S. Gould was first printed in Lewiston in 1862; and Thomas J. and John S. Butler, brothers, moved in from Walla Walla by pack train to start the *Boise News* in Idaho City in 1863. Also on their way to Idaho City were the Reynolds brothers—James S., Thomas B., and Richard W.—when they stopped in Boise. Boise discovered that they were carrying a printing press in one of their mule-drawn wagons, and persuaded them to stay. Within two weeks, on July 26, 1864, they turned off the first number of the *Idaho Tri-Weekly Statesman* that became a daily newspaper four years later.

James H. Goodhue, New Hampshire lawyer turned western journalist, bought the press, an old one, from the *Grant County Herald* of Lancaster, Wisconsin, of which he had been editor, and transported it up the Mississippi to St. Paul's Landing, where he proposed to start a newspaper for the inhabitants of the thirty-two log cabins of that Territorial Capital. His new friends convinced him of the impropriety of the *Epistle to St. Paul* as a title, so, on April 28, 1849, he started the *Minnesota Pioneer*, which on its fifth birthday was not only a daily newspaper but an institution of the great Northwest. Early newspapers of both St. Paul and Minneapolis live to convey today's news to the great-great-grandchildren of their original subscribers.

The press was late in reaching the Dakotas. The Sioux City *Democrat* was so far ahead of the wheels of the prairie schooners that Samuel Albright who started it in 1859 gave up the struggle—his press and types the loot of raiding Indians. The *Weekly Dakotian* of Frank Zieback lived from 1861, later absorbed its rivals in Yankton, and as the *Dakota Union* was a daily from 1875. In 1873 Colonel Clement A. Lounsberry rolled into Bismarck from the Minneapolis *Tribune* to start a *Tribune* of his own, the first newspaper for news-hungry immigrants in North Dakota published daily since 1881.

North Dakota's first newspaper was the *Frontier Scout*, irregularly issued from Forts Rice and Union in 1864 and 1865. The *Express* of 1874, later the Fargo *Forum*, and the Grand Forks' *Plaindealer* of the same year, afterwards merging with the later *Herald*, were also landmarks for news-hungry immigrants.

News in the Northwest could be cut by publishers to match the cloth supplied by subscribers. In Denver, A. W. Merrick and W. A. Loughlin loaded their equipment into a wagon, cracked a long whip, and set out for a destination undetermined, driving through more than four hundred miles of country familiar only to Indians, wild animals, and reptiles before coming upon Deadwood City. Within a week after breezing in, and before they had a roof they could call their own, the partners, on June 8, 1876, gave the camp the *Black Hills Pioneer*. The camp was famous as the terminal of Buffalo Bill's stage and the home of Calamity Jane Burke, who carried the mail to Custer, Montana.

From St. Louis by steamboat James Buchanan brought a printing press to Virginia City, Montana. With M. M. Manners he got out the first number of the *Montana Post* in late August of 1864. They sold all the first issue, 900 copies, for fifty cents apiece and after the second number "struck it rich" by selling out "lock, stock and barrel" for three thousand dollars. New owners, three times removed, took the press to Helena where it was lost in the fire of 1869. Scarcely had the Last Chance Gulch been renamed before Thomas J. Favorite and Bruce Smith gave Helena, on December 17, 1865, the *Montana Radiator*. The

Rocky Mountain Gazette was started in 1866, and in the same year R. E. and J. E. Fiske began publication of the Herald, a daily newspaper that was temporarily lost in the Record of 1900 and, since 1916, has been the Montana Daily Record-Herald.

While Free soilers were getting ready for the long trek to Kansas and henchmen of Old King Cotton were riding in from the Missouri border, hustling publishers supplied the northern Territory with newspapers which they had printed on the Idaho side of the Mississippi. Within two months after Franklin Pierce signed the Kansas-Nebraska Act, Bellevue had its Nebraska Palladium printed in St. Mary's, Omaha could read the Arrow from a press in Council Bluffs, and Nebraska City its News which was printed in Sidney.

Legacy of Sequoia, the author of the Cherokee alphabet, were the several Indian-language newspapers of the Reservation. In English the Oklahoma War-Chief of the 1880's defended the "rights of the earlier than the Sooners"; it was the enemy of transplanted Indians and target of the United States Army often in pursuit. The Territorial Advocate of Beaver in the no-man's land of the Panhandle of the late 1880's became with changing legislation the Herald.

From the Mississippi to the Great Divide settlement almost automatically produced newspapers. Newspapers preceded churches, and newspapers, counting noses, demanded schools. Boastful pioneers fondly regarded the arrival of the press as an evidence of a civic coming-of-age: an omen usually premature.

Naturally most of the midwestern press was of the boomer persuasion. The tub-thumpers by continuous boasting of climate, soil, waterpower, unrivaled accessibility, and the wealth and beauty of the country developed local pride to a veritable cult whose devotees were every subscriber profiting by the railroad, telegraph, industries, and capital, and who combined their efforts to lure settlers to the region. Such was the power of the boomer newspapers that there are still many pitiful tales told of men and women wandering in the unmapped wilderness looking for the fabulous towns and the town lots and the farms they had bought from rascals whose only credentials were faked super-boomer newspapers especially gotten up to relieve the victims of their money.

Grow or Bust was the motto of rival editors who celebrated every possible occasion with a Special Number. The big folios showed many woodcuts from drawings of obvious artistic license which pictured the curlicued and cupolaed homes of "our prominent citizens" of the "depot," the gates of the cemetery (invitingly ajar) and the exterior of the print-shop with Ye Ed in tight, big-checked trousers, gartered shirt sleeves, and handlebar mustaches, just about to lower the striped awning. Prominently boxed were the names of committees willing to supply further information. Every last boomer declared the town "already known throughout the country" and destined to become a world-famous center of wealth, culture, and elegance. And if the boomer philosophy always marched a few steps ahead of reality, every Annual proved consistently successful achievement.

In sharp contrast the newspapers of small cities and towns of New England gloomily, sometimes despairingly, reported that families and whole groups of families were abandoning the stony farms, their mills, dooryard factories, and the sea to go West. But in the same columns with inspired write-ups of the Annual Social Meetings of the Temperance Union they could—and did—flaunt the latest hard-cider drinking bouts which often called the constable from his warm bed. The antics of the insane or mischievous who paraded on roofs or capered on railway tracks were reported in detail, as were also the too-frequent visits of diphtheria and scarlet fever, the funerals, and the rare tragedies of violence. The story of a hired man who hanged himself out behind the pigpen left no detail untold.

Boomers, always practical, screened their local news to omit the evil and calamitous and diluted the tragic to "protect the name of our Fair City." The easy optimism of the times made virtues of the editorial blind spots that failed to detect rampant dishonesty in local government, pooh-poohed the implications of rising crime, and avoided mention of the obvious sources of epidemics. Boomers grew fat and lazy; they were content to drift on the profitable policies of their own inauguration—even unto Chicago's Century of Progress and beyond; and every instance where local newspapers failed to deal with matters not entirely secret to their adult circulation, they rubbed just a little thinner the fine-spun threads of confidence which are the only bonds between editors and readers.

Boosting the ugly town wallowing in the mud flats to the incipient metropolis it so soon became, John Wentworth of the Chicago *Democrat* combined super-booming with action, with notable results. As Mayor, Long John, six feet six inches tall and three hundred pounds of crusading energy, "cleaned up" in his own inimitable fashion. He advertised a dogfight and with a posse of thirty men armed with axes descended on the "dens," the shacks on the dunes that were headquarters for local and imported crime, and while the rickety colony was deserted, destroyed it. As editor he fought for more and better schools, a paid fire department, and a steam fire-engine; and he upheld Stephen Wright of the *Prairie Farmer* in his campaigning for parks and connecting boulevards for the town he boomed with letters to Eastern newspapers.

Editors glimpsed new frontiers in the 1850's although the issues leading to the Civil War established the confines of many pens. There were editors conscious that their newspapers were more than media for booming real estate and favorite sons, and there were editors whose intellectual honor rebelled against the meanness of a public demanding editorial conformance to the canons of civic pride at the expense of civic honesty.

James King of William, a newsman from the District of Columbia, where he added his father's given name to distinguish himself from other James Kings, made a fortune by an accidentally early arrival in California. His money gone, lost in one of the "failures" of the many early fly-by-night banking houses, he was filled with wrath and a reformer's zeal to eradicate greed battening on greed in the town where many men had gold coveted by a devious but determined few.

James King of William took the editorial chair of the new San Francisco *Bulletin* in early October of 1855. An unpretentious little folio, the *Bulletin* was less than a week old before it lashed out at older newspapers of the city, charging that The Press, the Watchman in the Tower was remiss in its responsibilities when it neglected to warn honest, decent citizens, for whom the *Bulletin* proposed to speak, of the undesirables left in the wake of the gold rush who had become silent partners of swindling bankers spending state and federal money to corrupt politics as a means of further access to the public purse. Palmer, Cook and Company were flatly accused of an alliance with the underworld and denounced as the Uriah Heaps of America. A Mr. Jones, calling next day to bluster and, if necessary, to bribe, found James King of William unimpressed, uncorruptible, and unremovable. The best the financiers could do was to stir up other newspapers in their defense, and James King of William soon had interesting news captioned: The Spirit of the Morning Press.

San Francisco gave its new fighting newspaper its blessing, and with circulation and advertising support encouraged the development of the unlovely theme of corruption in high places to make this the first major crusade against the power of ill-gotten money.

The *Bulletin*, looking into the career of James P. Casey, owner of the

Sunday Times and a politician of skyrocketing fortunes, exposed that expert ballot-box stuffer as an ex-inmate of New York's Sing Sing prison. Casey called next day to demand satisfaction, he was sensitive about these personal matters. He was thrown out of the newspaper's office but waited in the busy street until the editor stepped from his door—and shot him.

Casey took refuge in the station house, but Casey and his friends, the sheriff and the jailers were surprised when a few minutes after his arrival the building was surrounded by men shouting "Kill him! Kill him! Kill him!" Casey was removed in a wagon to the county jail for safe-keeping, and the crowd surrounding the Law and its prisoner were not unconscious of well-armed thugs pressing inward to positions of protection or rescue.

As the long funeral procession of the fallen soldier moved through San Francisco's thronged streets, black-draped and with flags half-masted, into the gates of Lone Mountain Cemetery on May 22, 1856, James P. Casey was swung from the hangman's noose. The *Herald*, opposing city housecleaning, expired, and the Vigilantes were reborn. The *Daily Evening Bulletin* continued with a new morning edition, the *Call*, until, succumbing to the great push of the Southern Pacific Railroad, it barely escaped extinction (the fate of the grand old *Alta California*) but survived to become the *Call-Bulletin* of William Randolph Hearst.

An extra of the *Dramatic Chronicle*, a *Daily Record of Affairs Local, Critical and Theatrical*, which had been established as a little theater give-away by the 'teen-age deYoung boys a few months previously, brought to San Francisco its first news of the shooting of President Lincoln. Up the wooden stairs of the "secesh" *Democratic Press* of Captain William Moss raced the "Feds"; types, type-forms, and papers were being hurled from windows in a fine frenzy when the police arrived to drag both Feds and Rebs off to cool in the calaboose. The newspaper was suspended but it reappeared the following June as the *Examiner* which a quarter of a century later was the organ of a politically-ambitious miner who struck it rich in the Comstock Lode—George Hearst.

Newspapers of the Confederacy, battered and starved, suffered again when the trials of peace reduced them to mere whispers of Southern integrity, and were almost extinguished by the carpetbaggers and other scalawags seeking their control. Leading the way to new frontiers in home counties Henry Watterson of the Louisville *Courier and Journal* campaigned for restoration of civic and legal rights for Southerners. And under the far-seeing Evan P. Howell and Henry W. Grady, one of the greatest of American journalists, the Atlanta *Constitution*, started in 1866 by Styles, Anderson, and Hemphill, with the cooperation of all newspapers from Richmond to New Orleans, led the South to new spirit, new peace, and new prosperity.

The Washington correspondent for the New York *Times*, James Simonton, in 1857 exposed a planned "land grab" which would have given almost all of the Territory of Minnesota to the Pacific Railway Company. Investigation retired four members of the House of Representatives, but the reporter's refusal to disclose the source of his information was punished by exclusion from that august institution.

Simonton's loyal editor, Henry Jarvis Raymond, died in 1868. Edward Wesley was retired, and only George Jones of the originating trio of the *Times* remained to uphold the honor of the city's best cheap-for-cash newspaper. Mr. George Jones gave his support to Louis J. Jennings when the affluence of New York politicians led that editor to the inquiry and criticism that finally pried the city administration free of the stranglehold of the country's most notorious pirates in public office.

The Tweed Ring in 1870 triumphantly reelected Governor John T. Hoffman and City Mayor Oakey Hall; the same election gave the city a Home Rule Charter that slyly made unremovable Controller Richard B. Connolly, President of the Board of Parks Peter B. Sweeney, and President of the Board of Supervisors William M. Tweed. The reinstalled Ring that had made the state legislature so pliant by "bribery, blackjack and blackmail," paid fantastically padded city bills of which sixty-five to eighty-five cents of each dollar went to their own pockets. But this Ring, which had the Federal Treasury as its next goal, began to take notice of Jennings' monotonous drummings.

To silence the *Times*, whose stories were becoming increasingly interesting to the rest of the country although passing unnoticed in other New York newspapers, a rumor of the offer of the tiger-hunter to a pro-Ring group was circulated. It was promptly scotched, however, by Mr. Jones, who then had hanging heavily over his head the danger of the Ring's acquiring control of stock held by the estate of Mr. Raymond.

Then an enemy of Tweed brought into Mr. Jones's office substantiating records from the County Auditor's office. The stunned Ring followed the only course it knew and offered five million dollars for their suppression. Thomas Nast (who created the Tammany tiger, replaced the old crowing Democratic rooster with a donkey, and gave the Republicans the elephant) was offered a half-million dollars to go abroad to "study art"; but he stayed home to draw for *Harper's Weekly* a cartoon entitled "A Group of Vultures Waiting for the Storm to Blow Over." And while they waited Jennings and John Foord analysed their windfall, sent the pro-Ring newspapers into a panic, and readied the public for the sorry reading that was to be theirs in September, 1871.

The Boss, electioneering, demanded only the justice that would prove him "innocent" and a majority of at least thirty thousand votes. The Tammany-owned *Transcript* and the Tammany-controlled *Star* wept that Tweed was "being tried in the newspapers." The *Herald* warned of riots, and the *Star* considerately published the home addresses of Jennings and Jones. The editor of the *Star* was Joseph Howard, Jr. Again the Reverend Henry Ward Beecher entered the scene, this time to declare in his stately fashion that he was sorry for Tweed, which very odd clerical tear was duly noted in the country's newspapers.

The Ring, repudiated at the polls, was smashed by the *Times* in less than two years. Tweed fled the country but he was recognized from Nast's drawings and was returned; Sweeney and Connolly also fled. Hall, who had been a Whig, a Know-Nothing, a Republican, and a Democrat, abandoned politics for journalism, and in London represented the *Herald* for his friend, the younger James Gordon Bennett.

The victory crashed into the newspaper offices with perfect timing. Editors and publishers who may have been blind, lazy, intimidated, or unwittingly in the hire of the master-minds of evil, or who took too seriously the idea that the public was looking for a "good-news news-paper" now rolled up their sleeves to clean the contaminated houses of local and national government. Newspapers risked their circulations, their advertising revenues, and (until it dawned on criminal intellects that one dead editor, publisher, or reporter was worth twenty live ones) their personnel to learn that the "power of the press" is measurable only by conviction, confidence, and cooperation of every newspaper's every reader.

Niggling newspapers refused the United States Senate the dubious privilege of concealing from taxpayers the scandals of the Crédit Mobilier. (The Crédit Mobilier was the construction company that syphoned to private pockets grants of the government to the Union Pacific Railroad and then, with inflated stocks, bought the compliance of Senators, Representatives, and the Vice President of the United States.) Exposés of land-grabs, of the planned back-pay grab, disclosures of the stealings of the Whisky Ring, and of official profiteering in sup-plies for Indian Reservations were developed on the foundations of facts that could not be denied. The proposed Press Gag Law to protect the political leeches so long and firmly attached to every government department exposed to the public the vital need for watchful and independent newspapers and completed the ruin of its sponsors.

Newspapers fought and won their battles with boodlers, with looters of the public domain, with tax thieves, and with the petty pilferers from public pork-barrels; they stirred apathetic, condoning, or conniving public officials into reluctant return to private life. Newspapers exposed and fought individual crooks, from solemnly sworn aldermen to solemnly sworn United States Senators, jailed the Ponzis of high finance, unmasked hoard-extracting crystal-gazers, unfrocked the fraudulent who would forever exploit the religiously credulous, and permanently retired the more blatant of medical quacks.

Crusades springing from editorial impatience with the progress of human decency, or from reporters' stories based on facts and campaigns plotted, planned or supported by newspapers, have in some measure affected the lives of almost all Americans from their cradles to their graves.

Newspapers crusaded for independence, for the Federal Union, for free bridges, and against debtors' prisons. Newspapers supported the fight against lotteries and campaigned to reduce the barriers to votes for every citizen.

Free lands, settlers, railroads, the telegraph were all realized by campaigning newspapers whose energies then turned to schools, fire-engines, sidewalks, water and sewage systems, gas and electric lighting of streets, roads and more roads, and the safer driving of automobiles.

The Safe and Sane Fourth of July can be credited to newspapers which in an effort to lessen the dangers of celebrations, campaigned for parks, benches, fireplaces, bridlepaths, municipal golf courses, swimming pools, and unpolluted beaches, rivers, and harbors. For Better Babies newspapers solicit free milk, medicine, sanatoria, summer cruises, camps, and vacations. For the aged and insane the newspapers have campaigned for better care, better food, and better beds in fireproof buildings.

Full measure of gasoline, full weight of purchased food, clean restaurant kitchens, sanitary bakeshops, inspection of meats, healthy cows, pasteurized milk in bottles are results of only a few of the many newspaper campaigns which have made American lives longer, safer, healthier, happier, and fuller.

News about news (a local news frontier of inestimable interest) was discovered and lost by editors and publishers who have stiffened into a comical pretense of ignorance of other newspapers and of news that might come from presses no farther away than the next block. A tangy undertone to all the day's news was supplied by the editorial game of tossing to editors for editorial comment items of obvious extravagance. News of a birth, reported in the Washington *Daily Chronicle* held the young mother to be "a charming beauty of bewitching grace," her father "a man of sterling worth," her mother "noble and glorious," and the new father "a young man who will go far and make his mark" went the rounds of editorial offices to gather comments completed by: "And if somebody doesn't want kicking we certainly have lost our social bearings."

But for color-loving, broad-visioned Americans the world-frontier-smashing feat of the younger James Gordon Bennett of the New York *Herald* eclipsed the toppling of sordid political and financial figures and the editorial treasure-hunts in the realms of news made by newspapers instead of reported by them.

The Crown Prince of American journalism sent Henry Morton Stanley, famous correspondent, to search for David Livingstone, missionary and explorer in Africa, unheard from for three years. From the outfitting of the expedition in Zanzibar news of mounting interest carried readers of the *Herald* through the Dark Continent to the scene of high drama in which Stanley stepped forward from ranks depleted by death, disease, and desertion to ask, as native drums at Ujiji on the shore of Lake Tanganyika pulsed faster, "Doctor Livingstone, I presume?" The frail white man answered "Yes," and all the world that could be reached by native runners, telegraph, and cable, thrilled to the news that gave Americans the heart-warming conviction of world-citizenship. Men and women in westbound immigrant wagons cheered.

It remained for Palmer Cox, later the Brownie Man, to celebrate with clever verse and pencil a not unimportant consideration in his *That Stanley*, published in 1872.

> . . . a dozen presses bright;
>   Flung off the *Herald*, day and night;
> So thick the crowd for papers flocked
> That streets and avenues were blocked.
>   While from a window hanging out
>   The *Herald* man beheld the rout,
>   And like a Prince did realize
>   The profits of his enterprise.

From this time on, newspaper publishers have supported by direct financing, by contracts for exclusive reporting, or by syndicated stories the exploration of the most remote corners of the earth. Their reward has been the news that never fails to satisfy American newspaper readers, and a sense of having contributed to the world's knowledge of the world.

VOL. XXIII., NO. 7,934.

THE DEADLY LIGHTNING.

SIX LIVES AND ONE MILLION DOLLARS LOST.

and entire was the destruction here that there is not a square inch of wood left—naught but a confused expanse of twisted iron bars. Just west of this are the rolling gear of two tank cars. The tanks were full of oil and it was evident that they had exploded, for pieces of them lie scattered around for a considerable distance.

North of this barrel warehouse is an avenue sixty feet wide, through which run two railroad tracks down to what is called the Standard Oil

Nameplate and Editorial, New York, May 11, 1883. Courtesy of New-York Historical Society.

In that cause and for that end solely the new WORLD is hereby enlisted and committed to the attention of the intelligent public.

JOSEPH PULITZER.

TRUE DEMOCRACY.

An intelligent newspaper must be independent. But it must not be indifferent or neutral on any question involving public interests. If it is a newspaper with the people and for the people, it must maintain those broad principles on which universal liberty is based, and oppose those abuses and evils the destruction of which was the mission of free institutions. Its rock of faith must be true Democracy. Not the Democracy of a political machine. Not the Democracy which seeks to win the spoils of office from a political rival. But the Democracy which guards with jealous care the rights of all alike, and perpetuates the free institutions it first established.

THE WORLD, under its new management, will maintain such a Democratic character. The political freedom the United States now enjoys sprang from a protest against organized privilegists claiming exclusive rights under the aegis of royalty. To-day, as time

𝔚orld

NEW YORK, FRIDAY, MAY 11, 1883.   PRICE TWO CENTS.

ETTI'S LAST NIGHT.	KEENE'S GREAT SACRIFICE.	WARD M'CONKEY HANGED.	DYNAMITE IN HAYTI.
HIS CELL-DOOR AND MANDING RELEASE.	HE SELLS A PICTURE AND MORT-GAGES HIS ESTATE.	Shooting from Under the Black Cap that His Executioners are Murderers. Pittsburg, Pa., May 12.—Ward McConkey was executed here to-day, in the yard attached to the County Jail, for the murder of George A. McClure in Dead-man Hollow, near McKeesport, Pa., on	THE REBELS USE IT TO KILL AND WOUND 100 PEOPLE. Government Troops Cut Off the Water

18

ON THE BREEZY SIDE

PLUG HATS, PRINCE ALBERTS, PICCADILLY WEEPERS, and embonpoints called "corporations," the money-mad who were stealing, raiding, building, dominating, and losing American enterprises, made New York of the gas-lighted opera and elevated steam-cars their capital. Seats in the United States Senate were occupied by their representatives, and Congressmen and Cabinet members amiably cooperated in plying the arts of the wily Jay Gould, the flamboyant Jim Fiske, the sanctimonious old Dan'l Drew, and other Big Fish confident that their ability to gobble up the Little Fish was the gift of an all-wise Nature.

One-time idealist of Brook Farm, Greeley's assistant on the *Tribune*, Lincoln's Special Observer with Grant, Stanton's Under-Secretary of War, and editor of the unsuccessful Chicago *Republican*, Charles Anderson Dana took editorial command of the New York *Sun* in January of 1868.

Under Dana the *Sun* was pledged to "study condensation, clearness and point"; and Dana promised that it would "endeavor to present its daily photograph of the whole world's doings in the most lively and luminous manner." The *Sun's* news was crisp, clever, and sparkling, laced with sensationalism, and balanced with the human interest of its founder. Editorially Dana, who declared he "would wear the livery of no party," strayed close to the cynical, perverse, and reactionary; the *Sun* neither saw, heard, nor said anything that might irritate the hippopotamus-like hides of the Tweed Ring until its omissions were the talk of New York excited by the revelations of the *Times*.

In the *Sun* Dana supported the first presidential campaign of General Grant, but four years later turned against him with the raucous "Turn the Rascals Out." He gave a cruel mock-support to "Doctor Greeley, the wood-chopper of Chappaqua" when in 1872 the old editor, ever politically ambitious, landed the nomination for president by the Liberal Republicans with Democratic endorsement. Greeley's platform promised reform and progress and he appealed to the emotions of the North and South with an invitation "to clasp hands across the bloody chasm."

Greeley's campaign was treated by most of the country's newspapers as something comic. "Old fool," "traitor," "ignoramus," and "crank" were among the milder epithets showered upon him by frankly distrustful editors, and to these humiliations was added an unnecessarily savage series of cartoons from the pen of Thomas Nast. So besieged with "calumny, acrimony, and ridicule" was the candidate that he confessed he "was not sure whether he was running for the Presidency or the Penitentiary." The campaign degenerated into a "race between husband and wife for the grave." On October 30, 1872, Mrs. Greeley, long an invalid, died. On November 6 the *Tribune* admitted Greeley's defeat. On November 7 it announced the editor's return to his office, and on the 8th published his last contribution. The old man, ill, sad, and discouraged, had learned he was no longer wanted on the newspaper that was his life, and in which, thanks to his generosity in sharing stock with employees and associates, he was helpless against their ingratitude. His mind failed and he died on November 29. The news that flashed across the continent met with a revulsion of feeling as deep as it was amazing;

editorial columns and readers' letter-columns alike were filled with a
spontaneous outpouring of affection and appreciation scarcely less than
the public emotion that followed the death of Lincoln. The world at
last acknowledged Horace Greeley as a very great American—honest,
unselfish, the true voice of thousands whose thinking he made articulate
and often forceful.

The New York *Tribune*, Bible of the Republicans, barely escaped the
itching fingers of Washington and New York boodlers. Schuyler Colfax,
Vice President tarred by the scandals of the Crédit Mobilier, was slated
to head the newspaper as the organ of the Big Fish! Options on the
newspaper's stock had been secured by William Orton, president of Jay
Gould's Western Union, when Dana, driving the rascals out of town
in his best style, made uncertain the plan for a newspaper devoted to
whitewashing the owner and the editor and their friends. As the deal
hesitated Whitelaw Reid found the financing that enabled him to save
the famous title from an inglorious end. Orton insisted on retaining one
share of stock and was a member of the board of nine trustees, smearing
the new management with "the Jay Gould taint."

After the next Presidential election, when the Electoral College made
its still disputed decision in favor of Rutherford B. Hayes just two days
before the expiration of Grant's tenure of office, Manton M. Marble,
able editor and sole proprietor of the New York *World*, gave up his
long fight for political elevation and sold out to his editorial assistant,
William H. Hurlburt.

Financed by Thomas M. Scott of the Pennsylvania Railroad the new
publisher, a Unitarian minister and a composer of hymns, called by the
Herald the Reverend Mephistopheles Hurlburt, continued to polish his
lofty editorial phrases with little attention to incoming news or outgoing
expenses until, three years later, came the day when the *World*, "thrown
in like a present with a pound of tea," was sold to Jay Gould along with
the Texas Railroad. Gould moved the newspaper to a new building into
which he had installed new presses. In this paper the financier then
claimed to have found a useful bludgeon in grabbing the Elevated Railroad "for its own good." Boston had already permitted the Gould-owned
Star to expire; and now New Yorkers resisted their opportunities for
"improvement" and the circulation of the *World* fell to about twelve
thousand copies a day, a drop which deprived the money-loving mogul
of about forty thousand dollars a year. In fact the *World* had become a
white elephant eating its master out of house and home.

In St. Louis, "Joey" Pulitzer, remarkable protégé of Carl Schurz and

Doctor Emil Pretorius of the *Westliche Post*, the leading German-American newspaper of the midwest, propelled himself about the town at breakneck speed with coattails flying and pad and pencil in hand for news while it was still news. Joey learned English, read law, tried politics, and found a handy nest egg in the purchase and quick resale of an expiring newspaper owning a valuable news-service franchise. And on the steps of the St. Louis County Court House on December 9, 1878, the St. Louis *Dispatch* was sold to the highest bidder, Joseph Pulitzer, for twenty-five hundred dollars.

The dejected *Dispatch* was subject to liens of nearly thirty thousand dollars; it held a title, claimed to be cloudy, to an Associated Press franchise, an assortment of worn-out types, and a plant rickety beyond repair. Within three days the *Dispatch* was united with the mechanically superior *Post*, and the new partners, Joseph Pulitzer and John A. Dillon, issued on December 12 the first number of the St. Louis *Post and Dispatch*. This was a folio printed seven columns to each page and remarkable only for its salutatory:

The Post and Dispatch will serve no party but the people; will be no organ of (Republicanism), but the organ of truth; will follow no caucuses but its own convictions; will not support the "Administration" but criticize it; will oppose all frauds and shams wherever and whatever they are; will advocate principles and ideas rather than prejudices and partisanship. These ideas and principles are precisely the same as those upon which our Government was originally founded and to which we owe our country's marvelous growth and development. They are the same that made a Republic possible and without which a real Republic is impossible. They are the ideas of a true, genuine, real Democracy. They are the principles of local self-government. They are the doctrines of hard money, home rule and revenue reform.

Further, as all St. Louis was to learn, these were fighting words, which backed up many a crusade to unhorse power and privilege to the great delight of the readers. The *Post-Dispatch* was owned by Pulitzer alone in about a year. And the reader-confidence already accepting the *Post-Dispatch* at something more than face value suffered a severe shock when in 1882 Colonel John A. Cockerill, managing editor, shot and killed in his office a locally prominent lawyer who had called to protest certain editorial statements concerning his partner who was then a candidate for Congress.

Leaving his newspaper six months later in the less impulsive hands of the steadier John A. Dillon, Pulitzer went East, and in New York learned that the World was barely managing to exist. The Biggest Fish of them all couldn't seem to sell his paper to the minnows for two cents a copy, five on Sundays.

By quick negotiation the old salvationist was sold for three hundred and forty thousand dollars, a sum far in excess of its value. But the World was cheap at any price, considering the satisfaction it gave Joseph Pulitzer when on May 11, 1883, he stood up and demanded to be counted among the illustrious, along with Charles Anderson Dana of the Sun, George Jones of the Times, Whitelaw Reid of the Tribune, James Gordon Bennett and his City Editor, William C. Reick, of the Herald, David M. Stone of the Journal of Commerce, president of the New York Associated Press, and Edwin L. Godkin of the Evening Post.

To New York Pulitzer conveyed his greetings and unusual promises; to every New York publisher he offered a challenge:

"The entire World property has been purchased by the undersigned, and will from this day on be under different management—different in men, measures and methods—different in objects and interests—different in sympathies and convictions—different in head and in heart. Performance is better than promise. Exuberant assurances are cheap. I make none. I simply refer the public to the new World itself, which henceforth shall be the daily evidence of its growing improvement, with forty-eight daily witnesses in its forty-eight columns. There is room in this great and growing city for a journal that is not only cheap, but bright, not only bright, but large, and not only large, but truly democratic—dedicated to the cause of the people rather than to that of purse potentates—devoted to the news of the new rather than the old world, that will expose all fraud and sham, fight all public evils and abuses—that will battle for the people with earnest sincerity. In that cause and for that end the new World is hereby enlisted and committed to the attention of the intelligent public. Joseph Pulitzer."

Supercilious eyebrows among the intelligent public after the first Sunday editorial of the new World may have been lifted higher as the newcomer impolitely complained of the odor of codfish permeating New York's aristocracy:

The new World believes that such an aristocracy ought to have no place in the Republic—that the word ought to be expunged from an American vocabulary. The World's aristocracy is the aristocracy of labor. The man who by honest toil supports his family in respectability, who . . . fights his way through life courageously . . . is the proudest aristocrat in the American Republic. Our aristocracy is the aristocracy of brains and labor . . . the genius that invents, the skill that accomplishes . . . makes its possessor an aristocrat for whom the new World will always be ready to speak.

The response of the public was almost instantaneous; Pulitzer sent for Colonel John A. Cockerill, employed new newsmen and new news methods. Within six months the rejuvenated title had the established newspapers of the town spinning dizzily in futile attempts to overtake, squelch, or oust the invader which was making off with their circulations from beneath their very noses. And in the early autumn of 1884 when the World ran off from its presses a full one hundred thousand copies and celebrated with one hundred guns fired in City Hall Park and a new silk hat for every employee, Colonel Cockerill could write with complacency:

It is certainly demonstrated that the Eastern public appreciates a style of journalism that is just a bit breezy while at all times honest, earnest and sincere, and a journalism that represents every day a laborious effort to meet the popular demand seasoned by just convictions.

Pictures—line cuts from mechanically made plates reproducing photographic negatives of the drawings of Valerian Gribayedoff and other artists—were the magnets that drew pennies from men and women who also found that the newspaper's editorials were alive and sensible to the American thirst for sensible comment on and reasonable explanation of the strange forces even then pushing concepts of the world into new lights and shadows. There were pictures of people in the news and of scenes in the news, pictures of ships, monuments, buildings, and bridges. There were maps and diagrams to make easy the assimilation of the news and, at last, "X marks the spot." Big pictures on the World's front pages vied with interesting groupings of smaller pictures to make the newspaper irresistible to prospective purchasers of any and all rival titles.

The World made a permanent impression on American newsmen when, in 1884, almost alone it provided the energy that elected Grover Cleveland in one of the country's most despicable campaigns: a feat that has since been frequently attempted but never with success. The Republican candidate, James G. Blaine, the "plumed knight" from Maine, was handicapped by the friendship of Jay Gould, doomed by the Rum, Romanism, and Rebellion speech of the Reverend Samuel D. Burchard (exclusively reported by Frank Mack for the Associated Press) and politically finished by Walt McDougall's drawing which appeared on the World's first page pictorially reporting the "Royal Feast of Belshazzer Blaine and the Money Kings." It was this campaign of the

World that either brought about, aided, or marked a sharp change towards the "monopolists" who had been glorified by a war-demoralized public as a later generation, after another war, was to glorify the gangsters.

Circulations of the World and the new Evening World that appeared to compete for New York's favors with the new Evening Sun swept into new thousands like a tidal wave, leaving publishers, editors, and owners of other newspapers, and especially Dana, frightened and furious. Dana led the attack with phrases smoldering with a hatred bred of fear, envy, and wounds of the purse. One of his masterpieces ended with ". . . it may shortly please the inscrutable Providence, which has chastened us with your presence, to give you that stern and dreadful signal—Move on, Pulitzer, move on." Pulitzer answered with an editorial captioned YES, HERE FOR GOOD and a new twelve-story skyscraper with a gilded dome that was paid for by the pennies of the public to which he gave his only allegiance. Becoming blind, Pulitzer never saw the World Building that looked down on the dwelling of the Sun and blocked the beautiful vista of the Brooklyn Bridge that had been the delight of Charles "Ananias" Dana.

The World campaigned for dimes for the pedestal which still supports the Statue of Liberty on Bedloe's Island. It sent a woman reporter to another island—Blackwell's—to report on the appalling conditions in the city-owned retreat for the insane. It sent Nellie Bly, the same Elizabeth Cochran, around the world; she lowered the time of Jules Verne's Phineas Fogg to seventy-two days, six hours, eleven minutes, and fourteen seconds; contests and coupon-clipping games hinging on this spectacular stunt were exciting and circulation-stimulating novelties.

The lively World that exposed rampant city boodling ventured out of its orbit to defend the striking steelworkers of Homestead, Pennsylvania, against the "private armies of the Pinkerton's" and the protective tariff which, complained the World, protected only the profits of the Iron Kings who imported cheap labor by the wholesale as slaves and would keep potential Americans ignorant and underpaid. The World grew to the stature of a national newspaper when in 1890 it withdrew its support from the Cleveland administration in protest against the jingoism threatening war with England over a boundary line between British Guiana and Venezuela, drawn in 1840 and after fifty years called a violation of the Monroe Doctrine. The newspaper's campaign for Peace by Christmas was a success, to the discomfiture of the government and those newspapers committed to seeing grave menace in the whipped-up dispute.

And high under the golden dome of Joseph Pulitzer's building, in the office of the San Francisco *Examiner*, William Randolph Hearst found a convenient location for the further study of the brilliant facets of journalism that made the New York *World* so outstanding a success. Here, too, was excellent hunting for talent; the westerner had quietly purchased the *Morning Journal* from John McLean, the Cincinnati publisher who had not done very well with the newspaper started in 1882 by Albert Pulitzer.

Raids began in earnest in 1890. No price was too high for this journalist whose indulgent mother had turned over to him several of his father's mining millions, and no defense was secure against the publisher who had bummed his way to the east bank of the Mississippi. He had crossed by firing the boilers of a ferry in return for his passage, and had since earned his every penny. Writers, artists, editors, and critics were lured from the *World* and other newspapers. Morrill Goddard, editor of the successful *Sunday World* and his entire staff went over to Hearst in a body. They were brought back, however, with juicier bait offered by S. S. Carvalho, Pulitzer's business manager, and another bid within twenty-four hours took them, including the office cat, back to the *Journal*, this time to stay. Goddard had more scope with Hearst to display his art in reducing the news of the day to the primer of sensationalism —sex, crime, love, hate, sympathy, suspicion—all of which he made palatable to even the most squeamish of his readers by quotations from the Bible.

An even more versatile specialist in the bizarre replaced Goddard on the Pulitzer staff. Arthur Brisbane had a fancy for Great Moral Lessons as palliatives for his sensation-soaked news, but the threat of a moral war against the *World* sent the inventor of tall-type headlines after his predecessor into the camp where enterprise was bolder. With Hearst Brisbane enjoyed a salary arrangement, also of his own invention, that made him a rich and cautious real-estate owner whose humorless editorials fluttered in the winds atop the pyramiding Hearst structure. Portentiousness was conveyed to the dullest minds by capital letters used in the manner of the underscoring of a maiden aunt.

A leering, one-toothed, vacant-faced character, ancestor of many of today's strips and panels, the Yellow Kid of Hogan's Alley was first drawn for the *Sunday World* by Richard B. Oultcat who went into Hearst's tents with Goddard. The Yellow Kid was replaced by a rival

Yellow Kid, by George B. Luks, who cavorted in the same Alley. The shapeless yellow garments of the twin Kids, advertised by Hearst on billboards, on sandwich men's boards, and on music-hall stages, branded both the *World* and the *Journal* and all their imitators as Yellow Journals.

The battles of Pulitzer and Hearst were more than circulation wars; they were the death struggles of giants who would acknowledge no master as long as one had talent and the other money. They forged the pattern of the journalism that spread the length and breadth of the land and affected and influenced even those editors and publishers who honestly despised the yellow newspapers for their pandering to the semi-educated with sensationalism expounded in primer English.

Tall types, flag-waving, red ink, and pictures were everyday necessities to the yellow newspapers. On Sundays their magazines were riots of color to which were often added free chromos for framing. If the *World* had a new color supplement, then Hearst promised the readers of the *Journal* "eight pages of iridescent polychromous effulgence that makes the rainbow look like a lead pipe." And under such spurs press builders and ink manufacturers devised new color presses and processes with wider color ranges more evenly and accurately applied.

The Sunday magazines of the yellow journals discovered the native American interest in science and catered to it with weirdly illustrated articles. They depicted the ice age returning to freeze the world into vast, cold stillness, the gases of the sun that would consume all the earth's life, and the unmanageable Gulf Stream busily manufacturing the climatic changes that would eventually play havoc with world population. Articles speculating on life on Mars and the possibilities of visiting the moon came to widely different conclusions, and respectable scientists, whose innocent statements were blown to hair-raising prophecies, protested being thus misrepresented, but editors took little notice.

The magazines of the Sunday yellow journals also reveled in the inverted snobbery of presenting lurid stories of the rich, the titled, and the socially prominent; family skeletons were exposed for the benefit of readers. The readers knew every diamond, ruby, or emerald tiara that brought bad luck to its owners and provided material for the great minds of the editorial plush. Female spies, smugglers, modern Robin Hoods, ghosts, and eccentrics who lived barricaded with their possessions in "castles" they shared only with cats, dogs, or goats were among the characters appearing week after week under different names, with different illustrations and different headings to, monotonously, just miss the promised super-sensationalism.

Reports of unverified probity extracted sympathy from readers of the *Journal,* who were horrified by the misery of Cubans under Spanish rule long before the rivals sensed the circulation-building values of a nice little war. The obligation of America to free Cuba from the savagery of General Weyler—the Butcher—and his body-and-soul destroying "concentration" was, strangely, something on which Joseph Pulitzer and William Randolph Hearst were agreed. And the war that Pulitzer and Hearst both prayed for, screamed for, and demanded in the flat, sepulchral tones of Doomsday, they both declared when the battleship *Maine* went down in Havana Harbor. A calm President, a deliberate Congress, and business unflurried by anticipation of profit were flayed as traitors until April 23, 1898, when war was at last formally declared by Congress. Then the publishers were found waiting with their armies of reporters, illustrators, and photographers.

Relayed from ship to shore, telegraphed or cabled from Key West, news of the Spanish-American War was "hollered in the streets" of New York from one dawn until another as publishers turned off as many extras as they could force from their presses. As many as forty editions in one day were printed at the height of this publishing folly, but only the *World's* W. W. Harden scored a news-beat when he cabled from Hongkong: "Dewey smashes Spain's fleet."

Talent at fabulous prices, yachts, tugboats, ferries, and small boats innumerable, plus the high costs of wired trivia made the war cost more than it was worth in noise-inflated circulations. The peace so heartily welcomed in the pressrooms found Hearst projected to a position that was a solid foundation for his political ambitions. Pulitzer, meeting the bills from earnings and impressed by the *Times* which, under Adolph Ochs's "All the news that's fit to print," had affected the town like a cool breeze on a hot day, retreated to normalcy.

The *World* under Frank I. Cobb, as under its greatest editor and owner, was the fine liberal newspaper needed in America. But, weakened by less decisive direction and by the complications of attempted rule from the grave, the Statue of Liberty that had replaced the press surmounting the globes at the nameplate disappeared with the *World* of Joseph Pulitzer on February 27, 1931. As a Scripps-Howard property the title was promptly merged with that of the gift of the Bennetts to New York, and the *World-Telegram,* more lately the refuge of Benjamin H.

Day's history-making penny *Sun*, now wears its combined responsibilities under the lighthouse of the great "E. W."

The greatest of American newspaper empires was erected on yellow journalism by William Randolph Hearst; but its titles stretching the length and breadth of the land have been reduced by the vicissitudes of time, depression, and a changing public. The Hearst Chain can still boast, however, great newspapers in great cities and also a steady climbing to higher levels of reader intelligence—an intelligence that weighs and accepts news and news-comments in modern contempt for ghosts.

The ghost, an unpleasant shade from the mind of Ambrose Bierce, poet, essayist, and Hearst columnist, was plainly seen in the New York *Journal* on February 4, 1901, not long after Governor Gobel of Kentucky was assassinated:

> The bullett that pierced Gobel's breast
> Cannot be found in all the West;
> Good reason, it is speeding here
> To stretch McKinley on his bier.

This shocking expression of the publisher who had supported the Free Silver Platform of William Jennings Bryan was followed by an editorial to the effect: "If bad institutions and bad men can only be got rid of by killing, then killing must be done."

Abuse of the President was constant and when McKinley was shot by anarchist Leon Czolgosz at the Buffalo Pan-American Exposition, the New York *Journal* was accused of inspiring the assassination. And for this conceited discrediting of the will of the people the Hearst newspapers have paid and paid; crusades, editorial sympathies, and political ventures alike feeling the tabu lingering on in underestimated public memory.

The Delta Democrat-Times, Greenville, Mississippi, January 9, 1952.

The Madisonian, Virginia City, Montana, January 11, 1952.

New Caanan Advertiser, New Caanan, Connecticut, January 11, 1952.

19

IN THE GRASSROOTS

LORD OF AMERICA'S FAR-FLUNG AND VARIEGATED grassroots newspapers, Ye Ed., stoop-shouldered, dyspeptic, always needing stronger spectacles and seldom solvent, has been—and is—one of the world's most happily and usefully employed men.

Editorial sanctums is what they called the semiprivate desks and chairs in cluttered offices redolent of printer's ink, kerosene, tobacco, and dust. They were always open to buzzing bluebottle flies in summer, sealed and superheated in winter, and permanently brightened with ancient calendars. Shiny hooks and spindles impaled orders for job-printing and bills payable and paid, which were packed away into barrels for storage in the barn.

Endlessly Ye Ed., the journeyman, the pressman, and the devil were cheered by practical jokes grown almost respectable by wear, and weekly all were flurried by cares of getting last-minute news composed, the types in their frames and to bed in a press usually afflicted with mysterious ailments and always of flighty disposition. Newspapers, at length printed, were then cut, counted, folded, wrapped, addressed, bundled into big baskets, and hurried to the post office.

Impatient customers waiting for the news did nothing to lessen publication-day nerves. Boy carriers, unnaturally quiet, waited for the newspapers which were awaited in turn in fretworked mansions with gazebos, in cottages clustering around churches, and in the tenements huddled beside the mill. Print-shops hurried to wrap up the papers and throw them aboard wagons or coaches, or they folded up freshly printed columns for the saddlebags of horsemen who would ascend the mountain trails or follow the stars across the lonesome prairie.

East or West, Ye Ed. has always been curiously the sum of his circulation, his newspaper the herald of all local pleasures to come, the record and memento of their passing, and the epilog of sorrow shared.

The steps leading to the offices of country newspapers have been worn by the feet of the local clergy calling with their weekly notices of sermons and services and the news. The Town Fathers came in person with the valued "legals"—and the news. For years merchants expected nothing less than editorial calls for their advertising; but when they dropped in to ask for special puffs for wares "just received," they too had news. Ladies, usually by twos, came in with items of the Baptist Strawberry Festival, the Methodist Sunday School Picnic, the meetings of the D.A.R., or the Temperance Union. Editorial ears were tuned for local gossip, editorial eyes were trained for the unusual, and the editorial presence was required at all local political rallies, celebrations, and town meetings.

Over the accumulated news countless country editors exercised talents far more sensitive and desirable than the ability to write. While editing the reports of others they instinctively chose the local news that made their newspapers essential to the home towns. News of births, deaths, and marriages, news of churches and schools, and the interesting comings and goings of home-town folks all unconsciously emphasized the unity of background of small communities and reflected just the amount of warmth in the welcome shyly extended to newcomers. Successful small-town newspapers have consistently left to mean-minded gossips the news that would hurt, and by this nice discretion readers judged their favorite editors.

Constantly the small-town press has tried to make itself useful to subscribers, printing addresses and proclamations of Presidents and governors. Long serials, short tales, anecdotes, and a poem or two made many issues worth saving, and there were always jokes and conundrums for clipping. Letters, often written from the state capital or from Washington by editors gone visiting, lifted entertainment from the unusual; and old-timers were interviewed to preserve the links binding the past to the future. This was the sort of thing that brought Dear Editor a shower of letters in response.

Successful country newspapers were always idiomatic, always using the words, terms, and phrases of the people the editor elected to serve; and the news was always colored by the character of the editor himself as vividly as were his editorials. News could be dry, crisp, and factual; it could even be mincing; and it has been known to lapse into a revolting coyness. News could also be (and consistently) peevish, sarcastic, and complaining. But most small-town subscribers have expected, and still receive, news reflecting in its choice and handling the tolerance of editors both wise and kind.

Humor has distinguished the country newspaper since its beginning. It was a dull week when country editors could not beguile smiles from country subscribers, and most of the humor was gentle fun. The annual reiterated comment on "the beautiful snow" that fell with such awful monotony, and with such awful monotony and aching backs had to be shoveled from paths, palled on subscribers weary of this annual editorial whimsy. Heavy dews which turned main streets into rivers to be negotiated only in mysteriously produced rowboats, and sun that baked apples on the trees comprised items all slanted towards the wryly comic. Humorous headings and asides signed Ye Ed. were folksy if not very funny, but this kind of humor creaked and groaned through the advertising columns. "CHARLIE ROSS has not been found, but YOU WILL FIND new cups and saucers in our new line of CROCKERY" and similar gems were considered worthy of fifty-two consecutive insertions.

All the rage in the late 1890's, the editorial fad for humorous warnings holds a kaleidoscopic review of the lighter side of small-town life and the proof that all country publishers are brothers at the type-cases.

The news was always the same; the characters were always the town's most respectable business and professional men, and settings varied with the seasons and locales. In New England: "Ye Ed. strongly advises anyone obliged to be absent from his property next Thursday to securely lock the doors and windows of house and barn. Main Street merchants will close at noon; they say they intend to hold their annual clambake." Guards with shotguns were recommended by midwestern and Southern editors "suspicious" that the banker, the feed-merchant, or the hardware dealer planned to raid cornfields or melon patches. Far western editors were terse: "Watch your cayuse." A more loquacious southwesterner reported "an expedition" being outfitted with "5 cases chew-tobacco, 4 burro loads of the stuff that busted Parliament and a fish-line. Ranchmen, beware! These folks sure are bad after chickens and ranch truck."

Favorite motto of the country press was "Independent in Everything. Neutral in Nothing." There were, and are, many small-town editors who share the mantles of the great and give their readers what they think they need, rather than what they know they want, and who scorn the innocuous little essays derisively called "think-pieces," so popular with metropolitan dailies. Small-town editors, independent of party claims, are usually brave enough to be independent of their subscribers too. And since the Cleveland-Blaine election contest, lone Republicans have plumped vigorously for their party candidates in zones solidly Democratic, and well-rounded phrases have extolled Democrats only to fall in the fallow ground of rock-ribbed Republicanism. Politically, Ye Ed. of the best tradition has always been on his own and willing to fight even paid-up subscribers—for his intellectual freedom.

The small-town boomers, dedicated to securing for their subscribers all the multiplying conveniences of the times, have changed the face of rural America. They have campaigned for waterworks and sewage-disposal systems; they have dwelt on the benefits of electric street-lighting, and have in time organized torchlight parades climaxed by speeches and the official "turning on of the bug-juice." They then began to campaign for electricity and gas for homes. They whooped up the new game of baseball and then fought for parks, diamonds, and bleachers; they took up collections for uniforms for players; and again successfully, they howled for trolley cars to replace the old gray mare, and for Saturday afternoon off for the sport they helped to make national.

The small-town newspapers most valuable to the country have been those leading the way to the elimination of the artificial boundaries of creed, race, and color. Small-town reporters and small-town cameras, in social, educational, and business news, have placed the Negro, the foreign-born, and their children in their rightful dignified positions in small-town American life.

Editors of grassroots newspapers have strained to preserve local beauty from industry's scars; more successfully they have saved local landmarks from the desecrating hands of "improvement." And all the time, regardless of wind, weather, science, or elections these are the editors who twang on the familiar strings of home-town news to produce that inimitable note that is news shared by friends.

In format Ye Ed. has usually condescended to please; the country newspapers expanded in sheet size with the blankets, shrank with the pennies, and again expanded with the yellow journals.

The spectacular successes of the New York *World* and the *Journal* influenced even the most remote of country weeklies. Front-page news arrived on front pages, and leading news articles in upper left-hand columns began to wear banked captions in tall types to "editorialize" as commonly as did their city cousins. And when national expansion boomed hamlets into towns and towns into cities, the more aggressive of small-town publishers turned to daily publication. Some of these newspapers are today irreplaceable in reader affection; others (their publishers' ambitions confused with prospects) went back to weekly publication, became links in growing chains, fell into the hands of monopolists from Maine to Montana, and died in dishonorable service of owners and editors interested only in swinging public sentiment to influence legislatures for the profit of stockholders. Some honorably failed.

A dash of the sensationalism of Pulitzer and Hearst was added to almost every country newspaper. To the boilerplate pictures of the famous were added those of the overdressed. Pictured also were their Fifth Avenue mansions, their Newport cottages of marble, the luxurious stalls of their race horses; and the illustrated news of international marriages was as frothy and as unsubstantial as the spun-sugar wedding bells atop the towering cakes—also pictured. It was the boilerplate that made the country sisterhood style-conscious and receptive to the practical patterns of Ebenezer Butterick. All the practical women's magazines began with his fashions and developed a profound national influence. Cartoons, mostly political, enlivened country newspapers. "Published by Permission of *Harper's Weekly*" or another of the many weekly news magazines, these gave a slightly spurious air of sophistication to local news laced with bucolic humor, spiced with lifted squibs and quips, and peppered with little black fists; but no doubt they flattered editorial customers.

Railroads carried more bundles and bigger bundles of the yellow journals which fascinated the country with their lively treatment of the news, with their pictures, magazines, comics and inserts; weekly the bundles were carried farther beyond the networks started by the penny dreadfuls; whole trainloads steamed from New York with loads lightened at every station. The foreign yellow newspapers supplanted the home-town weeklies and sometimes gained undisputed possession of new fields for the gospel of the Yellow Kid.

To the almost unbearable burdens of the newspapers of small cities was added the currency panic of 1907. Local news was "foreign" and uninteresting to the second generation of yesterday's immigrants, and unintelligible to those newly arriving. Countless country publishers, lost in strange towns suddenly sprung up around them, gave up the ghost, and newspapers important to only a few thousands of subscribers were no more.

In the best of times the country newspapers that all, at one time or another, belligerently warned advertisers and subscribers with "The Cash System is HERE to stay, and NO LET UP" made little headway in actually collecting cash from their advertisers. Advertising space was expected by the butcher and grocer who supplied Ye Ed's table. The dry-goods merchants at the Fair, the Boston Store, or the Paris Emporium advertised their bargains in return for thread, buttons, lace, percale, and corduroy supplied to the publisher's wife; and the shoe dealer who kept the feet of the publisher's progeny from the ground preferred to pay in shoes instead of dollars. Even the undertaker was willing to gamble the price of at least one first-class funeral in return for a weekly card.

Costs of newsprint, new types, inks, labor, and all the necessities of the most primitive of printing offices steadily spiraled from the beginning of the first World War; and many country publishers who had lived, and lived well, by barter were forced out of professional existence. In the past fifty years almost half of the country newspapers have vanished; the ten thousand or more which survived the transition to new news and publishing standards and economic changes are living tribute and undeniable testimony to the ruggedness of their bonds with their readers.

The newspapers of the grassroots reaching only home-town readers have already entered their great revival. Decentralization of industries, the outspread of city populations, and the ease with which out-of-town newspapers can be obtained almost everywhere, gives the country newspapers with their reporting of local funerals, weddings, schools, churches, stores, clubs, lodges, gardens, athletics, fires, and accidents—and of personal items—new values and new significance. This is the news straight from the uncontaminated wellsprings of American Democracy; its news of peace, sanity, and serenity provides the contrast necessary to intelligent evaluation of state, Washington, and world news of the day.

Youth, energy, brains, and training are turning to small-town presses; old mastheads are changing hands and new are in the building and the planning. Second-hand presses and rebuilt linotypes are already campaigning and crusading for the restablishment of American ideals. Small-town newspapers—both dailies and weeklies—are today making their communities happier for little children, and are satisfying the productive and comfortable and the aged. They never neglect home-town news, but watch for it, listen for it, search for it, and report it fully and honestly in that intimacy of understanding for which there is no substitute—that of country editor and subscriber.

They may never reward today's pioneers with stocks and bonds, too long the only symbols of success, but the dynamic newspapers of small towns that are already cutting new patterns in fine American living, promise interest-crammed lives and all the satisfactions of the most constructive of life careers.

PRESIDENTIAL EQUESTRIANISM.

Mr. Cleveland Riding the Administration Charger.

ACT I—*Scene I.*—THE MOUNT.

This special photogram to the TIMES, wired from Washington at enormous expense, is Short but sweet, and gives a graphic idea of Mr. Cleveland's appearance as he mounted the administration charger. A slight roughness in the lines is due to bumping against the insulators as it came buzzing along on the overland wires. Some readers may possibly think the rider's countenance should appear; but that will be presented later on.

Cartoon. The Times, Los Angeles, March 6, 1885. Courtesy of Bancroft Library, University of California.

20

THE ETHICAL PRESS

REACHING BACK INTO MEMORY, GRIZZLED EDITORS, publishers, and printers mark the Big Blizzard of '88 as the approximate birthday of the modern press: the mighty miracle pulsating to wired and wireless news, the phenomenon of daily collecting, editing, and printing within minutes reports of events transpiring halfway around the globe, and the upright press pledging Truth in all its columns.

"Fresh, brisk winds and fair," had been promised by Old Probabilities, the Government Weather Forecaster. "Clearing, brisk winds and warmer," expanded Professor T. F. Maury, meteorologist, under Personal Intelligence in the New York *Herald* that did not rely on the official word it printed on the same editorial page. But on Monday, March 12, when reporters ventured outside their doors, the snow that had started on Sunday was still tumbling from a darkened sky. Fighting their way through the drifts piling up in the motionless city to the nearest depots of "the Postal," reporters telegraphed their stories of the great storm to desks not very far away.

Few newspaper offices had telephones and newsmen favored the land lines now challenging the news-dictatorship of Jay Gould's Western Union. The Commercial Cable Company of those enterprising partners, the younger James Gordon Bennett and John W. Mackay of the Great Bonanza millions, had already brought down the costs of foreign news in brisk competition with the Atlantic Cable Company, which had gravitated into the possession of the monopolist. Gould had been forced to follow the advice of the *Herald* and "make himself less numerous" by fleeing to the safety of his yacht when men accusing him of tampering with telegraphed election returns threatened to hang him.

New York's celebrated sidewalks were lighted with the arcs of C. P. Bush. A few newspaper offices boasted the novel incandescent bulbs of young Tom Edison, and through most of New York's newspaper presses now ran wide ribbons of newsprint, almost entirely of wood pulp, from reels turned by the motors of Frank R. Sprague. But stuffy editorials about the remarkable wonders of the Great Electric Age were still printed from types composed by hand and stereotyped from the papiermâché molds made in newspaper offices. The Linotype of Ottmar Merganthaler and James C. Clephane had been used to set part of the New York *Tribune* for July 3, 1886, but its future success was still only the hope and belief of inventors and interested publishers. Another elusive promise was the half-tone process of photograph reproduction, which was also a blizzard-year gift to his country from Frederic C. Ives.

And now that its letters were no longer all capitals and its carriage no longer returned on its sewing-machine chassis by a foot-treadle, the typewriter, the invention of Christopher Sholes and Carlos Glidden was, in the New York office of the Associated Press, a warning of the changing of the guard.

More dramatic than escape from "private interests" seeking control of communication of the news was the explosion that shattered the old Associated Press of New York, a news monopoly from its origin. The Western Press Association was interested in the strange attitude of its New York masters towards the newer United Press Association, organized in 1882. Permitted to live and thrive by Western Union, its hitherto loyal ally, Western uncovered a little coterie syphoning Associated Press reports to United for sale to their rival newspapers and even financing new newspapers to provide more revenue for the same little group.

The original Association crumbled under the exposé of the scandals of secret deals. Cleansing the business of the collecting and distributing news to its core, Frank B. Noyes, Adolph S. Ochs, Joseph Medill, Victor F. Lawson, and Melville E. Stone led other publishers in the organization of the Associated Press of Illinois, now of New York. From 1892 news, not profit, has been the aim of the Association, whose operating costs are shared by its members who neither expect nor receive earnings or dividends.

The A.P. familiar to all newspaper readers is, in freedom from propaganda of government, politics, or commerce, matched by the U.P., or United Press, revived in name only by E. W. Scripps, and by the I.N.S., Hearst's International News Service, both commercial agencies.

It was largely in response to the pressure from the yellow journals that all the machinery for the production of newspapers moved towards new speed, capacity, and precision and the refinements in delicately adjusted controls that bettered the work of human hands. Every awe-inspiring, inspiration-stimulating improvement encouraged publishers to dream of circulations beyond reasonable counting. And every new and expensive press, soon the necessary investment of progressive publishers, required especially designed and constructed buildings to withstand their steady throbbing as they rolled off the news. Between the Big Blizzard and the opening of the First World War newspaper publishing was admitted to the ranks of Big Business with all the attendant risks and responsibilities.

No dull and drab procession planned by efficiency experts, Congressional committees, or the Welfare Clan was the transition of the newspaper of yesterday to that of today. It was a continuous salvo of fireworks whose set pieces, rockets, detonations, and whirligigs were applauded or booed into bankruptcy by the public that paid but a few pennies for each show.

Leading the confused and bewildered conservative publishers were the yellow journals. Frenzied in their power, their unlimited fields for exploitation, and their determination to dominate competition, the converts of the Yellow Kid created and fed the hysteria that demanded more news, shocking news, impossible news, news with scareheads and banners and appropriate pictures. The catch in this business of turning out the news in endless streams was painfully clear on those days when Grandfather Johnny Q. Public refused to believe that an important nugget of news lurked under at least one of the pretty shells of the head-line writers, and when great bales of unsold newspapers were beheaded and the "heads" returned for credit.

Searching for the sensationalism by which they lived, the yellow journals became keyhole newspapers that snooped and spied, peeked and pried without regard for the laws, rules, or rights of human privacy. Interviews were obtained by trickery or blackmail and trapped news-prominent individuals into foolish or stupid statements. Visits of the Gentlemen of the Press began to require witnesses, a stenographer, a lawyer, and/or a policeman.

Publishers whose ethical guides were the thin lines that kept them out of jail (until the public applied the brakes after the shooting of McKinley) continued to hold great circulations even after real or sim-ulated reform, giving rise to the publishing gospel in platitudes best expressed by Julius Chambers: "In every case the successful American journal has been built upon sensationalism, but it has been found, once established, that absolute accuracy and truth are the only bases for en-during success." This precept, unfortunately, failed to explain how to let go the tail, muzzle the bear, and lead it into other reader zones.

Risk to invested capital multiplied with the mounting costs of news-print, presses, tools, talent, wire, and feature services. Conservatism and caution were imposed on the press by hard facts, and puzzled publish-ers looking for guidance beheld success in terms so contradictory that confusion was worse confounded; the public granting life to newspapers was unfathomable, unpredictable, imperious, and inflexible.

In Kansas City, William Rockhill Nelson's *Star* crusaded vigorously for permanent civic improvements, gave its readers real news and hard-hitting editorials, and was "sworn by" all over the Sunflower State. In Denver the unregenerate Fred G. Bonfils and Harry H. Tammen, ex-lottery shark and ex-bartender, respectively, ran the *Post*, The Paper with the Heart and Soul, and from their office, locally known as the Bath of Blood, red ink spread in streamers, banners, and heads over this yellowest of yellow journals. And red blood splashed on blood-red walls and carpets to climax Sob Sister Polly Pry's campaign to release a state's prisoner accused, among other crimes, of cannibalism.

The *Post* of Boston, sensationally yellow under Edwin A. Grozier from the New York office of Pulitzer's *World*, rolled up its sensational thousands, while the *Transcript*, unaffected by the din and dyes of its noisier neighbor, steadily swung in its disciplined orbit.

"What's the matter with Kansas?" inquired William Allen White in the Emporia *Gazette*, which he made nationally famous by simple honesty and uncomplicated common sense. And the sage of Potato Hill, the neighborly Ed Howe, was doing right well with the Atchison *Daily Globe*. In San Francisco Freemont Older was successfully fanning the almost spent fighting spirit of the *Bulletin*. In Chicago Victor A. Lawson had made the *Daily News* (originated by Melville E. Stone) the sturdy defender of American labor and the pert competitor of the swelling *Tribune*. Adolph S. Ochs in New York, industriously aiming to fulfil his slogan of All the News That's Fit To Print, was making the *Times* an ample, comprehensive and accurate world-newspaper, while across the East River the Brooklyn *Eagle* under St. Clair McKelway was reader-strong and prosperous on a solid foundation of local news.

The Scripps chain was expanding, its local partners were entrusted with the perpetuation of the policies of its founder, who had bowed to neither wealth, society, politics, nor advertisers. The Hearst chain too was expanding, its hired executives providing sensations and policies as ordered by remote control, and always stirring sluggish competition into healthy activity. Other chains grew in numbers and in power; mergers were engineered, newspapers bought, and new newspapers started, of which every one had to fight to win and hold the public favor that money cannot command. And "patent insides" continued to roll off city presses for country consumption—some of which rested uneasily in city control.

Sunday news and Sunday newspapers fought long to win public tolerance. As early as 1796 Philip Edwards of Baltimore proposed, with a Specimen copy, a *Sunday Monitor* to an outraged public who permitted the project to go no farther. A year later, also in Baltimore, John Smith and Christopher Jackson managed to publish their *Weekly Museum* for twenty-five consecutive Sundays. In New York the *Observer* was offered on Sundays from 1809 to 1811; and here, twenty-five years later, that dashing young man of the penny dreadfuls, James Gordon Bennett, tried for Sunday circulation. Loudly David Hale of the Sabbatarian *Journal of Commerce* complained of the shattering of New York's peace and quiet and the annoyance to church-goers pestered by newsboys. "There ought to be a law," thundered Mr. Hale; there was a law, and Mr. Bennett's newsboys were arrested for disturbing the peace.

Sunday newspapers were elevating and literary novelties of Boston,

New York, Philadelphia, and Charleston, but without spectacular success. During the Mexican War news on Sundays was sometimes admitted to be useful; and during the War Between the States, when Sunday newspapers were first regularly issued by established dailies, they were, without public dispute, a necessity.

The modern Sunday newspaper of full news coverage, extra editorial weight, and entertainment in magazines and colored comics, originated in the flamboyancies of the competitive spirits and fertile brains of those master-tailors of the American newspapers—Joseph Pulitzer and William Randolph Hearst.

Business was the only consideration of the advertising managers of the yellow journals, and almost more important than profits was the importance of outselling all rivals. From the columns of the yellow journals—and even some more respectable journals—the advertisements of quack doctors and unsavory businesses were driven out by the combined pressures of public opinion and enforced law. Long snuggling in the columns captioned Personal, the same characters with no credit and little cash today seek their victims in the classified departments of a few American newspapers. Today accepting such advertising is considered criminally negligent.

Once in otherwise decent newspapers, physical symptoms and conditions were described with terror-inducing intimacy in the "testimonials" for patent medicines long the target of upright citizens. Welcomed especially in small-town newspapers for paying cash for space, the concocters of tonics fortified with firewater and soothing-sirups laced with laudanum, fastened their tentacles around those publishers who could be bribed, bullied, or cajoled into a "red-line" advertising contract that was self-canceling in event of legislation against their astonishing claims or exposure of the real ingredients of their nostrums, or the halting of their free selling of "sure cures" for every malady known to man. From the shelter of self-interested newspapers the patentees proposed to fight all restrictions. Newspapers and magazines supported an aroused public and backed leaders branded as cranks to secure, in 1906, passage of the Federal Food and Drug Act. For good measure a Post Office Act of a later date banned all puffs unless marked Advertisement, and then the Barons of Baking Powder and the Satraps of Soap joined the Princes of the Proprietaries in the seats of the ex-privileged.

Oldest of the bitter battles between newspaper publishers, their readers, and the general public is also its lingering grimmest. On New Year's Day of 1775, tips and presents to the Printer's Lads who Carry the Pennsylvania Journal to Customers made profitable the New Year's Verses thoughtfully provided by William Bradford. After a hundred years it was an agile as well as a stony-hearted subscriber who could avoid the bright eyes of carriers mentioned playfully by their publishers as "having mounted their Pegasus . . . so, kind Reader, be in readiness with those comfortable quarters." Encouragement of boy carriers—at the expense of subscribers—deteriorated into exploitation of boy labor in the first skirmishes of the penny newspapers, and reached its shabbiest in the pitched circulation battles of the tarnished knights of the Yellow Kid.

In the mid-1850's Charles Loring Brace found two young newsboys sleeping in an abandoned safe in lower Wall Street. He discovered that homeless lads were spending nights in empty barrels and packing-boxes or crouched over sidewalk gratings. They were up at daybreak and hollered the news, peddled, or polished shoes for money for food, tobacco, and drink. For these boys—runaways, boys lost by immigrants crossing the city, and boys coolly abandoned—Brace opened his Newsboys' Home where a bath and a clean bunk could be had for the night for six cents, food could be had for very little, and money in small sums was loaned to the young capitalists among whom Horatio Alger found his heroes.

Publishers of the yellow journals valued these little derelicts for their rugged persistence no less than for their pathos. Publishers whose carefree spending impressed the brazen of the brassy age given to vulgar display of ill-gotten wealth, added pennies from these boys to their inflated incomes. They forced them to take more newspapers than they could sell; if they were returned it was at a loss: a mean advantage practiced on the humblest employees of their gilded empires.

For lack of tenants the Newsboys' Home was closed and lately sold. City newspapers the country over are now largely the business of men at their own newsstands, and in the suburbs they are usually delivered over regular routes to regular customers by carrier-boys, true businessmen whose success depends on salesmanship, cheerful and prompt service, and good credit judgment. Almost all states now not only limit the working hours of young boys, but forbid their hawking newspapers in saloons, cafés, dance halls, and all-night restaurants. Times have changed, and the sympathy which newsboys once aroused has now frozen into scorn for the publishers who employ Little Merchants purely for their appeal to sentiment.

Almost as obsolete as the circulation managers who depended on sympathy—or scares—for sales are the old-time editors who once gave willing praise to uphold the advertising dollar, or innuendo to further an employer's political fortunes, or editorial pleas for legislation favoring investments of owners or publishers. Swinging to the other extreme are today's anonymous experts arriving at editorial conclusions by consultation and conference; they lack the flair of past preachers and pirates and, in their ivory towers too often turn the world away with chill news-analyses instead of firing it with needed sulfur and brimstone.

Vanishing, too, in the rise of ethics in newspaper publishing are the slanted headlines that either with deliberation or carelessness trap and indoctrinate the mentally lazy, the hurried, and the credulous. In their news headings otherwise reputable newspapers have knowingly coddled those of feeble moral fiber with promises of prosperity just around the corner, peace in industry, and peace between the nations. In headings, too, these newspapers have given aid, comfort, and alibis to undeserving presidents, dictators, bureaucrats, and bosses by deviating some degrees from the truth apparent in the immediately following text. Fatal to faith in both government and newspapers are the misleading leads, once accepted as wartime legitimacy, but now the symptom of corruption at the news-source.

Vanity, eternal vanity, will always spare the country the awful possibility of the Perfect Newspaper. To some willing to skip a few millenniums this would be a Good-news newspaper, containing nothing to disturb placid rumination. In a livelier news world editors and owners with yearnings for king-making can be depended on occasionally to illuminate slightly ludicrous spectacles. Editors and reporters let enthusiasm for bold, new creeds lead them to amuse, infuriate, irritate, or alienate friends and readers. Publishers aching for some slight advantage over competition's circulation or coverage, delight and mystify customers and customers' neighbors with presents of gold-encrusted china or white enamel saucepans for coupon-clippers; or they stage soap-box derbies, or indulge in sky-writing. And "Me too" promoters pompously present elegant publicity which they label Advertisement but which deceives no one over ten years of age.

Publishers, from their day-to-day experience with readers, advertisers, the general public, and that vast variety of special interests known to every press, have gradually evolved a code of ethics that is the sober acknowledgement that reader-relations are as binding as legal contracts. "Responsibility, independence, sincerity, accuracy and decency" are the high aims of newspaper leaders, the real strength behind today's roaring, rumbling, throbbing giants, which are continuously inking type-plates, printing both sides of newsprint spinning from reels automatically spliced onto reels rolling into place as newspapers, printed, cut, folded and counted, leave the presses in bundles on conveyor belts. Morning, evening, Sunday, and extra editions of many pages, move by tens of thousands with clocklike monotony to trucks, trains, and planes, on to newsdealers, newsstands, carriers, and post offices, to be read in a few minutes, or at most a few hours, by an ever news-hungry public that weighs its news, editorial, advertising, and mechanical achievements by constantly, if slowly, rising standards.

Nameplates:

Russkiya Vedomosti, Moscow, 30 June (13 July), 1917. Founded 1863.

Novoye Vremya, Petrograd, 26 October (8 November), 1917. Founded 1868.

Frankfurter Zeitung und Handelsblatt, Frankfurt-am-Main, 31 August, 1943. Founded 1856.

Vossische Zeitung; A Berlin paper of state and learned affairs, Berlin, 31 March, 1934. Founded 1704.

La Prensa, Buenos Aires, 26 January, 1951. Founded 1869.

Courtesy of Library of Congress.

21

CRY CENSOR!

FREEDOM OF THE PRESS, LIFEBLOOD OF THESE UNITED States, is the property of the people; restraint, regulation, or monitoring of news at its source, in transit, or at the presses, screens, or microphones, even though exercised by an elected administration or its appointees, is in direct violation of American spirit and American law; and each concession by law or relaxation of principle, no matter how small and freely made or granted under pressure, wears down the resistance of voters, legislators, and civic leaders as water wears away stone with its drip, drip, drip.

The itch to control the news is older than the press. Ever since some men began to communicate there have been contrary opinions to be suppressed, ideas to be advanced, power to be protected and perpetuated, and the credulous to be softened up. Only eternal vigilance can avert the wearing away of the rock from which all American freedom springs —the First Amendment to the Constitution which reads: "Congress shall make no law respecting the establishment of religion, or prohibiting the free exercise thereof; or abridging the freedom of speech or of the press or of the right of the people to peacefully assemble, and to petition the Government for a redress of grievances."

And many who signed the document beginning: "We, the people of the United States . . ." lived to see an administration of the government it instituted seeking to temper criticism by the Sedition Act punishing with fines and imprisonment the "publishing of any writing calculated to bring Congress or the Chief Executive into contempt or disrepute." Enforcement of this act politically destroyed its sponsors.

There was no censorship of the news of either the first or second War for Independence; and the government, embarrassed by the superior speed of the newspaper expresses, made no attempt to censor the reporting of the Mexican War. Censorship of the news of the War Between the States was without firm policy; the army and the newspapers wrangled constantly, and the public was always ready to defend hotly the traditional freedom of its news, to the obvious benefit of the Copperheads, and made no protest when the government took over the telegraph wires. Nor were there protests when the field order of General William Tecumseh Sherman reached Northern newspapers:

Not more than two newspapers will be published in Savannah; their editors and proprietors will be held in strictest accountability, and will be punished severely, in person and property, for any libelous publication, mischievous matter, premature news, exaggerated statements or any comments on the acts of the authorities. December 28th, 1864.

The government exercised no restrictions of censorship to delay the news of the war with Spain when no less than five hundred writers, artists, and photographers swarmed through blue Cuban waters on missions of finding—or stirring up—excitement to save the ballooning circulations of the yellow journals from deflation. Nor was military censorship a professional hazard twenty years later, when Richard Harding Davis, John McCutcheon, and other star reporters of Spanish-American hostilities were assigned to Watchful Waiting along the Rio

Grande. When the Marines landed in Vera Cruz, the bored Davis set out to interview President Huerta and landed in a Mexico City jail, but with news coverage comfortably complete. Suddenly these and other newsmen fled to home offices, to a port—any port, to a ship—any boat, and to Europe bursting into flames. Already new and sadder words were being added to American vocabularies.

Hurrying to posts in England, France, Belgium, Austria, Italy, and Germany, the men whose stories of the Kaiser's goose-stepping legions marching with iron heels over the face of Belgium and into France to be dramatically halted at the Marne held their compatriots poised in horror, and learned what censorship requires in wartime. Their reports of the courage of the French, the stamina of the English, the suffering of the Belgians, and of the German efficiency which seemed unconquerable to confused and unready allies, and their stories from bleak front-line trenches and devastated civilian homes, from hospitals and cantonments, were all censored by stern officers in uniform before the real news was "passed" and permitted to travel under the Atlantic. From the Allies came propaganda designed to play on warm American sympathies and from Germany poured the blustering threats of a fifth column with the damning support of the Hearst newspapers. President Wilson, reelected on "He kept us out of war" only a few months later, after the sinking of the Lusitania, led a war-minded, propaganda-reading, propaganda-absorbing, and propaganda-prepared people into overseas battle.

The Espionage Act of June 15, 1917, and the Sedition Act of May 16, 1918, curbed American free speech; military censorship limited free news in private letters from abroad and the Trading with the Enemy Act of October 6, 1917, not only controlled news going out of the country, but demanded sworn translations of articles in foreign-language newspapers which were permitted the use of United States mails. This too was at the discretion of the Postmaster General who was also given power to license and revoke licenses of English-language news media. The Committee on Public Information under George Creel combated the German fifth column with thousands of news releases. With advertising, posters, and films it supported the Red Cross and the Treasury Department in its financing of innumerable Liberty Loans.

The First World War, waged with new and devastating tools, brought new techniques of war reporting. Home offices employed military experts who drew broad pictures from the small glimpses secured by scattered correspondents, and pins with bright glass heads were moved across wall maps with remarkable accuracy, keeping pace with the lines of weary men under fire or holding a few hard-earned feet of France. Home troops in every American sector welcomed the Official Newspaper by and for the Soldiers of the A.E.F., the *Stars and Stripes*, with its robust humor and news from home, news of government, and of the Army. It led the many army newspapers that sustained the morale of high-spirited Americans and kept them reasonably content from home-training camps to front-line bivouacs under enemy fire, to the False Armistice, the True Armistice, Versailles, Occupation and—home.

Even before the War for Democracy was over the world, rejuvenated according to the optimistic, had fallen back into age-old furrows worn by the arrogant and predatory. Powers were again seized by force and cunning, and the scepters of czars, kings, and kaisers released by murdered, mutilated, or failing hands fell as prizes of ruthless conceit. Into jerry-built ideologies a new order of pipers lured by promises their victims and held them in tightening networks of control until they became enfeebled beyond resistance. The key to complete dominance was always the newspapers. Newspapers, in any form of dictatorship, had to be controlled, silenced, or killed; newspapers had to be seized if necessary but were preferably taken by logical, flattering deception, or by the jiggery-pokery of allocations of newsprint, or by "peoples' control of the presses," or other schemes making it impossible to determine the moment of the death of freedom under governments which could not stand the light of free news.

The bourgeois Russian press, the newspapers for the comparatively few who were able to read, were among the first casualties of the 1917 Revolution and the surviving papers were nationalized in 1919. Literacy, the great gift of the state to the followers of Lenin and Stalin, has been perverted by state-controlled newspapers whose every word is derived from the state as the fountainhead of truth and wisdom and whose aims and ends are the preservation of the same state by means of which news is designed to insulate its subjects against the discontent bred by knowledge of a freer, fuller world outside.

In Germany Handsome Adolph, who took from the hands of the dying Von Hindenburg the slack reins of that country's venture in democracy, in 1925 was responsible for an innocuous little law requiring only the registration and licensing of journalists. From this modest beginning Germany's newspapers were steadily squeezed until they were dry of independence and none remained but the tools of the Dictator who used them to glorify himself, to promote the fortunes of the National Socialist Party, soften public resistance, and mold German minds. Freedom, dignity, decency, and honor were gone.

For its criticism of the Italian Army, in 1945, *La Stampa* of Turin was suspended; it reappeared as *La Nuova Stampa*. Soon all Italian newspapers came under the iron thumbs of the party of black shirts and castor oil, and there were no free newspapers or free people left in the realm of Mussolini.

In Spain all newspapers opposing the Falange were confiscated. All journalists were licensed and all newsprint state-controlled. Even the Syndicalist newspapers now permitted by the Dictatorship are published under the watchful eyes of officialdom alerted to incoming English-language newspapers which might contain news of Spain. These are confiscated to prevent any seepage of extra-usual news.

La Prensa, one of the world's fine newspapers and the pride of Latin America, after writhing for months in the red tape and directives of a come-lately dictatorship, has been seized and its editor and publisher is in exile. *La Nación*, denied newsprint and hampered by difficulties of government manufacture, continues to publish, but is marked as another façade without foundation.

No European people has ever known that freedom of news which is accepted by all Americans as simply as they accept air and water. Only the British-born enjoy newspapers as free from government interference as those of America, and in these libel laws slow up the news, although a murder before the Courts has so pronounced it can be news as sensational as a similar tragedy reported by American newsmen. In England a voluntary censorship preserves the private affairs of Royalty from curious eyes and ears, and commoners in castle and cottage, whose teas have been enlivened by gossip none the less relished for being ascribed to "those awful American newspapers," have been more than once shocked to the marrows of their conservative British bones by tardily admitted truths.

Freedom of the American press, extended to foreign-language newspapers, was limited during the First World War by laws administered by the Post Office Department, and famous German organs of socialism disappeared together with others of divided loyalty. Of nearly a thousand daily and weekly newspapers in foreign languages, from Albanian and Arabic to Yiddish and Yugoslavic now being published in the United States, the Spanish lead in numbers of newspapers; but the highest circulations are among Italians and Germans. Natives of the Iron-Curtain countries—the Bulgarians, Czechoslovacks, Hungarians, Rumanians, Latvians, Lithuanians, Estonians, and even Russians—here enjoy news freedom unknown in their home countries.

The Second World War, the War wanted by no one but the dictators who manufactured it with the help of a captive press, was, for Americans, fought through clouds of military censorship and propaganda from Pearl Harbor to Hiroshima. Admitted to newspapers as news were the prophetic words of great minds who glorified the peace to come yet who—cut off from the wisdom of the people by censorship, the evil that spreads like a plague—let the prize slip through their fingers.

Even in times of peace only the First Amendment has preserved this keystone of all American freedoms. Endlessly men seek to find a loophole in the basic fabric, the unnoticed incident that can be exaggerated into some precedent leading to the control of the news. Political corruption in state, county, and city governments endlessly seeks to perpetuate power, profits, and monumental conceit by bribing a "good press" with jobs on public payrolls—accepted by not a few of the frailer newsmen. Endlessly city, state, and national administrations seek to shame, starve out, or altogether silence newspapers which criticize their weaknesses, inquire into the ties between politics and crime, or expose abuse of public trust on the part of elected representatives and executives.

Thirty years ago the City of Chicago sued the Chicago *Tribune* for ten million dollars, Mayor William Hale Thompson claiming the newspaper's stories of corruption had depressed city credit. In 1923, when it refused to open this Pandora's box, the State Supreme Court ruled that "the people have the right to discuss their government without fear of being called to account for their expressions of opinion."

The *Sunday Press* of Minneapolis crusading in 1931 against local gambling, exposed political corruption strong enough to bring down upon the state a "gag law" designed to suppress any and all "malicious, scandalous, and defamatory newspapers" as "public nuisances" by injunction. Penalties were provided for the recalcitrant, who could regain their inalienable rights only by convincing the court that they would, thereafter, conduct their publications "in the usual and legitimate manner." Interesting to all the nation's newspapers was the United States Supreme Court's decision that this threat of such limitless possibilities was contrary to the Bill of Rights. This decision thus set aside a state law which crippled a free press.

"A deliberate and calculated device in the guise of a tax to limit the circulation of information to which the public is entitled by virtue of Constitutional guarantee" was the opinion of the same Supreme Court when it judged Huey Long's levy of two percent of the gross revenues of newspapers of more than twenty thousand circulation as illegal and thus marked it as intended to destroy those New Orleans newspapers which dared to defy Louisiana's dictator.

In 1951, an International Conference on Human Rights resolved that commercial ownership of newspapers was an evil to be remedied by turning them over to responsible bodies representing politics, labor, and management as more likely than private ownership to provide accurate presentation of facts and healthy opinion. Yesterday witnessed the strange spectacle of appointed American leadership under the convoy of a Presidential appointee meeting to broadcast propaganda urging that America "return to old-fashioned secret diplomacy." For tomorrow an International Treaty on Freedom of Information that, if made the law, would bind American news to European and Asian politics, has been prepared, and not all the light streaming through the many windows of the United Nations building has disclosed an honest reason for this sacrifice.

The American newspaper will remain free to print news of its uncontrolled choice just as long as it holds itself the free partner of its free readers. Pliancy is its creeping danger and if independence, especially in Washington news, bends to accommodate politics, religion, society, wealth, industry, or labor in the day's news, independence is lost.

When Americans no longer trust their newspapers they will no longer concern themselves with the freedom of the press. And once the foundation of all American freedoms is delegated, surrendered, or abandoned, all Americans will lose their only means of protection against wrongs that will, inevitably, be inflicted by elected or appropriated power, and freedom will be regained only by the repayment of its original price—blood.

U.S. Afternoon Dailies At 32,225,000 Peak

By the Associated Press.

PHILADELPHIA, March 11.— Daily newspaper circulation in the U.S. last year nearly hit the all-time record established in 1950, the 84th annual edition of N. W. Ayer & Son's Directory of Newspapers and Periodicals disclosed yesterday. Combined circulation of English-language dailies reached 53,593,000 in 1951.

Evening newspapers increased circulation to 32,225,000, highest ever recorded despite newsprint shortages. The combined circulation of morning newspapers was 20,457,000 while the nation's three all-day dailies had a circulation of 911,000. Both figures are slightly below all-time peaks.

By the end of 1951 Sunday newspapers had a combined circulation of 45,906,000. Morning papers have added 15 per cent to their circulations and Sunday newspapers have added 19 per cent since World War II.

The New York Times.
March 12, 1952.

22

TO THE SKYWAYS

THERE ARE NEWSPAPERS THAT SEEM TO HAVE SOULS
as well as wills and determinations of their own, independent of publishers, editors, writers, and printers who come, and after lives spent
in their services, go. A hundred years ago Park Benjamin wrote: "The
souls of the *Tattler* and *Brother Jonathan* have been transposed into
the *Evening Signal*."

From the most inconspicuous of today's country weeklies to great
city dailies of national and international fame and importance, and all
so thoughtlessly called by friends and critics "the American press,"

American newspapers are essentially local—provincial and even paro-
chial—enterprises with roots and branches so firmly interwoven in local
scenes or areas whose histories are partly of their making, that few could
stand removal to the next counties.

Intimacy, not necessarily harmonious, has always been the key to the
successful American newspaper. Social, economic, and political experience shared by newsmen and readers supplies the permeating germ
necessary to circulation growth and strength, and this fundamental understanding that can be earned, cannot be bought or learned in any
school of journalism. Without this tacit bond a newspaper may be admirable in intent, brilliant in writing, flawless in typography and mechanical reproduction, and remain so synthetic that the pulse measuring
its vitality slackens and fails to respond to expensive surgery and drastic
stimulus. Fine old newspapers have been murdered by new owners with
the money to provide imported talent, and new newspapers whose publishers remain deaf to the overtones of healthy local relationships have
started out with promise only to die of malnutrition in the midst of
plenty.

Great circulations exact great penalties from newspapers; editorial
contact with the rank and file of readers thins almost to the vanishing
point and news, other than important or sensational, blurs and fades.
Wholesale omissions spare city editors the necessity of making the trig-
ger-quick decisions that a dozen times a day call for evaluations (never
neglected in newspapers of smaller circulations) of minor arrests, fires,
accidents, and other excitements so interesting to so many.

Letters from readers, crystal-clear vignettes of public sentiment, sympathy, scorn, and opinion, given dignified captions and appropriate
space, can command as high as eighty percent of reader-interest. Letters
are the perfect and not always flattering pictures of editors' congrega-
tions, and letters from readers glaringly expose, if omitted, publishing
claims of fairness. Omissions are also the perfect exhibition of the weakness that strains to please all and offend none of the many creeds, races,
politics, and crackpot interests too ready to deny to others the freedom
in which they themselves live. A dash of spice as well as an expression
of confidence in the loyalty of their readers was lost when editorial
etiquette, arthritic with age, stiffened into its present comical pretense
of complete ignorance of the existence of other newspapers and other
news channels; and an essential sap is doubly diluted when the feats of
esteemed colleagues in the next block are overlooked, or belittled, unwittingly to expose publishing claims to "fair and impartial" news.

It is news that makes a newspaper, creates opinions on men, events, and affairs, and also creates news and defines its evaluations. Entertainment daily grows more useful as well as more stimulating. Writers on art, literature, the theater, and music are now generally equipped with knowledge as technical as that required of experts on food, medicine, science, finance, aviation, or gardening. Society editors are now less impressed with the artificial boundaries of the elect, and, like the sports writers now concerned with other than specialists in pugilism, amuse and entertain others than enthusiasts of teas. Commercial news has new appeal, and even the real-estate news is escaping its long bondage to cubic and linear feet.

No one mourns the passing of those newspapers that are but ill-printed shambles of advertising held together by uninterpreted wire news and familiar syndicated features, without flavor, devoid of opinion, and as spineless as the give-away sheets thrown into suburban doors. There has been no public wailing when newspapers relying on uninvestigated sensations of doubtful truth have dwindled and disappeared in the chill indifference of the advertising dollar. Regrets mingle with relief when old-timers, stripped of every asset save old mastheads cease; and I-told-you-so's are the only obits for small-town newspapers unable to find any news.

Nothing seems to fill the void when a newspaper that is a patriarch of the American press succumbs to higher publishing costs, unable to meet higher prices for labor, talent, and newsprint. Readers in search of the news must then turn to other newspapers, and publishers in overlapping shopping areas expand their local news limits.

There is no substitute for reading, and the newspaper is not only the ideal news-medium but it is the acme to which all other methods of transmission (radio, television, and news-weeklies) are secondary. It is only the news in responsible newspapers in these news-saturated times that is the bulwark against the national devastation that rumor could spread from apprehension to panic, from panic to disaster of irreparable proportions with a speed frightening to contemplate.

America's news-hunger, older than the United States, is insatiable. The average American wants the latest news before he goes to bed, and the news is his first demand in the morning.

In its news-evaluations, news-selections, and news-presentation, in its editorial and editorial policies, in its make-up and mechanics, in its relations with employed labor and talent, in its acceptance of its responsibilities towards individual readers in need of better understanding of the world's problems, and in its duties towards civic health and the welfare of community, state, and nation, American newspapers have far to go before they reach the heights envisioned by editors and publishers as well as educators, the clergy, and the thoughtful public.

In our times we have seen American newspapers emerge from catch-alls of indiscriminately selected news and entertainment to orderly presentations of events and opinions in reasonable, readable, and understandable focus, the news for the most part fair, honest, and roundly informative, lightened by indexes, and simplified by summaries. Towards better newspapers, better reporting, and better defense of its readers, the entire American press is steadily progressing. Its lacks and its losses are compensated for by the growing national circulation of the great newspapers with their immense resources in financial, sports, national, and international reporting to supplement the small-town papers and the local news which represents American life, culture, and morality.

The first volume from Gutenberg's press opened learning to all the world. The press preserved folklore and with printed laws and precepts steadied both the state and the church. And printed newspapers were the dynamic force which won freedom, dignity, and honor for the common man. Free news has preserved in America those and other boons, and optimists not unreasonably cherish the prophecy of Samuel Bowles which was printed in the Springfield *Republican* on January 4, 1851:

The brilliant mission of the newspaper is not yet, and perhaps never will be, perfectly understood. It is, and it is to be, the High Priest of History, the vitalizer of Society, the world's high censor, the medium of public thought and opinion, the circulating life-blood of the human mind. It is the great enemy of tyrants, the right arm of Liberty and is destined, more than any other agency, to melt and mold the jarring and contending nations of the world into one great brotherhood, which, through the long centuries, has been the ideal of Christian and philanthropist. It's mission has just commenced.

END

BIBLIOGRAPHY

Baldwin, Hanson W. and Stone, Shepard, Ed., *We Saw It Happen*. New York: 1938.
Barrett, James Wyman, *Joseph Pulitzer and His World*. New York: 1941.
Bleyer, Willard Grosvenor, *Main Currents in the History of American Journalism*. Boston: 1927.
Brigham, Clarence S., *History and Bibliography of American Newspapers 1690-1820*. Cambridge, Mass.: 1947.
Bright, Charles, *Story of the Atlantic Cable*. New York: 1903.
Bruckner, Herbert, *Freedom of Information*. Indianapolis: 1949.
Buckingham, Joseph Tinker, *Specimens of Newspaper Literature With Personal Memoirs and Reminiscences*. Boston: 1850.
Bullard, F. Lauriston, *Famous War Correspondents*. Boston: 1914.
Chafee, Zechariah, Jr., *Freedom of Speech*. New York: 1920.
Clark, Thomas D., *The Southern Country Editor*. Indianapolis: 1948.
Cochran, Negley D., *W. E. Scripps*. New York: 1933.
Colden, Cadwallader D., *Memoir of the Celebration of the Completion of the New York Canals*. New York: 1850.
Colton, Walter, *Three Years in California*. New York: 1850.
Cooper, Kent, *Barriers Down*. New York: 1942.
Creel, George, *How We Advertised America*. New York: 1925.
Davis, Elmer, *History of the New York Times*. New York: 1925.
Elliott, Charles W., *A New England History*. New York: 1857.
Forman, Samuel Eagle, *Political Activities of Philip Morin Freneau*. Baltimore: 1902.
Fowler, Gene, *Timberline: Story of Bonfils and Tamman*. New York: 1933.
Fox, Louis H., *Bibliography of New York Newspapers, 1820-1850*. Chicago: 1928.
Franklin, Benjamin, *Autobiography*. Boston: 1897.
Fuess, Claude Moore, *Daniel Webster*. Boston: 1930.
Gamling, Oliver, *A.P.; A Story of the News*. New York: 1944.
Greeley, Horace, *Autobiography*. New York: 1872.
Green, John Richard, *Short History of the English People*. New York: 1895.
Green, Ralph, *The Iron Hand Press in America*. Rowayton, Conn.: 1948.
Gregory, Winifred, *American Newspapers, 1821-1936. Union List of Files Available in the United States and Canada*. New York: 1937.
Hallock, William H., *Life of Gerard Hallock*. New York: 1869.
Harding, George L., *Don Augustin y Zamorano, Statesman, Soldier, Craftsman and California's First Printer*. Los Angeles: 1934.
Hoe, Robert, *A Short History of the Printing Press*. New York: 1902.
Hough, Henry Beetle, *Country Editor*. New York: 1940.
Howe, Eber D., *Autobiography and Recollections of a Pioneer Printer*. Plainesville, Ohio: 1878.
Howe, Edgar Watson, *Plain People*. New York: 1929.
Hudson, Frederic, *Journalism in the United States*. New York: 1873.
Irwin, Will, *Propaganda and the News*. New York: 1936.
Isaacs, George A., *Story of the Newspaper Printing Press*. London: 1931.
James, George Wharton, *Heroes of California*. Boston: 1910.
Jones, Alexander, *Historical Sketch of the Telegraph*. New York: 1852.

Judson, Isabella Field, Cyrus Field, His Life and Work. New York: 1896.
Kainen, Jacob, George Clymer and the Columbian Press. New York: 1950.
King, William S., The Newspaper Press of Charleston, South Carolina. Charleston: 1872.
Kubler, George A., A New History of Stereotyping. New York: 1941.
Liebling, Abbott J., The Wayward Press. New York: 1947.
Livingston, Rutherford, John Peter Zenger. New York: 1904.
Lynch, Denis Tilden, Boss Tweed. New York: 1927.
Mabee, Carleton, American Leonardo: A Life of Samuel F. B. Morse. New York: 1943.
McMurtrie, Douglas C., Wings For Words. Chicago: 1940.
——, Various regional brochures on presses and printing.
MacNeil, Neil, Without Fear or Favor. New York: 1940.
Merriam, George Spring, Life and Times of Samuel Bowles. New York: 1885.
Morison, Stanley, The English Newspaper Between 1622 and the Present Day. Cambridge, England: 1932.
Mott, Frank Luther, American Journalism. Boston: 1942.
Munsell, Joel, Typographical Miscellany. Albany: 1850.
Murrell, William A., History of American Graphic Humor. New York: 1933, 1938.
National Cyclopædia of American Biography, The. New York.
Nevins, Allen, The Evening Post; A Century of Journalism. New York: 1922.
O'Brien, Frank M., The Story of the Sun. New York: 1918.
Oestreicher, J. C., The World is Their Beat. New York: 1945.
Oswald, John Clyde, Printing in the Americas. New York: 1937.
Payne, George Henry, The History of Journalism in the United States. New York: 1920.
Perrin, William Henry, The Pioneer Press of Kentucky. Louisville: 1888.
Plomer, Henry R., A Short History of English Printing, 1476-1898. New York: 1900.
——, Dictionary of Printers and Booksellers, 1668-1725. London: 1922.
Rich, Wesley E., The History of the United States Post Office. Cambridge: 1924.
Roberts, Brigham H., Comprehensive History of the Church of Jesus of the Latter Day Saints. Salt Lake City: 1830.
Rosewater, Victor, Cooperative News Gathering in the United States. New York: 1930.
Sandburg, Carl, Abraham Lincoln. New York: 1939.
Schachner, Nathaniel, Alexander Hamilton. New York: 1946.
Scharf, J. Thomas, Chronicles of Baltimore. Baltimore: 1874.
Seitz, Don Carlos, The James Gordon Bennetts. Indianapolis: 1928.
——, Horace Greeley. Indianapolis: 1926.
——, Joseph Pulitzer, His Life and Letters. New York: 1924.
Shaffner, Taliaferro P., The Telegraph Manual. New York: 1859.
Stoddard, Henry Luther, Horace Greeley. New York: 1945.
Stokes, I. N. Phelps, Iconography of New York. New York: 1915.
Stone, Candace, Dana and the Sun. New York: 1938.
Swanson, Neil Harmon, The Perilous Fight. New York: 1946.
Thomas, Isaiah, History of Printing in America. Worcester: 1810.
——, Revised Edition, with Author's Corrections and Additions. Albany: 1874.
Thompson, Joseph P., Memoir of David Hale. Hartford: 1871.
Van Stockum, W. P., Jr., The First Newspapers of England; Printed in Holland, 1620-1621. The Hague: 1914.
Villard, Oswald Garrison, The Disappearing Daily. New York: 1944.
Walker, Stanley, City Editor. New York: 1934.
Winkler, John W., W. R. Hearst, An American Phenomenon. New York: 1928.

NEWSPAPER

Advertiser, Cleveland, 133, Milwaukee, 149, Washington, 62
Advertiser and Commercial Intelligencer, 63
Alaska Times and Seattle Dispatch, 183
Alta California, 180, 182
American, Baltimore, 113, Herkimer, 148, New York, 98, 139
American Citizen, 96
American Daily Advertiser, 91
American Eagle, 172
American Farmer, 121
American Flag, 172
American Magazine, a Monthly View of the Political State of the Colonies, 26
American Minerva, Patroness of Peace, Commerce and the Liberal Arts, 61, 90, 95
American Pioneer, 172
American Royal Gazette, The, 54
American Turf Register, 121
American Star, 172
American, the National Advocate, and Statesman, 139
American Traveller, 123
American Weekly Mercury, 23, 24, 25, 26
Anglo-Saxon, 172
Appeal, 200
Argus, Albany, 112, 146, New York, 93, 96, St. Louis, 107
Arizonian, 185
Arkansas Gazette, 129
Arrow, 219
Augusta Chronicle, and Gazette of the State, 75

Aurora, General Advertiser, and Political, Agricultural Literary Journal, 88, 91, 92, 93, 94, 96

Balance, 97
Beacon, 107
Bee, Hudson, 97, New London, 97
Black Hills Pioneer, 218
Boise News, 217
Brother Jonathan, 267
Bulletin, Philadelphia, 174, San Francisco, 186, 221, 253

Californian, 179
California Star, 179, 180, 182
Call, 222
Call-Bulletin, 222
Centinel, 104
Centinel of Liberty, 62
Centinel of the North-Western Territory, 80
Chautauqua Gazette, 131
Cherokee Phoenix, 122
Cherry Creek Pioneer, 185-186
Christian Magazine, 120
Chronicle, Boston, 44, New York, 51, 96, Washington, 203
City Gazette and Daily Advertiser, 61
Clamor Público, El, 184
Claypoole's American Daily Advertiser, 60
Cleaveland Herald, 133
Colored America, 191
Columbian, New Haven, 130, Olympia, 183
Columbian Centinel, 88, 96

Commercial Advertiser, 95, 139, 141, 154, 199
Commercial-Gazette, 135, 198
Commonwealth, 104
Connecticut Courant, 39, 112
Connecticut Gazette, New Haven, 37, New London, 40
Connecticut-Herald, 130
Connecticut Journal and New Haven Post-Boy, 39, 130
Constitution, 223
Constitutional Gazette, 50
Corante, or Weekly Newes from Italy, etc., 10
Courier, Boston, 123, Charleston, 118, Portland, 123
Courier and Journal, 222
Courier Française, 62
Crepúsculo de la Libertad, 184
Cumberland Gazette, 76

Daily Advertiser, Albany, 148, Boston, 118, 119, New York, 60, 61, 139
Daily Advertiser, Political Historical and Commercial, 61, 85
Daily Avalanche, 199
Daily Chronicle, 226
Daily Citizen, 200
Daily Commercial Advertiser, 148
Daily Courant, 57-58
Daily Courier, 154
Daily Evening Advertiser and Tea Table Gazette, 62
Daily Evening Bulletin, 222
Daily Globe, 253
Daily Mirror, 121, 122
Daily Morning Chronicle, 209
Daily News, Chicago, 253, London, 210, New York, 199, 202
Daily Repository, 61
Daily Union, 201
Dakota Union, 218
Delaware Courant and Weekly Advertiser, 76
Delaware Gazette, or the Faithful Centinel, 76

Delta, 171
Democrat, Chicago, 147, 196, 220, Sioux City, 218
Democratic Free Press and Michigan Intelligencer, 134
Democratic Platform, 194
Democratic Press, 222
Deseret News, 183
Dessert, 62
Dispatch, 232
Domestick Intelligencer, or, Newes From Both Town and Country, 18
Dramatic Chronicle, A Daily Record of Affairs Local Critical and Theatrical, 222

Eagle, 202, 253
Eastern Argus, 109, 195
Eastern Herald, 76
East-Florida Gazette, 75
Emancipator, 192
Enquirer, Cincinnati, 135, Lexington, 107, Richmond, 112, 147
Essex Gazette, 44, 73
Estrella, La, 184
Evening Journal, 148
Evening-Post, Baltimore, 61, Boston, 28, 29, 35, 44, New York, 34, 60, 96, 122, 139, 154, 192, 233, Philadelphia, 59, Washington, 209
Evening Signal, 160, 167, 268
Evening Star, 209
Evening Sun, 235
Evening-Transcript, 156
Evening World, 235
Examiner, Lexington, 193, London, 152, Richmond, 95, 112, San Francisco, 222, 236
Express, 199, 202

Falmouth Gazette and Weekly Advertiser, 75
Farmer's Cabinet, 167
Farmer's Weekly Museum, 90

Federalist, 62
Federal Gazette, 116
Federal Republican and Commercial Advertiser, 111, 112
Flumgudgeon's Gazette and The Bumble Bee Budget, 177, 178, 181
Forum, 218
Free Enquirer, 122
Freeman's Journal, 104
Freeman's Journal, or, The North American Intelligencer, 55
Free Press, 134, 182
Free Society, 193
Frontier Index, 216
Frontier Scout, 218

Gazette, Albany, 51, Bennington, 94, Boston, 20, 21, 22, 35, 36, 44, Cincinnati, 135, 198, Buffalo, 130, 131, 148, Canandaigua, 109, Detroit, 128, 129, Emporia, 253, Erie, 131, Fredonia, 133, Knoxville, 80, London, 15, 18, 20, New-Harmony, 122, New-London, 40, New York, 31, 32, 34, 58, 93, 116, Norwalk, 212, Philadelphia, 23, 58, 59, Pittsburgh, 77, Rochester, 128, Scotio, 104, York, 58, Vincennes, 104, 105
Gazette and Commercial Reporter, 132
Gazette, and Country Journal, 67
Gazette, and Daily Advertiser, Alexandria, 63, Charleston, 60, 140
Gazette, and General Daily Advertiser, 62
Gazette Française, 53
Gazette of Maine, 75
Gazette of the United States, 68, 84, 85, 86, 95
Gazette, or, Country Journal, 36
Gazetteer, or Daily Advertiser, 61
Gazetteer, and Country Journal, 61
Gem of the Prairie, 148

General Magazine and Historical Chronical, for all the British Colonies in America, 26
Genius of the Lakes, 131
Genius of Universal Emancipation, 190
Georgia Gazette, 75
Georgia State Gazette, or Independent Register, 75
Globe, 147, 164, 208
Globe-Democrat, 107
Globe, The, 95, 154
Golden Age, 217
Grant County Herald, 217
Guardian of Freedom, 104

Hamilton Gazette, 104
Herald, Beaver, 219, Grand Forks, 218, New York, 90, 95, 106, San Francisco, 222
Herald of Freedom, 194
Herald of Gospel Liberty, 120
Hoch-Deutsch Pennsylvanische Geschict-Schreiber, Der, 26

Idaho Tri-weekly Statesman, 217
Idiot, 122
Illinois Emmigrant, 135
Illustrated Quadrule Constellation, 146
Independent Advertiser, 35, 38
Independent Chronical, 92, 94
Independent Gazette, or The New-York Journal Revived, 49, 84
Independent Gazetteer, or The Chronical of Freedom, 61, 96, 116
Independent Journal and The Daily Advertiser, 66
Index, 199
Indian World, 94
Inquirer, Nantucket, 166, Philadelphia, 203
Intelligencer, 107, 148

Journal, Boston, 198, Buffalo, 131,

Philadelphia, 58, 116, Providence, 120, 164
Journal and Courier, 130
Journal and Patriotic Register, 84
Journal of Commerce, 142, 143, 145, 146, 154, 155, 158, 164, 169, 170, 172, 192, 194, 199, 202, 233, 253
Journal, or, General Advertiser, 48
Journal, or Weekly Recorder, 84

Kansas Weekly Herald, 194
Kentucke Gazette, 79, 80
Kentucky Gazette, 79
Kingdom's Weekly Intelligencer, 17

Ladies Morning Star, 159
Leader, 215
Ledger, 59, 166
Liberator, 190, 192
Liberty Hall, and Cincinnati Mercury, 104, 135
Log Cabin, 167
London-Post, 19

Madisonian, 208
Man, The, 159
Manufacturers and Farmers Journal and Providence and Pawtucket Advertiser, 119
Market Day Advertiser, 59
Maryland Gazette, 23, 24, 35
Maryland Journal and Baltimore Advertiser, 43
Massachusetts Centinel; and Republican Journal, 67
Massachusetts Gazette, 41
Massachusetts Spy, or, Thomas's Boston Journal, 44
El Mejicano, 130
Mercantile Journal, 154
Merchants' Daily Advertiser, 62
Mercurius Alicus, 17
Mercurius Britannicus, 17
Mercury, Charleston, 191, 196, 197, Groton, 196, New York, 58, 198

Mercury and Universal Advertiser, 73, 74
Mercury, or, Weekly Advertiser, 38, 73
Michigan Essay: or the Impartial Observer, 106
Minnesota Pioneer, 218
Mirror and Ladies Literary Gazette, 121
Mississippi Gazette, 108
Mississippi Herald, 108
Missouri Democrat, 107
Missouri Gazette, 106, 107
Missouri Republican, 107
Missouri Reporter, 107
Mobile Gazette, 108
Moniteur de la Louisiane, 108
Montana Daily Record-Herald, 219
Montana Post, 218
Montana Radiator, 218
Morning Chronicle, 166
Morning Courier, New Haven, 130, New York, 141, 142
Morning Courier and Enquirer, 142, 143, 144, 145, 146, 160, 172, 174, 191, 192
Morning Express, 61
Morning Herald, 156, 157, 158, 159, 169, 170, 172, 181, 195, 197, 198, 200, 208, 209, 224, 226, 233, 250
Morning Journal, 236, 237, 238, 239, 245
Morning Post, 154
Morning-Post, 154
Morning-Post and Daily Advertiser, 60
Museum and Washington and Georgetown Daily Advertiser, 62

Nación, La, 263
National Advocate, 112, 140
National Gazette, 85, 86
National Intelligencer, 96, 110, 112, 208
National Police Gazette, 121

National Republican, 209
Nebraska Palladium, 219
New-England Courant, 21, 22, 73
New-England Chronical and Essex
    Gazette, 48
New England Magazine of Knowl-
    edge and Pleasure, 37
New-England Weekly Journal, 22,
    35, 36
New Era, 192
New Hampshire Gazette, 38
New-Harmony and Nashoba Ga-
    zette, or the Free Inquirer, 122
New-Jersey Gazette, 53
New Jersey Journal, 53
New Mexican, 184
New Mirror, 121
New Morning Journal of Politics,
    Literature and General Intelli-
    gence, 167
New York Gazette, Revived in
    Weekly Post-Boy, The, 34
New York Journal and Daily Patri-
    otic Register, 61
New-York Mercury, 51, 53
News, Norwich, 180, Sidney, 219
News-Letter, 19, 20, 21, 35, 44, 45
Niagara Journal, 131
North-American, 60, 178
North-Carolina Gazette, Hillsbor-
    ough, 76, 77, New-Bern, 35, 36
North-Carolina Magazine, or, Uni-
    versal Intelligencer, 36
Northern Spectator, 167
Nugget, 185

Observator, 153
Observor, 253
Oklahoma War-Chief, 219
Oregon Spectator, 181, 182
Oregonian, 183
Orleans Gazette: and Commercial
    Advertiser, 108

Pacific News, 180
Packet, 62, 66

Packett, and Daily Advertiser, 48,
    60, 66, 166
Packette, 58
Palladium, 118
Paquette, 37
Patowmack Guardian and Berkeley
    Advertiser, 80
Payo de Neuve Méjico, El, 184
Pennsylvania Chronicle, and Univer-
    sal Advertiser, 43
Pennsylvania Evening Post, 47-48,
    59
Pennsylvania Evening-Post and Daily
    Advertiser, 59
Pennsylvania Freeman, 193
Pennsylvania Gazette, 25, 26
Pennsylvania Journal, 52, 255
Pennsylvania Mercury, 55
Pennsylvania Packett; and Daily Ad-
    vertiser, 60
Penny Magazine, 152-153
Penny Post, 38
Perfect Occurrences, 17
Phenix, 135
Philanthropist, 190
Philadelphische Zeitung, 26
Picayune, 170, 171
Plaindealer, 218
Plain Dealer, 133
Plough Boy, 121
Polar Star, Boston Daily Advertiser,
    62, 116
Polynesian, 182
Porcupine's Gazette, 89, 95
Post, Boston, 252, St. Louis, 232,
    Washington, 209
Post-Boy, 38, 40
Post-Boy and Advertiser, 44
Post-Dispatch, 232
Post-Gazette, 103
Prairie Farmer, 221
Prensa, La, 263
Press, 197, 209
Prophet, 179
Public Intelligencer, 18
Publick Occurrences, Both Foreign
    and Domestick, 19, 20, 45

Public Ledger, 59, 60, 158, 166
Puget Sound Dispatch, 183

Rebel, 200
Recorder, Boston, 121, Richmond, 95
Register, Baltimore, 179, New Haven, 130
Reporter, 107
Republic, Buffalo, 105, St. Louis, 107
Republican, Chicago, 230, Springfield, 120, 154, 203, 270, Santa Fe, 184
Republic of the Rio Grande, 172
Review, 152
Rhode Island Gazette, 22
Rivington's Gazetteer, or, the Connecticut, Hudson's River, New Jersey and Quebec Advertiser, 51
Rivington's New-York Gazette, and General Advertiser, 54
Rivington's New-York Gazette, or, the Connecticut, Hudson's River and Quebec Weekly Advertiser, 50
Rivington's Royal Gazette, 51, 54, 58
Rocky Mountain Gazette, 219
Rocky Mountain News, 185
Royal American Gazette, 51
Royal Pennsylvania Gazette, 51
Royal South-Carolina Gazette, 51, 75

Seaman's Friend, 182
Sentinel, Laramie, 216, Milwaukee, 149
Shawanoe Sun, 194
South-Carolina and American General Gazette, 75
South-Carolina Gazette, 27, 60
South-Carolina Gazette and Daily Advertiser, 60
South-Carolina Weekly Gazette, 27, 60

South-Carolina Weekly Journal, 27
Southern Confederacy, 202
Southern Sentinel, 199
Spectator, London, 152, New York, 95
Spirit of the Times—The American Gentleman's Newspaper, 121
Splifincator, 159
Squatter Sovereign, 194
Staats Courier, 59
Staats-Zeitung, 197
Stage Coach Register, 123
Stampa, La, 263
Standard, 200
Standard and Democrat, 192
Star, Boston, 231, Kansas City, 252, New York, 224, Tucson, 185
Stars and Stripes, 262
Statesman, 139
Stewart's Kentucky Herald, 104
Summary, 40
Sun, Baltimore, 158, 166, New York, 95, 155-156, 157, 158, 159, 164, 165, 166, 167, 169, 230, 235, 239
Sunday Chronicle, 209
Sunday Courier, 144
Sunday Press, 264
Sunday Times, 222
Sunday Tribune, 148
Sunday World, 236

Tattler, London, 152, New York, 160, 267
Telegraph, 148
Telegraphe, 61
Telegraphe, et le Commercial Advertiser, 108
Territorial Advocate, 219
Territorial Enterprise, 183-184
Texas Gazette, 130
Texas Republican, 130
Time-Piece, 108
Times, Boston, 158, 166, London, 124, 144, 210, New York, 173, 193, 197, 198, 200, 202, 203,

223, 224, 230, 231, 233, 237, 253, Sitka, 183

Times, and Patowmack Packet, 80

Transcript, Boston, 154, 253, New York, 98, 156, 157, 158, 159, 166, 224

Tribune, Bismarck, 218, Chicago, 147, 148, 196, 203, 253, 264, Minneapolis, 218, New York, 167, 168, 169, 172, 193, 197, 198, 200, 201, 202, 209, 230, 231, 233, 250

Tree of Liberty, 104

True American, Lexington, 193, Philadelphia, 62

Trump of Freedom, 132

Union, 208

Union: New Orleans Advertiser and Prices Current, 108

United States Recorder, 93

Universal Instructor in all the Arts and Sciences, and Pennsylvania Gazette, 24, 25

Verdad, La, 184

Vermont-Gazette, or, Freeman's Depository, 74, 75

Vermont Gazette and Green Mountain Post-Boy, 74

Vermont Journal and Universal Advertiser, 74

Virginia Gazette, 24, 50

Virginia Gazette, and Richmond Daily Advertiser, 62

Virginia Gazette: or, The Norfolk Intelligencer, 49

Visitor, 198, 217

Washington Pioneer, 183

Wasp, 97, 98

Weekly Advertiser, 40

Weekly Advertiser, or, Pennsylvania Journal, 26

Weekly Dakotian, 218

Weekly-Journal, 32, 34, 35

Weekly Museum, 253

Weekly Oregonian, 182, 183

Weekly Post-Boy, 34

Weekly Register, 109

Weekly Rehearsal, 28

Weekly Times, 130

Western Imigrant, 107

Western Journal, 107

Western Sun, 104

Western Spy, 104

Westliche Post, 232

Whig, 200

Wisconsin Free Press, 149

Wochentliche Staatsbote, Der, 47

Woman, 159

Working Man, 122

Working Man's Advocate, New York, 122, St. Louis, 107

World, 174, 197, 199, 202, 203, 231, 233, 234, 235, 236, 237, 245, 252

World-Telegram, 238

GENERAL AND NAME INDEX

Abell, Arunah S., 166
abolitionists, 192-193
Adam brothers, 124
Adams, James, 76
Adams, John, 76, 92, 95, 97
Adams, John Quincy, 96, 122, 147
Adams, Samuel, 35, 36, 44, 76
Adams, W. H., 194
Adet, 92, 94
advertising, first advertisement on, 24
  increasing costs of, 145
  use of "testimonials," 254
advertisements, of tourist trade, first,
  131
Alexander, James, 33
Alien and Sedition laws, 94, 216,
  260-261
Allen, John, 14
Allen, Robert S., 6
almanacs, early, 12, 14, 19
Ames, Fisher, 102
Ames, John, 123
Anderson, 223
Anderson, John, 50
Andros, Sir Edmund, 15
anti-slavery societies, 190, 191
Aguiler, Santiago, 178
Albright, Samuel, 218
Applegarth, 124
Armstrong, Henry, 206
army newspapers, 171-172, 262
Arnold, George, 123
"Artemus Ward," 201
Associated Press, 250, 251
Atkins, Samuel, 14
Atree, William, 156

Bache, Benjamin Franklin, 88, 89,
  91, 92, 93, 94
Bache, Mrs. Benjamin F., 94
Badger, Willard, 123

Baily, Francis, 55
Bailey, William, 193
Bain, Alexander, 206
Baker, N. A., 216
Banker, Aza D., 166
Barber, Joseph, 130
Barnes, Henry, 134
Barnum, Phineas T., 105
Baur, Andrew, 124
Bay, Jacob, 55
Bay Psalm Booke, 12
Beach, Alfred E. and Moses S., 172
Beach, Moses Y., 164, 167, 168
Beecher, Henry Ward, 203, 224
Belmont, August, 199
Benjamin, Park, 160, 267
Bennett, James Gordon, 118, 144,
  154, 156-158, 160, 164, 165,
  166, 168, 169, 172, 174, 175,
  199, 201, 207, 208, 209, 233
Bennett, James Gordon, 224, 226,
  250, 253
Benton, Thomas Hart, 107
Berkeley, Sir William, 13
Berry, A. M., 182
Bierce, Ambrose, 239
Biglow, Horatio, 118, 130
"Bill Arp," 202
Binney, Archibald, 81
Birkenhead, John, 17
Birney, James C., 192
Blaine, James G., 234
Blair, Francis, 147, 164
Blake, Henry Ingram, 118
Blaeu, Willem Janszoon, 9
Bonfils, Fred G., 252
Book of Genesis, 12
Books, early printed, 9
boosters, newspapers as local, 219-
  220
Boring, Wayne, 7

Boyle, John, 45
Boudinot, Elias, 122
Bourne, Nicholas, 10
Bowles, Samuel, 120
Brace, Charles Loring, 255
Brackenridge, Hugh H., 78, 104
Bradford, Andrew, 23, 24, 26
Bradford, Fielding, 79
Bradford, James M., 108
Bradford, John, 78, 79
Bradford, Thomas, 35, 62
Bradford, William, 14, 23, 26, 31, 32, 34, 41, 60, 62, 67, 116
Brady, Matthew, 202
Brannan, Samuel, 179, 180
Brooker, William, 20, 21, 23
Brooks, 141
Brooks, Erastus, 164, 172
Brooks, James, 164, 172
Brooks, Noah, 201
Brough, John, 135
Brougham, Lord, 152
Brown, 61
Brown, Beriah, 183
Brown, Charles, 201
Brown, Godwin Cotton, 130
Brown, John, 194, 195
Brown, Rev. John W., 104
Brown, Matthew, 62
Browne, Junius Henri, 200
Bruce, David, 125
Bryant, William Cullen, 139, 192, 199
Buchanan, James, 218
Buckingham, Joseph T., 123
Buckley, Sam, 58
Buell, Abel, 54
Buellaas, Jesse, 112
Bunce, George, 61
Burchard, Rev. Samuel D., 234
Burke, John D., 62
Burr, Aaron, 104, 145
Burroughs, Edgar Rice, 7
Bush, C. P., 250
Butler, Nathaniel, 10, 17
Butler, Thomas J., 217
Butler, John S., 217

Byers, William B., 185

cable, establishment of the, 210-211
Calhoun, John C., 147
California, 178-181, 184, 221-222
Callendar, James T., 95, 96, 97
"Camillus," 91
Campbell, John, 19, 20, 21
Capp, Al, 7
Carey, Mathew, 68, 106
Carlisle, David, 89
Carpenter, James, 131
Carpenter, Joseph, 104
Carroll, Charles, 41
Carter, John, Sr., 67
cartoons, political, 36
  first series of, 67
Carvalho, S. S., 236
Casey, James, 62, 93
Casey, James P., 221, 222
Caxton, William, 9
censorship, 259-265
  early English, 10, 18
Chambers, Ephraim, 25
Chambers, Julius, 252
Charles I, 11
Charless, Joseph, 106
Chestham, James, 96, 97
Childs, Francis, 60
Childs, Nathan, 61
Church, John, 73
church papers, 120-121
circulation battles, 168, 171
Civil War, 197-203
  blockade effect of, 199, 200
  Confederate newspapers after, 222
Clapp, W. W., 118
Clay, Cassius Marcellus, 193
Clay, Henry, 106, 135
Clayland, Thomas E., 61
Claypoole, David C., 60, 66, 91
Clephane, James C., 250
Clinton, DeWitt, 137
Clowes, John, 17
Clowes, William, 152-153
Clymer, George, 123
Cobb, Frank I., 238

Cobbett, William, 89, 92, 93, 95, 96
Cockran, Elizabeth, 235
Cockburn, Admiral, 112, 113
Cockerill, John A., 232, 234
code of ethics, modern, 256
coffee houses, dissemination of news
    in, 115, 116
Coffin, Charles C., 198
Colburn, Richard T., 200
Coleman, William, 96, 97
Coles, Christopher, 117
Colfax, Schuyler, 231
Collins, Grace, 53
Colorado, 185
color printing, early, 23
Colton, Walter, 178, 179
Comestock, Seth, 130
comic strips, 236
commodities, as subscription pay-
    ment, 64, 75, 107, 129, 133
Compton, T. G., 199
Congress, first verbatim report of, 96
    opened to newsmen, 86-87
Congressional Record, 86
Connecticut, 37, 39-40
Constitution, first published, 66
Continental Congress, 58
Cooper (of the London Times), 124,
    152
Cooper, Samuel, 36
corante, 10
Cornell, Ezra, 168, 206
Cornish, Samuel S., 191
Cosby, William, 32, 33
Cotton, Godwin Brown, 108
country editions, reprints as, 90
country newspapers, 241-247
court journals, 96, 208, 209
Cowper, 124
Cox, Palmer, 226
Craig, Daniel H., 166, 207, 212
Craighton, Edward, 216
Crédit Mobilier, 224, 231
Creel, George, 261
Crisis, The, 52
Croker Papers, the, 123
Cromwell, Oliver, 18

Craske, Charles, 212
Croswell, Edwin, 146
Croswell, Harry, 97, 98
Crow, 123
crusades, rise of newspaper, 220-223,
    235
Cummings, Alexander, 174
Curtis, C. H. K., 60
Cyclopœdia, Chambers, reprinting
    of, 25

dailies, first, 59-61
    patrons of, 63
Dale, Robert, 122
Dana, Charles Anderson, 230, 231,
    233, 235
Danforth, Samuel, 12
Danner of Nuremberg, 9
Dauby, Augustin G., 128
Davis, 184
Davis, James, 35
Davis, Jefferson, 198
Davis, Matthew, 144, 145
Davis, Richard Harding, 260, 261
Davis, Thomas, 76
Dawson, Moses, 135
Day, Benjamin Henry, 154-158, 164,
    199
Day, Calvin, 108
Day, David M., 131
Day, John, 10
Day (Daye), Matthew, 12
Daye, Stephen, 12
"Death-Bed of a Deist, The," 62
Declaration of Independence, 50th
    anniversary of, 139
    reporting of, 47, 48
DeForeest, Henry, 34
Delany, James, 33
de la Rosa, José, 178
Delaware, 76
Dennie, Joseph, 90
Dickenson, John, 66
dictatorship, censorship under, 262-
    265
Dictes and Sayengis of the Phyloso-
    phers, The, 9

Dillon, John A., 232
Dirks, Rudolph, 7
distribution, 119
    London Plan of, 153
Dix, John A., 202
Dobbins, Thomas, 61
Dockrill, Joseph, 178
Donatus, Ælius, 8
Dongan, Thomas, 13
Draper, John, 40
Draper, Margaret, 45
Draper, Richard, 41
Dred Scott decision, 195
Drew, Daniel, 229
Drinkwater, Paul, 109, 130
Driscoll, Dennis, 75
Dryer, T. J., 182
Duane, William, 94
Duclot, Louis, 108
Dunlop, John, 47, 58, 59, 60, 66
Dunlop, William, 60

Eades, Benjamin, 36, 43, 44
Earl of Dunmore, 49
Earl of Rivers, 9
Earl of Stanhope, 81, 152
Edison, Thomas A., 250
Edson, Gus, 7
Edson, Peter, 6
Edwards, Philip, 61, 253
Eliot, John, Rev., 12, 13, 148
Elizabeth of England, 10
Ellis, Albert, 148
English, David, 62
epitaph of Franklin, 69
Erie Canal, 128, 137, 138, 146-147
Espionage Act, 1915, 261
Evans, George Henry, 122, 159
express riders, 145
extraordinaries, 63

"Fabious," 66
Farewell Address of Washington, 91
farmer papers, 121
Faulkner, William, 180
Favorite, Thomas J., 218
Faxon, Henry W., 105

Faxon, Theodore S., 206
Federalist papers, reprinting of the,
    66
Fenno, John, 68, 84, 85, 86, 88, 89,
    95
Ferguson, Robert, 76, 80
Fessendon, Thomas, 90
Field, Cyrus, 210, 211
Fierer, Charles, 80
Fisher, Bud, 7
Fiske, James, 229
Fleet, Thomas, 27, 28, 29, 35, 44
Flemming, 45
Fletcher, Benjamin, 14
Folwell, Arthur, 7
Fontaine, J. B. L. S., 108
Foord, John, 224
foreign language press, 26, 47, 108,
    122, 148, 219, 232, 263, 264
foreign news, early source of, 63
Forney, John W., 209
Forrest, 148
Foster, Theodore, 184
Fouldis, 152
Fourdrinier, 123
Fowle, Daniel, 35, 38, 55
Fowle, Zachariah, 38, 42
Fox, Fontaine, 7
Franklin, Ann, 38, 44
Franklin, Benjamin, 22, 24, 25, 26,
    34, 35, 36, 37, 38, 43, 58, 60,
    67, 68, 69, 72, 88
Franklin, James, 20, 21, 22, 68, 72
Franklin, James, 38, 73
Freamer, James M., 171
freedom of the press, 83-84
    gag laws and, 263-264
    Hamilton's conception of, 98
Freeman, Edmund, 80
Freeman, Frederick K., 216
Freeman, Legh, 216
Freeman's Oath, 12
French Revolution, 92-93
Freneau, Philip Morin, 61, 85, 86,
    87, 88, 93, 95, 208
Funk, Charles, 26
Funk, Samuel, 26

Gaine, Hugh, 51, 58
Gales, Joseph, Sr., 96
Gales, Joseph, Jr., 96, 110
Gallatin, Albert, 87, 105
Galle, 9
Galloway, Joseph, 43
Gannon, M., 165
Garrison, William Lloyd, 190
Gansefleisch, Johann, 9, 54, 81
Gates, J. M., 216
Ged, William, 152
Genet, Charles E. E., 90
"Genevese Traveller," 144
George, Henry, 159
Georgia, 75
Giel, John, 36, 41, 44
Gilpin, Thomas, 123
Gisborne, F. H., 209, 210
Glidden, Carlos, 250
Glover, Jose, 11-12, 73
Gobright, Lawrence A., 203
Goddard, Katherine, 61
Goddard, Mary Katherine, 43
Goddard, Morrill, 236
Goddard, Sarah, 43, 67
Goddard, William, 41, 42, 61
Godkin, Edwin L., 233
Goodhue, James H., 217
Goodman, Joseph T., 184
Goose (Vergoose), Elizabeth, 27
Gordon, Thomas, 32
Gospel of Matthew, 12
Gould, A. S., 217
Gould, Jay, 229, 231, 234, 250
Government Printing Office, 209
Grafton, Richard, 10
Grady, Henry W., 222
Graham, David, 61
Graham, W. W., 144
Grant, U. S., 230
Great Lakes, water travel on, 131
Greeley, Horace, 154, 167, 172, 173,
    174, 193, 195, 196, 197, 198,
    201, 212, 213, 230, 231
Green, Bartholemew, 13, 20, 40
Green, Charles D., 62
Green, Duff, 107

Green, John, 40, 41
Green, Jonas, 35, 41
Green, Samuel, 12, 13, 22, 39, 130
Green, Samuel, Jr., 13, 14
Green, Thomas, 36, 37, 39, 130
Green, Timothy, 13, 39, 43, 73, 74
Green, Timothy, the third, 40
Green, William, 54
Greene, Charles, 154
Greenleaf, Thomas, 61, 84, 88, 89,
    93, 95, 96
Gridley, Jeremiah, 28
Griswold, Roger, 94
Griswold, Zachariah, 130
Grout, Jonathan, 116
Grozier, Edwin A., 252
Gribayedoff, 234
Guess, George, 122
Gutenberg. See Gansefleisch, Johann

Hale, David, 142, 143, 144, 172,
    253
Hale, Nathan, 118, 119
Hall, Ebenezer, 44, 48, 116
Hall, Francis, 139
Hall, John, 77, 78
Hall, Oakey, 223
Hall, Samuel, 44, 48, 73
Hallock, Gerard, 142, 143, 144, 172,
    173, 199
Halstead, Murat, 198
Hamilton, Alexander, 66, 84, 85, 88,
    91, 96, 97, 98, 104, 145
Hamilton, Andrew, 33, 34
Hammond, Charles, 135
Hancock, John, 48
Hanson, Alexander C., 112
Harden, W. W., 238
harbor news, 143-144, 145, 165
Harris, Benjamin, 18, 19, 45
Harris, Eli, 130
Harris, Isaac H., 122
Harrison, William Henry, 208
Harvard, John, 11
Harvard College, 11, 12, 48
Hasselback, Nicholas, 43
Haswell, Anthony, 74, 75, 94

"Hawser Martingale," 154
Hayes, Rutherford B., 231
Hayward, 156
Hearst, George, 222
Hearst, William Randolph, 222, 236, 237, 238, 239, 245, 251, 254
Hemphill, 223
"Henry Homespun, Jr.," 121
Henry, Patrick, 41
Hicks, John, 44, 51, 58
Hinkle, Joseph, 106
Hoe, Robert, 125, 138
Hoffman, John T., 223
Holden, William, 200
Holt, Charles, 93, 97
Holt, Elizabeth Hunter, 84
Holt, John, 37, 43, 48, 49, 61, 84
Holt, John Hunter, 49
Hood, John H., 108
Horner, 60
horse express, 144, 145, 164, 168
Hosmer, George W., 198
Hough, George, 74
Houghton, Richard, 164
House, Royal S., 206
Hovey, 184
Howard, Joseph, Jr., 202, 224
Howe, Admiral, 49
Howe, Eber D., 132, 133
Howe, Ed, 253
Howe, General, 49, 51
Howell, Evan P., 222
Hudson, Frederick, 164, 172, 173
Hughes, Rev. John, 201
Hull, James, 131
humor, rise of, in newspapers, 123
Humphreys, Daniel, 55
Humphreys, James, 59
Hunt, Thomas, 33
Hunter, William, 37
Huntress, The, 122
Huske, Ellis, 35
Hutchens, John, 119
Hutchinson, Governor, 36

Illinois, 147-148, 219-220, 264

Indiana, 104
Indian-language newspapers, 122, 219
inks, colored, 23
    for color printing, 237
    home-made, 55
International News Service, 251
Iowa, 217
Israel, John, 103
Ives, Frederic C., 250

"Jack Downing of Downingsville," 123
Jackson, Andrew, 96, 108, 123, 127, 135, 142, 144, 147, 164, 208
Jackson, Christopher, 253
Jackson, Solomon M., 154
James, Alfred, 183
Jay, John, 60, 66, 91
Jay Treaty, 90, 91
Jefferson, Thomas, 48, 85, 86, 95, 96, 97, 103, 107, 112
Jennings, Louis J., 223, 224
Jernegan, William L., 183
job-printing, by newspapers as side-line, 64, 102
Johnson, Andrew, 203, 209
Johnson, James, 75
Johnson, Marmaduke, 13, 14
Johnston, Joseph E., 215
Jones, 184
Jones, Alexander, 207
Jones, George, 223, 233
Jones, Merriwether, 95
Jones, William Carey, 217
"Josh Billings," 202, 283
Journal of Continental Congress, 86

Kalendarium Pennsylvanienne, 14
Kansas, 194, 252-253
Kansas-Nebraska Act, 193, 219
Kansas Territory. See Kansas
Keemle, Charles, 107
Keimer, Samuel, 24, 25
Keith, George, 14
Keller, Friedrich Gottlob, 212
Kelly, 148

Kelly, Madison, 133
Kelly, Robert S., 194
Kendall, Amos, 164, 192
Kendall, George Wilkens, 170, 171
Kent, Frank, 6
Kentucky, 79-80, 103
Key, Francis Scott, 113
Killen, Jacob A., 76
King of William, James, 221
King, John, 217
Kneeland, Samuel, 21, 22, 36, 39
Knight, Charles, 152, 153
Knox, Thomas H., 198
Koening, Friederich, 124
Kollock, Shepherd, 53, 61

labor press, early, 122
Lang, John, 62, 93, 116
Larkin, Isaac, 93
Larrabee, C. H., 183
Lawrence, David, 6
Lawson, 141
Lawson, Victor A., 253
Lawson, Victor F., 251
Lee, Henry, 111
Le Fevre, Raoul, 9
Leggett, A. A., 165
Leggett, William, 192
L'Estrange, Roger, 18, 153
Letters of Cato, 32
letters to newspapers, 52
letters, to the editor, 65, 66, 85
Lewis, John A., 184
Lewis, Morgan, 97
Lewis, William, 51, 53, 58
libel, cases under Alien and Sedition
    laws, 94-95, 97
  English law applied to, 97-98
  Zenger trial for, 32-34
Life of Mohammed, serialized, 36
Lincoln, Abraham, 105, 196, 197,
    198, 199, 203, 231
Lingan, General, 111
Lippmann, Walter, 6
literary supplement, first, 62
"Little Sermons of the Lay Preacher,"
    90

Livingstone, David, 226
Locke, David R., 201
Locke, Richard Adams, 157
Logan, Andrew, 133
London Plan of distribution, 153,
    156, 159, 161
Long, Huey, 265
Loughlin, W. A., 218
Louden, John, 138
Louden, Samuel, 66
Louisiana, 264-265
Louisiana Territory, 103, 106, 108,
    129
Lovejoy, Elijah, 192
Luks, George B., 237
Lumsden, Francis A., 170
Lundy, Benjamin, 190
Lynde, 156
Lyon, James, 108
Lyon, Matthew, 94, 95, 108
Lyons, Leonard, 6

McAllister, Hector, 50
McCarthy, Dennis, 184
McClellan, George B., 203
McCutcheon, John, 260
McDougall, Alexander, 42
McDougall, Walt, 234
McElrath, Thomas, 172
McElroy, John, 183
Mackay, John W., 250
McKelway, St. Clair, 253
McKnight, Sheldon, 134
McLean, 62, 66
McLean, John, 236
McLean, J. R., 135
Madison, James, 66, 85, 96
Mack, Frank, 234
Maine, 75-76
Mallinson, Frank, 202
Manners, M. M., 218
Marble, Manton M., 199
Mallet, Elizabeth, 57, 58
Marvel, Andrew, 41
Maryland, 23, 35, 45, 111-113
Mary Tudor, 10
Mason, Stevens Thomson, 91

Massachusetts, 11-13, 14-15, 19-22, 28-29, 34-35, 36, 37, 40-41, 42-45, 48, 55, 67, 116-118, 120, 124
Mather, Cotton, 22
Mather, Increase, 15
"Matthius the Prophet," 158
Mansion, Colard, 9
Marschalk, Andrew, 108
Maxwell, William, 80, 104, 142
Mecom, Benjamin, 37, 38
Medill, Joseph, 148, 196, 251
Meeker, Jotham, 194
Mein, 45
Merchants Reading-Room, 117
Meredith, Hugh, 25
Mergenthaler, Ottmar, 250
Merrick, H. W., 218
Merrick, John L., 185
"Messrs. Colon and Spondee," 90
Mexican War, 170-173
Michigan, 106
Midwest, the, 219-220
See also under individual states
Milk for Babes, 12
Miller, Heinrich, 47, 48, 58
Miller, Isaac, 108
Miller, James M., 106
Miller, John, 60, 119
Miller, Nathaniel, 44, 51, 58
Miller, Peter, 26
Miller, Samuel, 108
Minnesota, 218
Mississippi Territory, 108
Missouri, 231-232
Missouri Territory, 107
Moffatt, Darius, 108
Monroe, James, 96
Monster of Monsters, The, 38
Montana, 218
Morgan, William, 98
Morning Newspaper Association, 141, 142, 143
Morton, William, 60
Morris, George P., 121
Morris, Lewis, 33
Morrison, Archibald M., 199

Morse, Samuel F. B., 168
Moss, William, 222
"Mrs. Silent Dogood," 22
Muley Malack letters, 140
Mullaly, 210
Munsey, Frank, 95
Murphy, 61
Musgrove, Philip, 21
"Mustang," 171
Mutiny Act, effect of, 42
Myers, S. M., 194

Napier, 124
Nast, Thomas, 223, 224, 230
Nebraska Territory, 216
Needham, Marchmont, 17
"Nelly Bly," 235
Nelson, William Rockhill, 252
Newell, Robert H., 201
New England, 11-13, 14-15, 110, 220.
See also under individual states
New Hampshire, 38, 90
news books, coffee-house, 116, 117
newsboys, 254-255
news-hawker, 59, 153, 155
newspaper chains, 253
newspapers, as a political organ, 98-99
first American, 19
influence on national unity, 107
news picture, first, 23
news letters, 65
New Testament, 13
New York, 13, 14, 31-34, 48-49, 50-54, 58, 60-62, 66-67, 84-85, 97, 105, 109, 117, 122, 130-131, 137-147, 151, 153, 172-173, 191-192, 201, 206, 223-224, 229-231, 233-235, 250, 255
New York Associated Press, 173
New York Press Association, 206, 207, 211
Nicolls, Richard, 13
Newell, William, 159
Niles, Hezekiah, 109

Noah, Mordecai Manuel, 140, 141, 142, 144, 160
North Caolina, 35-36, 76-77
North Dakota, 218
Northwest Territory, 104
Norwell, Joshua, 107
Noyes, Crosby S., 209
Noyes, Frank B., 251
Nuthead, William, 13

Ochs, Adolph S., 238, 251, 253
Ohio, 103-104
Oldbody, Ann, 159
"Old Boy in Specs," 144
"Old Oaken Bucket," 121
Old Testament, 13
Older, Freemont, 253
Oram, James, 138
Oregon, 181-182
Oregon Territory. See Oregon
O'Reilly, Henry, 206
"Orphus C. Kerr," 201
Orton, William, 231
Osbon, O. S., 197, 200
Osborn, Charles, 190
Osborn, W. J., 194
Oswald, Eleazer, 61, 84, 96
Othman, Frederick C., 7
Otis, James, 36
Oultcat, Richard B., 236
Oury, W. S., 185

Pablos, Juan, 11
Pace, Henry, 95
Pagenstetcher brothers, 212
Paine, Thomas, 52
paper, cost of, 55, 81, 123, 212
paper-making, 55, 123, 212
    Dutch Engine, 55
paper-mills, 24, 78
    subsidy for, 55
Parker, James, 34, 37, 41, 42, 51
Parks, William, 23, 24, 35
Parmlee, 155
party press, first, 84
    patterns of the, 90-91
    subsidized, 88

Patterson, Leonard, 61
Paul Pry, 122
Pearson, Drew, 6
Pegler, Westbrook, 6
Penn, Shadrock, 107
Penn, William, 14, 77
Pennsylvania, 14, 22-23, 25-27, 36, 41, 43, 47-48, 52, 54-55, 58-62, 66, 68-69, 77-79, 81, 103, 123-124, 193
Pentland, Ephrim, 104
Percival, James, 131
"Peter Porcupine," 89, 92, 93, 95, 96
"Petroleum Vesuvius Nasby," 202
Philips, Eleazer, 27
Phillips, H. I., 6
Pickering, Timothy, 92, 108
Pickett, Charles, 177, 178
picture, half-tone process for, 250
Pierce, Franklin, 219
Pierce, Richard, 14, 19
Pierce, William, 12
pigeon carriers, 166, 210
Pinckney, 93
Pittock, Henry L., 183
Platt, Kin, 7
policy, pre-Revolutionary, 44
policy statement, of Elizabeth Mallett, 57-58
    of Franklin, 21
Polk, James K., 208
Pony Express, 186
Poor Robin's Almanac, 22
Porter, Royal S., 123
Porter, William T., 121
Postal Act, of 1792, 72
postal service, demand for, 73
post-offices, demand for, 73
Post-Offices, Goddard's, 43
Post-Master General, first, 43
Post Roads, early, 72, 73
Present State of New-English Affairs, 15
presses, advances in, 212
    at beginning of Revolution, 54
    color, 237

presses (cont.)
  Columbian, 124
  cylinder, 124
  first American, 11, 12, 13, 73
  Gutenberg, 8-9
  hand, 184
  Hoe, 125
  improvements on, 9-10, 81
  Linotype, 250
  in Mexico, 11, 130
  in Peru, 11
  as prizes of war, 48, 49, 58
  Ramage, 81, 183
  religious origins of, 148
  on shipboard, 49, 53, 181, 211
  Stanhope, 124
  Stearn, 124
  stereotypes, 125
  Washington, 124
Pretorius, Emil, 232
prices, early newspaper, 153-154
Priestly, Joseph, 88
Printer, James, 13
Printer to the King, 50
printers, Indian, 13, 122
Prynne, William, 18
public printers, 14, 24, 27, 49, 73,
  129, 209
Pulitzer, Albert, 236
Pulitzer, Joseph, 231, 232, 233, 235,
  236, 237, 238, 245, 253, 254

Quigley, Joseph, 36

railroad, transcontinental, 216-217
Ramage, Adam, 81, 101
Ramsey, Dave, 155
Raymond, Henry Jarvis, 173, 193,
  223
Recueil des Histoires de Troyes, Le,
  9
Reed, Ebenezer, 128
Reid, Whitelaw, 198, 231, 233
Reick, William C., 233
reporter, first professional, 118
Rhode Island, 22, 38, 42, 68, 110

Rhode Island Society for the En-
  couragement of Domestic In-
  dustries, 119
Revere, Paul, 44
"Reverend Mephistopheles Hurl-
  burt," 231
Reynolds, James S., 217
Reynolds, Thomas B., 217
Reynolds, Richard W., 217
Rhett, Robert B., 197, 198
Ricardi, Antonio, 11
Richards, Daniel H., 149
Richards, Willard, 183
Richardson, Albert D., 200
Richmond, William, 119
Rind, William Alexander, 62
Ritchie, Alexander, 208
Ritchie, Father Thomas, 112, 147
Rives, John, 164
Rivington, James, 50, 51, 54, 58
Rittenhouse, William, 14
"Robert Rusticoat, Esquire," 97
Roberts, George, 146
Robertson, Alexander, 51, 58, 59
Robertson, James, 51
Rogers, Gamaliel, 35, 55
Ronaldson, James, 81
Roosevelt, Eleanor, 6
Roulstone, George, 80
Royall, Anne Newport, 122
Ruark, Robert C., 67
Rush, Benjamin, 95
Rush Light, The, 95
Russell, Benjamin, 67, 88, 89, 92,
  94, 95
Russell, David, 74
Russell, Joseph, 40, 41, 44
Rust, Samuel, 124, 138

Sackette, R. T., 108
salaries, apprenticeship, 132
  early, 52, 68
  of editors and writers, 135
Salisbury, Guy H., 148
Salisbury, Hezekiah, 109, 132
Salisbury, Smith H., 148
Salisbury, Smith W., 109, 132

Sargent, Winthrop, 108
Schurz, Carl, 231
Scripps, E. W., 251
Scull, John, 77, 78, 103, 104
Scott, Thomas M., 231
Searle, Ambrose, 51
Sears, Isaac, 50
Seaton, William W., 96, 110
Sedition Act, 1918, 216
Semple, Robert, 178, 179
sensationalism, 158, 160, 236, 237, 252-254
Sequoia, 122
Servel, M., 165
Sewall, Samuel, 14
Seward, William H., 165
Shaw, Henry, 202, 203
Sheldon, John P., 128, 129, 134
Sheppard, Horatio D., 154
Sherman, William Tecumseh, 198, 202, 260
Sholes, Christopher, 250
Simmons, Azariah H., 166
"Simon Simple," 122
"Simon Spunky," 90
Simonton, James, 223
size, and format effect of, on sales, 146
    changes in, 154
Skillman, 141
Skinner, John S., 113, 121
slavery, 189-195
Sleeper, John S., 154
Smalley, George Washington, 203, 211
Smith, Alexander, 33
Smith, Bruce, 218
Smith, Charles, 202
Smith, Rev. Elias, 120, 121
Smith, Francis, O. S., 207
Smith, Garritt, 196
Smith, John, 253
Smith, John E., 75
Smith, Seba, 123, 154
Smith, William, 33
Smith, William Harrison, 96
Snowden, Samuel

South, the, 189-203, 260.
    See also under individual states
Southard, Samuel, 208
South Carolina, 27
Southwest, the, 129-130, 184
Southwick, Solomon, 121
Sower, Christopher, 26, 54, 59
Spanish American War, 238
special correspondents, first, 166
Spiegle, Dan, 7
Spooner, Alden, 73, 74, 129
Spooner, Judah-Paddock, 73, 74
sporting papers, 121
Sprague, Frank R., 250
"Spy in Washington," 144
Stamp Act, 1765, effect of, 41
Stanley, 156
Stanley, Henry Morton, 226
Star Chamber Acts, 11, 18
Star Chamber Court, 10, 11
"Star-Spangled Banner, The," 110
steamboat, importance of, 134
Stedman, Edmund, 197
stereotype, advances, 153
    for papier-maché molds, 250
    invention of, 125
Stillman, Isaiah, 131
Stockwell, Stephen N., 154
Stokes, Benjamin M., 108
Stone, David M., 233
Stone, Melville E., 251, 253
Stone, W. L., 139
Story, Enoch, 55
Storey, Francis V., 154
Stout, Elihu, 104, 105
Stowe, Harriet Beecher, 192
strike, first, 68
Stringfellow, John H., 194
Stuart, John, 62
Styles, 223
Sullivan, Mark, 6
Sunday extra, first, 53
Sunday, editions, 254
    publication on, 253
    strict observance of, 142, 143
supplements, in color, 237
    first literary, 62

Surveyor of the Press, 18
Suydam, John V., 148
Sweeney, Peter B., 223

Talleyrand, 93
Tammen, Harry H., 252
Tappan, Arthur, 142, 143, 190, 191
Tappan, Lewis, 142
taxes, as censorship, 264-265
  early newspaper, 39
  effect of, 152
telegraph, Electro-Magnetic, 168,
  169
  growth of, 206-207
  French, 117
  Omaha to Salt Lake City, 216
  by semaphore and flag, 116
  "visual," 118
telegraphic news, dominance of, 172-
  173
Tennessee, 80
That Stanley, 226
Thayer, Eli, 194
Thompson, Ephraim, 97
Thompson, William Hale, 264
Thomson, Charles, 48
Thomas, Isaiah, 37, 42, 44, 67, 69,
  72, 74
Thornton, Jessy Quinn, 181
Tillock, 152
Timothy, Elizabeth, 27
Timothy, Lewis (Louis Timothée),
  27,
Titcomb, Benjamin, 75
Titcomb, Benjamin, Jr., 76
Topliff, Samuel, Jr., 117, 118
Tourney, 138
Tousey, Sinclair, 159
Towne, Benjamin, 43, 47, 59
Townsend, George A., 203
Trading with the Enemy Act, 1917,
  261
transportation, problems of, 72
travellers' press, 123
Treadway, Daniel, 124
Trenchard, John, 32
Truth Advanced, The, 14

Tucker, Luther, 148
Tucker, Ray, 6
Tully, John, 19
Tweed Ring, 223, 224
Tweed, William M., 223, 224
Twyn, John, 18
Tyler, John, 208
Tyler, Royall, 90
type foundries, 54, 55, 81, 184
types, black-letter, 10
  English-letter, 55
  from Gothic matrices, 54
typewriter, invention of, 250
T Vault, W. G., 181

United Press Association, 250, 251

Vail, Alfred, 168
Van Dam, Rip, 32, 33
Vermont, 73-75
Verplank, Johnston, 98
Villard, Henry, 197
Virginia, 13, 24, 41, 49-50, 53

Wagner, Jacob, 112
Wait, Thomas Baker, 75
Walker, Lynde M., 154
Walter, John, 124
War Between the States, 197-203
War of 1812, 111-113
Warren, Joseph, 36
Washington, 96
Washington, D. C., 62, 112
Washington, George, 48, 51, 52, 54,
  84, 85, 86, 90, 91, 92, 97
Watterson, Henry, 222
Webb, James Watson, 142, 143,
  144, 156, 160, 172, 174, 191
Webb, T. D., 132
Weed, Thurlow, 148
Webster, Noah, 90, 91, 92
Wells, John, Jr., 75
Wells, John J., 124
Wells, Robert, 75
Wells, William C., 75
Wentworth, John, 147, 196, 220
Wesley, Edward, 223

Western Associated Press, 211
western frontier, 128, 131-135, 148, 178-187, 215-219
Western Press Association, 250
Western Union, 250, 251
Weyler, General, 238
Wharton, Thomas, 43
Wheaton, Henry, 112, 140
Wheeler, 148
White, William Allen, 253
Whitmarsh, Thomas, 27
Whitney, W. K., 183
Whittier, John Greenleaf, 193
Whole Book of Psalms, The, 12
Wiley, 183
Wilke, Franc B., 198
Wilkes, Ziba, 131
Willard, Frank, 7
Williams, Barney (Bernard Flaherty), 155
Williams, Jonathan, 184
Willington, Aaron S., 118
Willis, Deacon, 121
Willis, Nathaniel, 80, 104
Willis, Nathaniel, Jr., 108, 121
Wilson, 152
Wilson, Alexander, 211
Wilson, Woodrow, 261
Winchell, Walter, 7
Winchester, Jonas, 180
Winship, Winn, 104
Winthrop, John, 11, 12
Woodruff, William Edward, 129

Woodward, Samuel, 121
Wiener, George W., 155-156
Wollard, Isaac B., 184
women, publishers and printers, 34, 43, 57, 67, 159
Wood, Benjamin, 199
woodcuts, 38, 76, 133
"Woodman, Spare that Tree," 121
World War I and new reporting techniques, 261
World War II, 264
Wright, Frances, 122
Wright, Stephen, 227
Wrightson brothers, 184
Wrightson, William, 185
Wyoming, 216

Yankee Doodle, derivation of, 40
yellow journalism, 236-237, 251-252
Young, Brigham, 183, 216
Young, Chic, 7
Yundt, William, 61
Young, John Russell, 197
Youth's Companion, The, 121

Zamorano, Don Augustin Vincente, 178
Zenger, Catharine, 34
Zenger, John, 34
Zenger, John Peter, 8, 36, 37
arrest of, 32
trial, 33-35
Zumarraga, Don Fray Juan, 148